KILLING AND SAVING

KILLING
─── A N D ───
SAVING
Abortion, Hunger, and War

JOHN P. REEDER, JR.

The Pennsylvania State University Press
University Park, Pennsylvania

Library of Congress Cataloging-in-Publication Data

Reeder, John P., 1937–
    Killing and saving : abortion, hunger, and war /
John P. Reeder, Jr.

        p.   cm.
    Includes bibliographical references (p.   ) and index.
    ISBN 0-271-01028-2 (cloth : acid-free paper)
    ISBN 0-271-01029-0 (paper : acid-free paper)
    1. Right to life. 2. Assistance in emergencies. I. Title.
    K3252.R44 1996
    179'.7—dc20   93-2510
                                                              CIP

Published by The Pennsylvania State University Press,
Barbara Building, Suite C, University Park, PA 16802–1003

It is the policy of The Pennsylvania State University Press to use acid-free paper for
the first printing of all clothbound books. Publications on uncoated stock satisfy the
minimum requirements of American National Standard for Information Sciences—
Permanence of Paper for Printed Library Materials, ANSI Z39.48–1992.

For Jane, Nick, and Kate

Contents

Acknowledgments

I want to thank all the students in courses at various institutions with whom I have debated the issues, and all the colleagues over the years who have offered insightful criticisms. Vaughn Allen, Healan Gaston, Amy Johnson, Christine Lehmann, Zachary Lesser, and Jennifer Pelli were particularly helpful in the end. Several student assistants have helped with the bibliography and references. Kathleen Pappas and Jane Simmons have seen me through numerous revisions. Susan Lundgren expertly copyedited the manuscript.

Introduction

Contrary to Alasdair MacIntyre (1984) and others who assert that modern Western morality is in disarray, torn by incommensurable moral views, I believe there is much agreement at the level of "considered moral judgments" about taking and saving human lives. We have, in other words, a considerable overlap in regard to which sorts of killings are prohibited and which sorts of savings are required. Various traditions, theistic and nontheistic, have shaped Western morality and overlap on these crucial issues.

These overlaps in judgment amount to a moral tradition in their own right, a tradition that does not deny that part of our duty is to maximize the good (lives or the length and quality thereof) but that also constrains maximization within certain basic duties or rights.[1] Alan Donagan (1977)

---

1. The tradition usually never allows maximization to override basic duties or rights. Compare the view expressed by Nagel (1972) that maximization and basic duties or rights may simply constitute incommensurable moral considerations, one of which on certain occasions we may have to disregard.

2 KILLING AND SAVING

argued that this tradition limits what we may do even to help others—as strands of Western tradition have interpreted Paul's statement in Romans 3, one may not do evil even that good may come. This book defends the coherence of this tradition against critics such as James Rachels (1986) and Helga Kuhse (1987) who attack some of its cardinal notions, such as the moral significance of the distinction between killing and letting die and the principle of double effect. I do not defend the "sanctity of life" in the form Kuhse criticizes and I agree with many of Rachels's specific moral judgments; nonetheless, I revise and hence attempt to maintain a tradition they want to abandon.

The various traditions that overlap, however, do not always agree on how basic duties and rights are to be conceived. They do not agree, for example, about the nature of our responsibility to aid others or the extent— the cost to ourselves—to which we should do so. And they do not agree about how basic duties or rights are to be justified. One tradition—let us call it the Enlightenment tradition—justifies basic duties or rights as what we have by virtue of certain human capacities, such as the capacity to reason consistently, as the product of agreements between actual or hypo- thetical agents, or as the fruit of our capacity to identify sympathetically with others.[2] Another tradition—the neo-Aristotelian—roots basic duties or rights in certain virtues, principally justice, which are part of human good.[3] Still another tradition anchors basic duties or rights in the relation of human beings to God; the duties or rights humans should observe are ways of honoring God's dominion over or love for humanity.

I believe that the disagreements can only be explained finally in terms of the beliefs by which duties or rights are justified, ultimately the worldviews of which these moral traditions are a part. I note some of these deep struc-

2. Cahill (1980, 285–87) is correct that the natural rights tradition often does not ac- knowledge a positive right to aid, but see Little (1986) on the version of the tradition that does. The tradition can also recognize sociological and metaphysical senses of the claim that persons are essentially social. See Hollenbach (1979, 13ff.) and Reeder (1990).

3. Despite these differences in justification, the overlapping traditions I gather here share a normative outlook that can be contrasted with a utilitarian approach such as Nielsen's (1973; 1990). Roughly speaking, Nielsen is prepared to sacrifice some lives in order to maxi- mize the number of lives saved (unless there are other relevant consequences to be factored into the calculation of the greatest good of the greatest number). The consensus I work out of, however, limits the circumstances in which innocent life may be sacrificed to save a greater number; that is, innocent life may be sacrificed only when the right to life is yielded, nothing is lost, there is nonvoluntary or involuntary pursuit, or double effect obtains. Maximization alone is not sufficient. For a representative view, see Brody (1975, 12–18) on maximization. It could be, however, that a normative view such as the one I propose here has a higher-level justification in an appeal to the preservation of certain values for all. See Chapter 5, notes 1 and 16.

tural differences and make some suggestions, but I do not try here to adjudi-
cate questions about the "foundations" of duties or rights. Following
Michael Walzer's methodology in *Just and Unjust Wars* (1977, xv–xvi,
53–54), I explore the "superstructure" of moral convictions.[4] I do not try,
in other words, to justify the convictions I systematize; that is a task for
another day. I hope it is useful simply to chart some basic points at which
our convictions converge and diverge, the "our" signifying not a single
"common morality" but a set of overlapping traditions (cf. Kagan 1989).[5]

My aim, therefore, is to present a coherent account of a set of overlapping
judgments about taking and saving lives. The account I present here draws
from the various traditions. I reflect the views of others, but I also shape
the meaning of the rights not to be killed and to be saved as I think they
should be understood. My account owes much to Philippa Foot and Judith
Thomson, but on some questions—for example, the extent of our duty to
aid others—it resembles theological views more than contemporary versions of the Enlightenment traditions. I express my account in the vocabulary of rights, in contrast to an ethic of duty or obligation not correlated
with a right that can be yielded.[6] For example, some theologians hold that
as a trustee of God one has a duty not to take life, and that we do not
possess the dominion to release others from that duty; in medical contexts,
therefore, we do not have a "right" to life that we can yield or waive.[7]
However, in my account I incorporate the notion, which still other theologians accept, that one can even yield the right not to be killed; in this
theological vocabulary, humans are delegated the dominion to make that
decision.

The cases I deal with have mainly to do with abortion and infanticide,
starvation, and war. Each of these problems arises in the context of broader

---

4. I have sought at most a "narrow reflective equilibrium" between general convictions
and judgments on specific cases. Presumably a full account of rights would also offer some
notion of their justification in terms of a wider network of beliefs. For discussion of the issues,
see, for example, Gewirth (1978; 1993), Little (1986; 1993), and Outka and Reeder (1993).

5. Anyone who doubts the considerable overlap between someone like Kuhse and recent
Roman Catholic moral theology should read McCormick, for example, on the criterion of
relational potentiality and his refusal to dichotomize the "sanctity" and the "quality" of life
(for example, 1981a, 383–401). The overlap I have in mind need not consist in the view that
there is some common content and rationale in and behind our moral views. Some religious
thinkers and "Enlightenment" moralists have claimed this, but it is also possible that a more
modest sense of a common morality exists, namely, a partial overlap of content and reasons.
I believe this overlap exists, and I attempt to organize and shape it here; I focus mainly on
content, however, and only make suggestions about rationale or justifying reasons. On issues
regarding a common morality, see Outka and Reeder (1993).

6. See Childress's (1986) excellent analysis of the concept of a "right to life."

7. See Brock (1979) on rights-based, in contrast to duty-based, theories.

issues about social existence: sex and reproduction, the distribution of natural and social goods, and political community. I also touch on euthanasia. I do not pretend to offer a fully adequate discussion of these moral problems; my aim is only to attempt to locate the issues on a normative map. Other cases are introduced, some of which have been very real in human history—for instance, collaboration with tyranny—and some that, though conceivably real, have been invented by ethical thinkers to help us clarify our thinking.

Some feminist writers have objected to the use of abstract or hypothetical examples, however, on the grounds that it is characteristic of women to insist that moral situations must be examined as they actually are (cf. Parsons 1979; Gilligan 1982; Noddings 1984). Even hypothetical cases, however, tell a certain sort of story. As Eric Mack (1985) notes, one must spell out a particular history in order to determine when deaths of the "innocent" are permitted; thus there is no hard-and-fast line to be drawn between "abstract" and "narrative" approaches to moral issues even where rights are invoked.

The deeper question, which I do not address here, is whether the discourse of individual rights is morally viable in the first place. Some contemporary critics argue that the notion of rights possessed by persons as such, by anyone regardless of historical context, is fatally flawed, and should be supplanted by alternative moralities, for example, one of love or caring.[8] Other critics insist that, at the very least, individual rights must be supplemented by other distinct moral perspectives. In regard to abortion, for instance, critics have argued that the language of rights distorts the moral situation, or at best represents only one sort of relevant consideration or perspective. Respect for the rights of persons as such represents one virtue, and caring, another, each expressing a different facet of moral experience.[9] Elsewhere I argue that these dimensions (along with notions of human good

8. A benevolence or love ethic has a history as one strand of the Enlightenment (with roots in Judaism and Christianity), and it has recently been taken up by feminist thinkers.

9. Levi (1987) criticizes Thomson's use of hypothetical examples because they do not express the point of view of actual women with unwanted pregnancies, for whom the question whether the fetus's right to life implies a duty to bear is a nonissue; rather, says Levi, the only real issue is the woman's right to make reproductive decisions (1987, 35). But this position is actually close to Thomson's, for her starting point is the woman's right to decide what happens in and to her body; Thomson's point is that if the woman has decided not to provide life support for a fetus (because she does not want it, believes she cannot care for it adequately, or whatever) she exercises her own right to control her body and she does not violate any general negative right not to be harmed the fetus is said to have. For other criticisms of a rights approach to abortion, see Parsons (1979), Gilligan (1982), and Churchill and Simán (1982).

or flourishing) are not related as distinct and irreducible perspectives, but are interwoven in various interpretations and ways of life (see Reeder 1994). Here I propose only that, however people weave together different dimensions of the moral life, the language of rights can express some basic convictions that many share.

I first present a sketch of a basic right not to be killed and a right to be saved; collectively, one can refer to these rights as the "right to life" (Feinberg 1980a), although some writers restrict the phrase to the negative right not to be killed (Thomson 1984). I speak of the two as distinct rights, but I suggest that in more than one tradition a certain commitment to the welfare of the individual underlies both the negative and the positive injunctions. (To maintain the flow of the main argument, I assume in the text that individuals have full moral status; in the Appendix I argue that the issue of status cannot be decided without reference to substantive moral beliefs.)

I then deal with four sorts of circumstances arising in various cases in which I argue that we kill but do not violate the right not to be killed: yielding, nothing is lost, the pursuer, and double effect. One could say that under these conditions or circumstances the right not to be killed is overridden or justifiably infringed; I suggest, however, that we can write the conditions into the meaning of the right itself.

Finally, I also argue that outside of these sorts of circumstances and two sorts of exceptional occurrences (a moral dilemma and a Nazi-like "supreme emergency") there are no others in which we are morally justified in killing, even in order to save; the right, once qualified, is absolute.

My aim, then, is to weave a general view of killing and saving that covers a number of circumstances and is applicable to a variety of cases. If there is any merit here, it is in trying to forge a coherent account that encompasses several disputed theoretical issues and moral problems. My argument builds out from a number of authors, especially Brody, Donagan, Foot, Ramsey, and Thomson, but I have not attempted to give a detailed or chronological account of their views. I try to synthesize and modify as I go along. I do not attempt to compare my view systematically with all the current writers who deal with these matters or to respond to all relevant objections. I try in the notes to indicate some of the writers who have developed ideas similar to mine, and some who take a different tack. The philosophical and theological literature is immense, and I leave many authors unacknowledged, some of whom I have read, and others I have not. For these omissions I offer apologies. I regard my effort here as an unfinished conversation.

1

The Right Not to Be Killed and the Right to Be Saved

I argue for a negative right not to be killed and a positive right to have one's death prevented, to not be allowed to die. My first task is to propose that there is a sensible distinction between two sorts of actions: killing, and allowing to die or letting die. We need to know what we are contrasting when we speak of killing over against letting die before we can ask whether the distinction has moral significance and, if so, what sort. A narrow notion of the distinction equates it simply with the difference between commission and omission: one kills if one unplugs a respirator, one lets die if one does not start it up. A broader notion I adopt here links the distinction to a difference in two types of situations: in the one, the agent brings about a causal process sufficient to cause death; in the other, the agent refrains from preventing or continuing to prevent some other antecedently obtaining lethal process.[1] I adopt this broader notion because the narrower one sug-

---

1. For discussion of the view that the distinction between killing and allowing to die expresses the distinction between acts (commissions) and omissions, see Brock (1986, 118ff.). "When I kill someone, I act in a way that causes that person to die when they would not

gests that the moral question is simply about whether a commission—unplugging a respirator, for example—is equally as justified as an omission, for example, not putting someone on the respirator in the first place. The more significant issue in my view has to do with another contrast: if both not starting and also stopping a treatment (for example, a respirator) are sometimes justified, then *ceteris paribus* is a lethal injection also justified? The contrast at issue, in other words, is between refraining to prevent some antecedent lethal process either by not starting or stopping aid, and introducing some new cause of death.

After discussing the broader notion of killing and letting die I then address the question whether the distinction has moral significance.[2] Normatively I try to hold together the view that the right not to be killed is more stringent than the duty to save with the conviction that in some circumstances it is as wrong to let die as it is to kill.

Killing and Letting Die

Consider these definitions of O. H. Green (1980, 198), which are intended not only to reflect but also to sharpen ordinary usage. Green's first case,

---

otherwise have died in that way and at that time. When I allow someone to die, I omit to act in a way that I could have acted and that would have prevented that person dying then; that is, I have both the ability and the opportunity to act to prevent the death, but fail to do so" (1986, 118). Thus turning off the respirator would be "killing." On another view of the killing/allowing-to-die distinction: "If you kill someone, what you do is to initiate a deadly causal process that leads to the person's death. If you allow someone to die, you allow a deadly causal process which you did not initiate to proceed to its result of a person's death" (1986, 121). On this view, one acts (commission) when one turns off the respirator, but one also allows to die (1986, 121–22). This second view is close to Green's (1980) in that it turns on whether the agent initiated the "deadly causal process." Brock (1992, 13ff., 186–87) argues for the act/omission interpretation of the killing/letting-die distinction, in part because what I call here the broad view would commit us to saying that a "greedy son" who disconnects his mother's respirator merely allows her to die (see also Brock 1986; 1989, 340ff.). For Brock, what the son does is an unjustifiable act of killing. (The killing would be justifiable under other conditions, such as the patient's consent.) Cf. McMahan who argues that an "enemy" who turns off a respirator kills, not because of the enemy's motive, but because the enemy did not initially provide aid (1993, 254ff.). I prefer, however, to say that the greedy son or the enemy lets the patient die, but unjustifiably. However, I think that the moral questions would remain even if, for purposes of a theory of action, one preferred another view. For instance, even if one called taking a patient off a respirator a justified killing, as opposed to a letting die, the question would remain whether killing in the sense of lethal injection is also morally justified.

2. I agree with Bennett (1981) that the distinction should not incorporate moral content. For a critique of the notion that there are two tasks, first, to get clear about actions, causes, effects, and so on, and second, to ask about their moral significance, see Duff (1982, 7ff.);

which I call Category 1, expresses the notion of letting die as refraining from preventing some antecedent process:[3]

A lets B die if, and only if,

 (1) there is a condition c which is sufficient to cause B's death unless A or some other agent does something s which will prevent B's death from c, and A is aware that this is the case,
 (2) A did not bring about c,
 (3) A refrains from doing s, and
 (4) B dies from c.

In Category 1, A (the agent) did not bring about the death-causing condition; the agent refrains from giving or continuing to give someone life-saving aid—for example, not going to the aid of a drowning swimmer or breaking off a rescue.

Green next introduces a case, call it Category 2, which describes a sort of killing, one that also involves refraining to prevent death:

A kills B when A refrains from preventing B's death if, and only if,

 (1) there is a condition c which is sufficient to cause B's death unless A or some other agent does something s which will prevent B's death from c,
 (2) A brought about c,
 (3) A refrains from doing s, and
 (4) B dies from c.

(Green 1980, 198)

Green introduces Category 2, the killing by refraining category, to deal with the sort of case where A brings about c—for example, someone puts a dog in a pen without food, "thereby insuring that . . . not feeding the dog would bring about its death." According to Green, the agent in this case *kills* the dog. But if "the man had refrained from feeding a hungry

---

see also Casey (1971, 168–69), Chandler (1990, 420–22), and Ladd (1979, 178–79), who argue that moral considerations affect whether we describe an action, for example, as letting die.

3. Bennett (1981; 1983; 1994) develops an account of positive and negative instrumentality in contrast to a "causal" account. For other interpretations, see Dinello (1971), Otten (1976), Russell (1977), Audi (1978), and Feinberg (1984a, 159–61, 172, 257–58 n. 34). On Bennett's earlier argument (1971), see Anscombe (1966, 208).

dog in the street, so that the dog died as a result, the man would not have killed it but rather let it die. He would have done nothing to bring it about that the dog would die unless he fed it" (ibid.).

Finally, Green describes a paradigm case (my Category 3) of killing that does not include refraining:

A kills B without refraining from preventing B's death if, and only if,

(1) there is a condition which is sufficient to cause B's death,
(2) A brought about c, and
(3) B dies from c.

In Category 3, A brings about the death-causing condition; there is apparently no opportunity to intervene once the lethal process is begun, and thus A, who started the process, has no choice as to whether to intervene or refrain from intervening (ibid., 196). In Category 3, one straightforwardly takes an action that results in death—for example, one gives a patient a lethal injection and there is no antidote.

In categories 1 and 2, the agent refrains from saving B, which on Green's assumption and mine is an intentional act of omission. I think Green's Category 2 should also refer to a situation where the agent *intentionally* puts the dog in the pen: the agent not only refrains from feeding the dog (in this respect the case is like an instance of letting die), the agent also intentionally brought about the condition c sufficient to cause death. The agent who intentionally administers poison and does not administer an antidote seems every bit as much a "killer" as an agent who gives a poison that has no antidote. If the agent intentionally brings about condition c, then we refer to Category 2 as an instance of killing.

We would want to distinguish Category 2, then, where the agent intentionally brings about condition c, from other cases where the agent may have played some causal role but did not intentionally bring about the death-threatening situation. For example, an agent could unintentionally give a poison to someone else; the agent would have brought about condition c but not intentionally. In this case the agent who refrained from giving the available antidote would let die. We would let Green's Category 1 (letting die) cover cases where the agent either had no causal role or, if the agent did bring about condition c, did not do so intentionally. As we see in the discussion of abortion in this chapter, the woman who plays an unintentional causal role in bringing about the pregnancy lets the fetus die if she refrains from providing it life support; she unintentionally plays a partial causal role like the person who unintentionally puts the dog in the kennel. The question, nonetheless, will be whether she has a moral responsibility to prevent its death.

Finally, to complete our modifications of Green's definitions we would perhaps want to say that in Category 3 the agent kills when the agent intentionally brings about the death-causing condition c. Thus Category 3 will be symmetrical with respect to Category 2. What we rule out in our definition of killing in Category 3 is the unintentional causing of c; we do not refer to cases where we unintentionally bring about c as instances of killing. If I give you a poison unintentionally and you die, I do not kill you; rather I brought about your death. We strain ordinary usage, but we are now talking about intentional actions in categories 1, 2, and 3.[4]

Here, then, are Green's definitions with my changes:

Category 1: A lets B die if, and only if,

(1) there is a condition c sufficient to cause B's death unless A or some other agent does something to prevent B's death from c, and A is aware that this is the case,

(2) A did not bring about c, or did not intentionally bring it about,

(3) A refrains from doing s, and

(4) B dies from c.

Category 2: A kills B when A refrains from preventing B's death if, and only if,

(1) there is a condition c sufficient to cause B's death unless A or some other agent does something s which will prevent B's death from c,

(2) A intentionally brought about c,

---

4. Green's view is that letting die (not preventing death) must be intentional (since it consists only of an act of refraining) but killing need not be; one "can do something unintentionally which causes another's death or do something intentionally which causes another's death without intending to cause death. In either case the act is unintentional killing" (1980, 197). Kuhse (1987, 48–49) argues that killing and letting die can be unintentional (when the letting die is an omission, but not a refraining). However, she suggests that for purposes of discussion both be assumed to be intentional. See her definitions, which are also adapted from Green (1987, 51). My sense is that we could use one or another set of definitions of killing and letting die (which refine ordinary usage) so long as they help us focus on the crucial distinction between initiating a deadly sequence and failing to prevent or continue to prevent some antecedent threat. For example, we could define letting die broadly as omission (omitting to aid or to continue to aid), and then consider intentional omission, i.e., refraining, as a subcategory. This would be symmetrical with Green's definition of killing, which can be either nonintentional or intentional.

(3) A refrains from doing s, and

(4) B dies from c.

Category 3: A kills B without refraining from preventing B's death if, and only if,

(1) there is a condition c sufficient to cause B's death,

(2) A intentionally brought about c, and

(3) B dies from c.

With these modifications, then, we can let Green's definitions stand as heuristic devices. Nevertheless, we would do well to make some further clarifications. First, before proceeding to questions of moral responsibility proper, exactly what falls under the letting-die category? For Green, allowing to die involves refraining; turning off the respirator is a commission that is part of a larger omission or refraining; the doctor refrains from continuing to prevent the patient's death.[5] (Both omissions and commissions are actions or doings in a broad sense.)

Not starting and stopping medical treatment, then, are both instances of letting die: "When a physician turns off the respirator he thereby refrains from continuing to prevent the patient's death and lets the patient die. . . . When, on the other hand, a physician administers a lethal injection, he does something which is sufficient to cause the patient's death and kills him" (Green 1980, 199).[6] Thus, not starting treatment is like not going to rescue someone who is drowning; stopping treatment is like breaking off a rescue; both are instances of letting die because one refrains from preventing death. Helga Kuhse (1987, 49–50) puts this point well:

> An agent can refrain from preventing death by *doing* something—
> for example, turning off an artificial respirator, removing an intrave-
> nous drip, telling the nurse not to administer antibiotics, and so on.

5. Cases of letting die as Green defines them are not confined to instances in which a disease will inevitably cause death and all one could do is "prolong" life; letting die includes cases where the death-causing disease could be cured but treatment is refused. See Audi (1978, 44 n. 1).

6. For Green, refraining seems to be a special class of omissions: ". . . a person refrains from performing an action if, and only if, he has the ability and opportunity to perform it and is aware of this but does not perform the act and is also aware of this" (1980, 197, 198). Zimmerman, on the assumption that refraining is close to or the same as intentionally omitting, says that Green's definition is too weak, for the person might be vacillating and not have come to a decision not to do the thing (1981, 549), which for Zimmerman is a necessary criterion of intentional omission.

Similarly in a non-medical setting: I can refrain from preventing the drowning swimmer's death by removing my hand that held her head above water. If I neither pushed the drowning woman in, nor in any other way positively contributed to her being in the water, I have not killed her if she drowns following the removal of my hand: I let her die. The same applies in the medical setting: if a physician turns off an artificial respirator sustaining the victim of an accident, who is unable to breathe by herself, she has not killed the patient but let her die. In turning off the respirator, the physician refrains from continuing to prevent the patient's death and allows the patient's death to occur as a causal consequence of a medical condition not of her making. The patient would have died earlier from the medical condition, for which the doctor is not causally responsible, had the doctor not halted the flow of events that would, without her intervention, have led to the patient's earlier death. It is true that the patient would not have died when she did had the doctor not turned off the respirator, but it is equally true that the doctor's refraining could only result in the patient's death because of, and in conjunction with, the patient's medical condition. Whilst turning off an artificial respirator thus involves the physician in *doing something,* it is essentially different from an act of killing, such as giving a lethal injection. When the doctor administers a lethal injection, she initiates a course of events that is, under the circumstances, sufficient to bring about death.

Second, as we see in Chapter 4 on double effect, intentionally bringing about a situation that causes death is not the same as intending the death, and this fact bears on the moral assessment of particular killings. I may bomb a military target intentionally as a means of winning a war and kill noncombatants in the process, but I do not necessarily intend the deaths of noncombatants that result from my bombing. Again, we strain ordinary usage: if I kill, I intentionally bring about a condition sufficient to cause death, but I do not necessarily intend death as end or means.[7]

Note also that one can let die without intending death itself as means or end. To fail to start, or to stop, treatment in order to avoid the suffering that the treatment causes, knowing that death will in all likelihood result, is different from aiming at death itself in order to end the patient's agony. In the former case, the treatment itself causes the suffering but ending treatment also causes the end of life; in the latter case, one has to end life

7. See note 4.

intentionally (by ceasing treatment) as the means of ending suffering caused by the disease. In both cases, however, one lets die or allows to die because one either does not start or stops the process that would have prevented death (at least temporarily).

Finally, note that in Green's definitions letting die and killing include B's actual death; the actions are defined so that they include the result.[8] In cases of letting die, however, where one refrains (intentionally) from saving B—from doing the s that will prevent B's death—it is possible that someone else could save B, and in that case B would not die; one would have refrained from saving B, but B would not in fact have been let die.[9] In the case of killing in sense 3, there is presumably no empirically available possibility of saving once the condition c is inaugurated—there is no antidote for the poison, or the speeding bullet can't be stopped. However, it is at least possible that A or someone else could intervene (Superman or Superwoman could stop the speeding bullet!), so that here as well we can distinguish between intending to take a course of action that kills and having killed. Nonetheless what we are evaluating in categories 1, 2, and 3 are intentional actions we assume will have certain results.

The Right Not to Be Killed and the Right to Be Saved

Assuming a distinction between killing and letting die, Philippa Foot says that

> justice has to do with what men *owe* each other in the way of noninterference and positive service. . . . Wherever a man acts unjustly he has infringed a right, since justice has to do with whatever a man is owed, and whatever he is owed is his as a matter of right. (1978, 44–45)

---

8. Audi says that not saving from a death-threatening cause does not entail letting die since the individual "need not die" (1978, 48–49). See also Rachels (1979, 167). Morillo (1977, 35) discusses taking "letting die" either in a "results" sense (someone dies) or in an intentional sense (someone is left to die).

9. Kuhse (1987, 77) notes that death is only a matter of probabilities in cases of killing as well as letting die.

For Foot, rights are based on the virtue of justice (1978, 3).[10] There are negative rights of noninterference, including the right not to be harmed or killed, and there are rights of positive service.[11] Rights to positive service generally arise from "contract or public arrangement"—for example, the services of doctors or firemen (1978, 46)—although she notes that children have a right to support from their parents and aged parents a right to their children's help (1978, 47):

> Where everyone may have the duty to leave someone alone, it may be that no one has the duty to maintain his life, or that only some people do. (1978, 48)

Foot thinks that the starving have a right to be fed in the sense that they have "claims" that should be considered, but they do not have a general right to which someone else's duty corresponds (1978, 46–47). There is no general right to be aided even in life-threatening situations.

There is, however, the virtue of charity "which attaches us to the good of others" (1978, 45):

> An act of charity is in question only where something is not demanded by justice. (1978, 45)

Charity overlaps with the negative and positive duties of justice, so that some actions—for example, failing to care for a parent—would be both unjust and uncharitable; but charity also goes beyond justice, leading us to refrain from harms and to provide benefits not demanded as a matter of right (1978, 44–45ff.).[12]

10. See Brock (1979, 95–98) on goal-based, duty-based, and rights-based moral theories. Duty and virtue theories can have a place for rights; but they are derivative from general principles (Donagan's respect for rational creatures) or virtues (Foot's virtue of justice).

11. My inclination following Gewirth (1978) is to take life as a species of well-being (in contrast to freedom) in respect to which one has a certain negative and a certain positive right. Others would posit a basic right of sovereignty or self-determination that covers bodily integrity as well as liberty of action; one has a right to noninterference (or to aid) in these two respects.

12. Green claims that obligations in regard to killing and letting die depend on considerations such as justice and charity (and not on "inherent features of the killing–letting-die distinction") (1980, 201), but he challenges Foot's view that there are "general noncontingent connections" (1980, 200). As regards charity, Green takes Foot to say that ordinarily—that is, given a minimum of basic goods and the absence of evil such as intractable pain due to illness—life is a good. But Green's view is that there is no minimum that grounds a noncontingent connection between life and good (1980, 200); whether life is a good depends on how various things are valued. Thus presumably there is no noncontingent connection between charity (which promotes good) and life. But the right to aid could be noncontingently connected to life if the right is so defined; the right holder who does not find life good could

Is charity optional? At one point Foot says that we can extend the notion of duty to include what we should do for others out of charity as well as from rights to positive service (1978, 27). This would seem to make charity required, on the assumption that what is a duty is not optional. Nonetheless, she says (1978, 27) that duties of charity are "owed only in a rather loose sense, and some acts of charity could hardly be said to be *owed* at all." Perhaps she means that charity is required when it overlaps with justice, but in other cases it is not. If charity were required for any range of actions, and it were a duty, it could still be distinguished, however, from the sort of duty that is a matter of justice and hence of rights.

Similarly Judith Thomson assumes that what one ought to do out of kindness or "Minimally Decent Samaritanism" is something distinct from rights, and hence, I assume, justice. She is willing to acknowledge, in addition to the right to life (the negative right not to be killed) and rights we confer on others by pledging or promising our help, an "ought" of Minimally Decent Samaritanism—for instance, one ought to give someone lifesaving aid if the aid can be provided at a very low cost to oneself (if pregnancy lasted only a week, or if all it would take to save my life would be Henry Fonda crossing a room "to place a hand briefly on my brow") (1984, 182, 183). (Let us use "Minimal Samaritanism" as shorthand for Thomson's phrase.) I take Thomson to be saying perhaps that Minimal Samaritanism is something required, although not based on a right, in contrast to Good—or even Splendid—Samaritanism which is supererogatory (1984, 184–85). Or she could mean that Minimal Samaritanism is something one ought to do—there are good reasons for being kind—but not something required at all; on this reading, even Minimal Samaritanism is optional. In any case, Minimal Samaritanism is not a right to a benefit subject to fair or just distribution; even if it is not optional, it falls outside the sphere of justice.[13]

---

waive the right. As regards justice, Green insists that in light of the right not to be injured or killed it would be "unjust to take the life of an innocent man against his will" (1980, 200–201), but because some people do not want to live, the relation between justice and killing is contingent. I would again express Green's moral point as the agent's ability to waive the right. The right itself would thus not depend on the agent's particular wants, and thus Foot is correct to say that the connection between justice and killing is noncontingent. Noncontingency does not signify that the meaning of the right is immune from revision; the connections are noncontingent given certain concepts of the rights. On the sense in which one can violate someone's right "without harming him, and even in doing good," see Foot (1981, 159).

13. Melden (1977, 17) also does not think others generally have a right to our aid; we don't blame those who are unkind in the same way that we blame those who violate rights (23–24). See also Murphy (1973) who holds we have a right to noninterference but not to aid; following Kant, Murphy sees the former as a "perfect" duty, the latter as "imperfect"; one does not have a right even to be saved from attack.

Thomson gives two reasons why Minimal Samaritanism is not a right. First, we should distinguish situations in which, for example, two boys are given a box of chocolates and each has "clear title to half," and situations in which the box is given to one boy who may be "greedy, stingy, callous—but not unjust" if he does not share. Second, if we call Minimal Samaritanism a right, then we make having a right to something depend on how easy it is to provide it. But rights, she says, should not depend on how hard it is to respect them (1984, 183). Do I really have a right to be saved if the rescuer should help only when it can be done with minimal inconvenience?

The force of the chocolate box analogy, however, depends on whether we assume that no one has a general "title" to aid from any one else. Thomson assumes that a right to be aided derives only from specific promises or gifts. But if certain of our resources were not morally regarded as our private possessions but held jointly with others, then it could be that others have a title or right to our aid. The resources with which we could aid others could be like the chocolate box given to both boys, rather than the private possession of one. Moreover, even if resources are privately and justly owned, we could still have a duty to use part of our resources to help others get or keep basic goods; the duty to save could be derived from this general "right to positive service." If the boy who had no chocolate needed it for health or life, not merely to increase happiness, then the one who had more than he needed could have a duty to help.

And as for the objection that having a right to something should not depend on the difficulty of providing it, it seems to me that Thomson's intuition can be saved but one can still speak of a general right to aid. Once the level or cost of aid is decided, then agents have a right to that level of aid; no further deliberations about difficulty are required; one has a right to aid of that sort. Yet if Thomson still objects that rights are rights to something, without regard to what it costs the one who upholds the right, then I would respond as follows. Even negative rights presuppose judgments about costs and how they should be distributed.[14] If my taking one of your kidneys (without your consent) to save my life is prohibited because of your rights, then a particular version of the right to bodily integrity has been assumed. Not only your life but your bodily parts are protected; you

14. Kagan (1989) claims that if one cannot independently justify constraints against doing harm, then any view that limits aid only on grounds of its cost to the giver would be committed to an option to do harm, for refraining from harm can be costly. As Kagan argues, the limitation on giving is usually supplemented by an independent constraint on doing harm. Kagan examines various justifications for the constraint and finds them wanting. See the Conclusion.

are not required to sacrifice your organ to save me; I must bear the cost of respecting your right, as it were. The reason the right-holder has a right to something without regard apparently to how much it costs to respect it is that the definition of the right already incorporates a judgment about which costs are and are not required in order to aid others.[15] Thus negative rights also rest on assumptions about costs to the one who has the right and the one who respects it.

I speak, therefore, in contrast to both Foot and Thomson, of a right to be saved as well as a right not to be killed. I opt here for that strand of Western tradition that puts such aid under the rubric of justice. Even if there is a distinctly different moral dimension of love or caring, I am going to assume that we have a general right to be aided, over and above any specific rights based, for example, on contracts or promises, at least where certain basic goods such as life are at stake. At the very least I would insist that we are *required* to give lifesaving aid. And I want to posit a *right* to such aid because I argue subsequently that agents are not wrongly allowed to die when they refuse lifesaving treatment. A right, as I use the term, is in Joel Feinberg's (1980b) terminology "discretionary" and not merely "mandatory"; it not only signifies that others have a duty toward you, but that you can waive their fulfillment of that duty.[16]

I do not attempt to provide the grounding for this right. It may be that an actual convention or agreement based on reciprocal self-interest is the only feasible basis for such a right (see Reeder 1982). Alan Gewirth (1978) attempts to ground the right to be rescued on the same requirements of agency and reason that establish negative rights. Perhaps Foot's virtue of justice could be expanded to include it. It could even be interpreted along with the right not to be killed as an expression of charity or love, understood as the foundational virtue (see Dyck 1972; Reeder 1992). No matter how the right is justified, we must still draw a firm distinction between "what we owe people in the form of aid and what we owe them in the way of noninterference" (Foot 1978, 27). This distinction is drawn *within* the sphere of justice.

15. Feinberg (1984, 126, 132–33, 140, 162–63) endorses and defends a right to aid when "without unreasonable cost or risk to oneself or others," one can prevent "harm, or an increased degree of harm." Those who deny a right to aid based on justice, Feinberg believes, have confused advancing someone's interests beyond the status quo ante (conferring a benefit in this special sense) and preventing a drastic fall below it (1984, 135–36); Feinberg treats the former as benevolence which should not be legally required, but the latter (a "benefit" only in the general sense of favorably affecting interests) as a matter of justice and properly the subject of legal regulation.

16. For the view that aid is an obligation or duty see Arthur (1977); cf. Aiken (1977). Cf. Davis (1988, 320–21) on the distinction between rights and decency, and Cahill (1984, 267) on a duty to help not based on a promise or contract.

Thomson on Abortion

Let us look at Thomson's view of abortion to see how the distinction between interference and aid applies to this crucial case. The duty not to kill pertains to certain instances of what in the last section I call "killing." Although a failure to save may not necessarily result in death (someone else may intervene or condition c may not in fact be lethal), the duty to save is a duty in certain circumstances not to refrain from the action that could prevent death. I am trying to decide when killing and not saving are wrong—when killing, in other words, is a prohibited form of interference and saving is a required form of positive service.

Thomson's interpretation of abortion incorporates a distinction between the negative right to life (the right not to be killed) and any positive right the fetus might have to life support. Thomson argues that the issue is whether the woman owes the fetus life support, not whether she violates its right not to be killed. She assumes for the sake of argument that the fetus is a moral person who has such a right. She wants to show the conservative that even if the fetus is a moral person with the right to life, that right is not violated under certain conditions when the woman withdraws her life support, for the woman has a right to decide "what happens in and to her body."

Her argument goes as follows. Abortion is not a matter of violating a fetus's right to life (the right not to be killed), but of withdrawing aid. In cases of rape and contraceptive failure (nonintentional pregnancy), where the woman has not committed herself to bear the fetus (conferred on it a special right to aid), she does not violate any right of the fetus to aid.[17] What the woman does is morally parallel to pulling the plug on a famous violinist:

> You wake up in the morning and find yourself back to back in bed with an unconscious violinist. He has been found to have a fatal kidney ailment, and the Society of Music Lovers has canvassed all the available medical records and found that you alone have the right blood type to help. They have therefore kidnapped you, and

---

17. Cf. Kamm (1992, 90) on whether voluntary pregnancy creates responsibility. See also Wicclair (1981, 342), who challenges the view that the woman has, on the basis of their role in her biological system, a "permanent and exclusive right of ownership" over the bodily parts that also sustain the unborn. Thomson, I believe, does not assimilate the woman's right over her body to a property right, but even if she did, it could still be the case that the woman had a duty to use her property to provide for the fetus. Nonetheless Wicclair raises the important issue of the nature and justification of the claim-right Thomson posits.

last night the violinist's circulatory system was plugged into yours, so that your kidneys can be used to extract poisons from his blood as well as your own. The director of the hospital now tells you, "Look, we're sorry the Society of Music Lovers did this to you— we would never have permitted it if we had known. But still, they did it, and the violinist now is plugged into you. To unplug him would be to kill him. But never mind, it's only for nine months. By then he will have recovered from his ailment, and can safely be unplugged from you." (1984, 174)

Thomson speaks of not "killing" the unborn unjustly, but on my definitions she can be read as saying that the woman lets the fetus die; and she in fact says that if the fetus can be removed without it dying, one must do so, for the woman is only entitled to separate it from her life-support system, not to ensure that it dies. Thus Thomson argues that unless the woman has intentionally become pregnant and hence committed herself, in the sense of a promise or pledge, to bearing the fetus, no right to aid is infringed.[18] Moreover, she also argues that the independent consideration of Minimal Samaritanism calls for a low level of aid that does not extend to the cost of pregnancy.[19]

I would amend Thomson's view, as noted in the previous section, by

18. Thomson, I believe, argues that either intentional pregnancy (inviting the people-seed)—which is like a pledge, promise, or commitment—or the failure to take reasonable precautions, places a special obligation on the woman, that is, confers a special right of assistance on the fetus. She does not in her classic paper, however, deal with conditions that might be attached to such commitments, for example, whether the obligation ceases if the pregnancy becomes life-threatening. My sense is she would assume such a condition. She did not deal as well with the question, regarding intentional pregnancy, whether the woman can change her mind, that is, whether the commitment however defined is revocable or irrevocable. The example of a desire to abort in the seventh month in order not to postpone a trip is introduced as a failure of Minimal Samaritanism (1984, 186–87).

19. Michaels (1984) argues that in our society there are moral and legal duties at the level of cost of Good Samaritanism, for example, the moral and legal duty to defend one's country (1984, 216ff.). Michaels (1984, 220–21) notes that the cost to both woman and fetus must be considered and observes that in many cases aid at great cost is not required in order to bring the fetus to term. Michaels, however, agrees finally with MacIntyre (1984) that we do not have a "moral community"; we lack a "clear, let alone shared, sense of our obligations to one another" (Michaels 1984, 223). For an attempt to show that U.S. law does not require rescue at great cost, and an argument that on equal protection grounds women should not have to help the fetus in cases of rape or contraceptive failure, see Regan (1979). Cf. Ramsey (1973, 225) on Grisez's (1970b, 343) view, directed against Thomson, that not to bear could be a failure of an "obligation . . . to do good to another when we can and there is no serious reason not to do it." For objections to "'Good Samaritan'" approaches, see Davis (1993, 750–55).

adding a general right to lifesaving aid. The violinist example is supposed to show that the violinist has no right to aid because no voluntary commitment was made. Strictly speaking, however, the violinist example only shows us a case where no special right to aid created by a voluntary commitment exists. It could still be the case that there is a general right to aid. Even if there were, however, the cost required of the giver could still be minimal and hence not extend to pregnancy.

Let us now look at major objections to Thomson's views. First, do not some abortions "kill"?[20] My sense is that some methods of abortion do "kill."[21] Some methods of abortion are more like strangling a drowning swimmer (who hangs on your neck or shoulders, and hence threatens your own life) than they are like pushing off the swimmer's arms.[22] When one pushes the swimmer away, one lets the swimmer die, like removing a patient from a respirator; but to deny the swimmer your help you may have to kill. Even where the woman kills, however, Thomson can still argue that the right not to be killed is not violated. If I have no duty to help the drowning swimmer, either because I did not commit myself to help or because the cost exceeds what the general right to be aided requires, I can kill if necessary to avoid giving aid. Even if Thomson were to admit a general right to aid she could still say that if saving someone demands my life, I am entitled not only to withdraw aid and let die, but to kill if necessary because the cost is too great in either case. And if I do not unjustly

20. Foot (1984, 184–85) argues against Thomson that the woman does not fail to save but originates a fatal sequence in the act of abortion, as opposed to cases where we allow to continue a fatal sequence we did not begin. Foot would be right to say that some abortion procedures initiate a new "fatal sequence," but I do not think that Thomson's moral argument need be limited to removing or detaching the fetus which then dies, in contrast to "killing" in order to remove. Cf. Brody (1975, 29–30) and Devine (1978, 109ff.). Cf. also McMahan (1993, 269ff.), who responds as follows to Foot's objection to Thomson that abortion is not a letting die but a killing, since it originates a fatal sequence and does not merely remove a barrier to an antecedent threat: there are cases where someone "naturally" needs help on an ongoing basis, rather than being exposed to a "distinct" or "deviant" threat; for example, children need this sort of aid and so does the fetus; thus, one can let a child or a fetus die.
21. See Kamm (1992, 21–22, 82) who distinguishes four sorts of abortions. First, the fetus is simply removed but dies without support; second, a solution ejects the fetus, and in the process kills it; third, as in the craniotomy, the fetus is attacked but its death is not intended as the means; fourth, the death is intended. See McMahan (1993, 268) on the distinction between abortions that kill and "extractive" abortions that let die.
22. Cf. Kamm (1992, 22ff.; 84–86, passim) who argues that it is sometimes permissible to kill to avoid saving as well as to let die. See also her discussion (1992, 75) of Brody's objection (1972) and Thomson's reply (1973). On the case for pushing away the drowning swimmer, see McMahan (1993, 251–52) and Malm (1989, 254–55) to whom McMahan refers (1993, 252 n. 5).

kill, I do not violate the right to life.[23] As I argue in Chapter 3 ("The Pursuer"), the fetus who must be killed lest the woman bear an unjust burden (assuming Thomson's view of positive duties and their extent), has in effect become an involuntary threat whose demand on the woman's resources exceeds what she owes; the fetus cannot be merely removed or separated from those resources; now the death of the fetus must be procured in order to effect the separation.

Killing could also be justified when the cost is less than life, assuming that only minimal help is required. Compare another swimming case. You have gotten your hands on my shoulders, but this does not threaten my life. It does mean, however, that I must stand on a bed of sharp coral. To save you, I will have to suffer severe injuries. I am a dancer and saving you will not only cause me pain and inconvenience, but very likely damage my career. If killing this swimmer is justified, then *ceteris paribus* so is killing the fetus when it demands more aid than the woman owes. Thus, so far there is no obstacle to Thomson's thesis that a woman can withdraw aid or even kill the fetus. If the woman could not simply unplug the violinist, he too could be killed.

Another objection to Thomson's thesis is this: the woman is kidnapped in the violinist example, and hence that case is parallel only to rape where the sexual act that put the fetus in its dependent position is not voluntary; hence no special right has been granted. (I assume that most cases of incest are also coercive.) However, although the pregnancy in cases of contraceptive failure is unintentional, say the critics, the sex act presumably is voluntary and the voluntary sex act confers on the fetus a special right of support. Because the sex act was voluntary, the woman is not entitled to let die *or* kill.[24] Where the sex is voluntary, say the critics, there is a special moral responsibility or obligation for the pregnancy. The critic, in sum, grants to

23. Parent (1980) notes that Thomson abandoned the "moral specification" view of the right to life (the right to life is the right not to be killed unjustly) used in her 1971 abortion essay in favor of the idea that rights are sometimes justifiably infringed but not violated (Thomson 1976). See Chapter 5 for further discussion.

24. Lichtenberg (1982, 32) and Russell (1977, 92–93) argue that if one "nonnegligently" and "accidentally" endangers someone, one has no special moral responsibility, no greater duty to prevent harm than anyone else does. Carrier, however, argues being "partly responsible" and being the only one who can help creates an obligation to help (1975, 388–89). Nicholson also argues against Thomson that a voluntary act of sexual intercourse commits the individual to a special duty to provide bodily assistance (1978, 55, 57, 59–60) because one causes the fetus to be in the dependent position. In the case of rape, however, the act is not voluntary and no such duty is owed (1978, 50ff.). Cf. Camenish (1976, 137–38) and Meilaender (1987, ch. 5). See Feinberg and Levenbook (1993, 224–45) and Kamm (1992) for a detailed and illuminating dissection of these issues.

Thomson that in rape the woman is coerced not only into helping but also into creating (along with the rapist) the need for help (the violinist in contrast already needed help before the kidnapping); the critic also grants that because of the coercion no special responsibility is created. The critic insists, however, that when sex is voluntary the woman's partial causal responsibility creates a special obligation.

Mary Anne Warren puts the principle this way:

> There is room for the anti-abortionist to argue that in the normal case of unwanted pregnancy a woman has, by her own actions, assumed responsibility for the fetus. For if x behaves in a way which he could have avoided, and which he knows involves, let us say, a 1 percent chance of bringing into existence a human being, with a right to life, and does so knowing that if this should happen then that human being will perish unless x does certain things to keep him alive, then it is by no means clear that when it does happen x is free of any obligation to what he knew in advance would be required to keep that human being alive. (1984, 107–8)

The issue, then, is whether voluntary sex confers a special positive right to support on the unborn (considered as a moral person with the right to life in the negative sense).

Warren suggests another case as an analogy to unintentional pregnancy:

> Suppose, then, that violinists are peculiarly prone to the sort of illness the only cure for which is the use of someone else's bloodstream for nine months, and that because of this there has been formed a society of music lovers who agree that whenever a violinist is stricken they will draw lots and the loser will, by some means, be made the one and only person capable of saving him. Now then, would you be obligated to cooperate in curing the violinist if you had voluntarily joined this society, knowing the possible consequences, and then your name had been drawn and you had been kidnapped? Admittedly, you did not promise ahead of time that you would, but you did deliberately place yourself in a position in which it might happen that a human life would be lost if you did not. Surely this is at least a prima facie reason for supposing that you have an obligation to stay in bed with the violinist. (1984, 108)

Warren says that the music lovers did not "promise" to bear the burden if the lot fell their way. What then is the basis of the obligation? That you agree? Just the fact that you put yourself voluntarily into a situation (you "agree" to the lottery) where whether someone lives might depend on you, seems to be sufficient to create a prima facie obligation. Warren says that in any case this situation is unlike the case of the unborn in one important respect, namely, that it is a matter of helping or not helping an existing person, not of bringing one into being. The woman takes a chance of bringing a person into existence who will be dependent on her and only her for survival.

However, does this difference, she asks, make a moral difference? Would it *lessen* the woman's responsibility? Warren returns to her original "intuition":

> My own intuition, however, is that x has no more right to bring into existence, either deliberately or as a foreseeable result of actions he could have avoided, a being with full moral rights (y), and then refuse to do what he knew beforehand would be required to keep that being alive, than he has to enter into an agreement with an existing person, whereby he may be called upon to save that person's life, and then refuse to do so when so called upon. Thus, x's responsibility for y's existence does not seem to lessen his obligation to keep y alive, if he is also responsible for y's being in a situation in which only he can save him. (1984, 109)

She correctly sees that the issue is whether, if through a voluntary act you play some causal role such that a person becomes dependent on you and only you for survival, you incur a special responsibility, that is, you confer a right on that person to your help. Warren thinks you do, but has no explanation why. The crucial point seems to be not that someone is brought into existence but that someone is made solely dependent on someone else for survival.

For Thomson, of course, positive rights are created only by voluntary commitments.[25] Rape is the most obvious case (parallel to a person kid-

---

25. According to Gibson, Thomson argues in her abortion essay that the right to life is a right not to be killed unjustly; the fetus is aborted and hence killed unjustly if and only if it has a right to the woman's body; some fetuses don't have such a right, and hence some fetuses don't have a right to life; thus Thomson's version of the right to life is inconsistent with the conservative's premise that all persons (including fetuses) have the right to life (1984, 134; cf. 136–37). Thomson in my interpretation wants to say that the right to life does not include a positive right to what one needs to live; one does not have that sort of right unless others have undertaken some special obligation to provide it. Thus if no such right exists, it does no injustice to the fetus under certain conditions if it is aborted (removed from the womb) and dies as a result; the negative right to life is not violated. I also argue that even if the fetus must be killed in some circumstances, Thomson can still argue that the *right* not to be killed has not been violated.

napped and hooked up to the violinist) where the woman has not committed herself. Thomson also argues that no commitment has been made when "reasonable precautions" have been used; you have no obligation to let people-seeds grow in your house if you have put the best screen you can find on your windows. Thomson admits that in contraceptive failure the woman had a causal role in bringing about the fetus's existence in a condition where it cannot survive on its own. But her conviction is that if reasonable precautions are taken (the pregnancy is unintentional), the woman's partial causal responsibility does not confer any special right to be helped.

My view is that Thomson is correct. Even if by one's voluntary non-negligent action one unintentionally makes someone else dependent for life support (whether they previously existed or not), one does not confer a special right above and beyond the general duty to aid. Consider another case. You voluntarily drive on the highway often; you take all reasonable precautions to keep your car in good shape; however, on one occasion your brakes fail and you hit another car causing it to go off the road and to burst into flames; someone is inside the car but cannot get out without your help. Does the partial causal role of the driver whose brakes fail confer a special right to be rescued on the person in the car? My intuition is that it does not. If there is a general right to be rescued then it applies, but the driver's causal responsibility does not confer a special right of support. The driver owes no more than if someone else's car had caused the accident.[26]

The assumption here is that sex and driving, like opening the window to get air in Thomson's people-seed example, are activities that do not in themselves, because they are especially risky, create special responsibilities for untoward consequences for others who have not assumed similar risks (in contrast, see the discussion of potholing in Chapter 2). The objection could be raised, however, that the fetus is not sufficiently like the person in the car who needs to be rescued. The person is not at fault but he or she at least took the risk of driving or riding as an intentional agent. To strengthen the driving example, therefore, the case could be altered so that the one to be rescued is an infant, who owes its presence in the burning car to the purposive activities of others.[27] If one's view is still that no special

26. See Kamm's (1992, 61, 95–96, 178) use of a similar driving analogy. Here, unlike the case of the violinist, the innocent party would not need help were it not for our car. Hence if not aided the innocent dies, it is made worse-off than it would have been were it not for the accident. See also Kagan (1988a) on the issues regarding the idea that "the person who harms another has a special obligation to correct the harm. . . ."

27. I owe this objection and suggestion to George Damoflis. A defender of Thomson (against the Warren view that voluntary sex creates a special duty) might also argue that no special obligation should fall on the woman since the man also participated in the sex. Warren and others who make the voluntary-sex-creates-responsibility argument could reply in turn, however, that both parties have obligations, although in the nature of the case now they are not

obligation is created, then *mutatis mutandis* partial causal responsibility for pregnancy would not create a special obligation either. Even if the person in the burning car will be worse-off if you do not help than he or she would have been if the accident had not occurred, the argument is that for a range of ordinary activities we do not incur special responsibilities for unintended consequences simply because we have a partial role in creating the situation in which someone needs our help.[28] To uphold Thomson's assimilation of rape and unintentional pregnancy, one has to argue, then, that no special responsibilities are created simply because unintentionally one plays a causal role in the creation of a situation where a person needs our aid.

Even if Warren were correct, however, the woman would not necessarily have a duty to bear the child if doing so would cost her life.[29] It would be open to Thomson still to insist that any right the unborn acquires through voluntary intercourse would not require the sacrifice of her life. For example, suppose Thomson granted that the unborn acquires a right to use the woman's body because of her voluntary intercourse. During the course of the pregnancy the woman develops hypertension so that to continue the pregnancy will endanger her life; the unborn can endanger the woman not only through its movements, but through its very presence. To those who believe that voluntary intercourse confers a special right to life support (makes the woman "responsible" to bear the child) Thomson could propose an exception where pregnancy will cost the woman's life.[30]

(unfortunately) equally burdensome. Should technology someday allow men to bear children (transplanted uterus and fertilized egg), then presumably some just procedure for assigning the duty could be devised.

28. Trammel (1975, 135; see also 1978; 1979; 1980) argues that "the more directly involved X is for Y's needing to be saved, the more responsible X is for helping to rescue Y." See Kuhse's critique (1987, 74–80). Note the complexity of the factors here—both how the need arises and how the helper comes to help, where human causes are concerned, can be described as voluntary or coerced, and intentional or unintentional. Note also how careful one has to be in speaking about whether someone who is not aided is "worse-off": If aid once given is removed, then the person is no worse off than before the aid was given relative to the condition in which they need aid, but in another sense, if aid is not given, then the person is worse-off relative to their condition before the accident. One factor relevant to the revocation of a commitment is whether if you initially help and then withdraw you make it difficult or impossible for others to step in; thus in this additional sense, to be aided, then to have aid withdrawn, could make a person "worse-off." See Kamm (1992) on these complexities.

29. Some interpreters see "self-defense" as an argument independent of Thomson's basic points about rights and Minimal Samaritanism. See Gibson (1984, 132–33). On my interpretation, however, she intends the "trapped in a tiny house" case to fall under her major rubrics. See Thomson (1984, 177) on the case where the one who helps the violinist will die; see also (1984, 178–79).

30. On not giving up life and limb to save a newborn (*a fortiori* the unborn), even when one intentionally creates it, see Kamm (1982, 113–14).

Suppose a critic argued that voluntary intercourse with reasonable precautions may not confer a special right to life support, but at least *extends* what the woman ought generally to give by way of aid. Substantively these come to the same thing, but the critic may think it important to distinguish the idea that a special right is created from the notion that what one ought generally to do for others varies according to the voluntary causal role one has played in bringing about the situation. Although the woman did not intentionally cause the situation, the intercourse was voluntary and therefore the woman should give more than she ordinarily would. The woman should do more than the general right to be aided usually requires.

My view is that the contingency of being a partial cause of a person's being in need of aid (by way of one's voluntary but not negligent action) does not increase the cost the rescuer should undergo. To return to the car example, I owe no more to the person in this car by way of a general right to aid than I would owe if I had simply come across a burning car. I would not require of the driver whose brakes failed *more* than the ordinary duty. As long as we include driving or riding in the ordinary activities of life, as opposed to other situations where one takes special risks that lessen the duty of others or increase one's own, then the cases are symmetrical. Partial causal responsibility through nonnegligent voluntary action does not remove the events from the natural lottery, and thus only the ordinary level of aid is required. I conclude that voluntary intercourse with reasonable precautions does not increase the cost of aid owed. Thomson could say, moreover, that even if one's duty were increased in cases where one plays a causal role, there is no reason to suppose that the increase would extend all the way to comparable cost, that is, the woman's life.

Does negligence either create a special right or increase the amount of aid ordinarily owed? Consider a couple who are negligent about contraception, who we do not excuse because of age or other mitigating factors, and who either out of culpable ignorance, or out of indifference or recklessness (see Feinberg and Levenbook 1993, 223), do not take reasonable precautions to avoid unintended effects. My sense is that a failure to take reasonable precautions does increase responsibility whether we express this as a special right or an increase in the aid we should ordinarily provide. If the standard of aid is low, then negligence perhaps could require help up to comparable cost to the giver; if the standard is high, even already at the up-to-comparable cost level, then negligence could increase responsibility to a level at or beyond comparable cost. For example, if I negligently brought a child to swim in a dangerous place, I might feel that I should even give my life if the child gets in danger.

I propose, then, a general right to aid, but I defend Thomson against the objection that some abortions are killings, and the objection that causal responsibility through voluntary action, that is, voluntary sex, either imposes a special right to aid, or increases what we should do by way of a general right to aid. The remaining issue, however, whether or not we introduce a *right* to lifesaving aid, is the standard of aid required. Even if one continues to distinguish Samaritanism from a right as Foot and Thomson do, the further question is whether the "minimal" standard is correct. It could be that Henry Fonda ought to come from California, and not merely from across the room, to put his hand on one's fevered brow; since it is the fetus's life that is at stake, perhaps the woman should bring it to term. A high standard of Samaritanism would presumably *ceteris paribus* require pregnancy with all its costs in order to save life. At what cost then to oneself should one aid others?

Thomson could argue, correctly, it seems to me, that rape nullifies the duty to aid (wherever the level is set); one need not stay hooked up to the violinist even for a minimal period. But for cases of contraceptive failure (voluntary sex, but unintentional pregnancy), the woman is in the position, *mutatis mutandis,* of the driver of the car whose brakes fail and who finds himself or herself in the position of being the only one who can help the victim of the accident he or she unintentionally caused. One could argue that if the driver had been kidnapped, parallel to rape, the general duty to aid would be nullified; but where the driver's driving is voluntary, then the question is the *level* of aid owed: at what cost should the driver extract the victim from the burning car? At what cost should the woman aid the fetus?

Here we see some traditions draw apart. Thomson's strong negative right and minimal standard of aid can be explained, for instance, by Gilbert Harman's (1977) theory of morality as a system of actual conventions based on reciprocal self-interest. Even the wealthy and powerful need strong negative rights, but they need aid much less than the poor and weak do; a minimal standard of aid is a plausible compromise (see Reeder 1982). For Alan Gewirth (1978), however, rights are based on what any agent needs regardless of the natural or social lottery. Thus, if any agent needs, wants, and claims from others not only noninterference but provision for aid, in order to have basic freedom and well-being, then a stronger doctrine of aid can be expected; regardless of their place in the natural and social lottery, agents will want there to be a duty to give aid up to the level of comparable cost so that the freedom and well-being of all are equally enhanced. The determination, then, of the standard of aid will depend on how we try to justify the rights or duties we acknowledge. I favor, although I cannot defend it here, a high standard of aid: roughly, we should be prepared to redistribute our resources, our bodies, or our property so that others have essential goods such as life, up to the point of comparable cost to ourselves. For my purposes here, however, the question of the standard of aid can be left open. Even a low standard, as I note subsequently, would require more aid to the starving, for example, than many give. Furthermore, some people may acknowledge a more onerous standard where property is concerned, perhaps even up to comparable cost, while not accepting a similar standard for bodily injury, for example, the gift of a kidney or limb (see Chapter 4 where I discuss a paralysis example). In any case, the consensus insists that giving life is not required.

In conclusion, Thomson attempts to determine what a woman might owe the unborn by way of a special right to positive service or what Minimal Samaritanism calls for. Her discussion assumes that the unborn is parasitic or dependent on the woman; the unborn needs help to survive. Thus Thomson seems to be emphasizing an aspect of what Davis calls the "asymmetry" between the fetus and woman (Davis 1984a, 205ff.). For Thomson there is symmetry as well and it resides in the fact that rights and Minimal Samaritanism apply (by hypothesis) to them both as moral persons. Thus, Thomson's argument handles the fetus's dependence as a feature of a particular case, as opposed to a moral view that in light of that dependence would not grant the same moral status to fetus and woman. Thomson is chiefly dealing with appropriations of aid where the woman has not committed herself to help (and hence in her view no special right to aid has been established), and where the aid needed goes beyond the standard of Minimal Samaritanism. I defend her view that no special right is created without the woman's commitment (in cases of contraceptive failure as well as rape) and argue that the woman is entitled to kill as well as let die. I posit, however, a general right to aid as opposed to a nonrequired "ought" or even a duty not correlated to a right, and I suggest that a high standard of aid would presumably *ceteris paribus* require pregnancy.

If a higher standard of aid were assumed, one that would require pregnancy, and no other considerations override Samaritanism in a particular case, then Thomson's attempt to deal with the conservative by assuming moral status would fail. Warren argues that since voluntary sex seems to create a special responsibility, the defender of abortion in cases of nonnegligent unintentional pregnancy has no option but to deal with the question of the moral status of the fetus. Thomson's argument is vulnerable, however, not in what she says about special responsibilities, but in her view of aid as *minimal* Samaritanism. If the fetus is attributed full moral status (as Thomson does for the sake of argument) *and* if a standard of aid were assumed that extends to the costs of pregnancy, and if *ceteris paribus* obtains, then Thomson's argument would not work, at least for nonnegligent unintentional pregnancy; she would be forced, as Warren argues, but for a different reason, back to the question of moral status (see the Appendix).

Thomson, however, could try to avoid going back to the question of moral status—and hence to continue to address conservatives who assume it—by saying more about aid. Since she does not posit a general *right* to aid, as I suggested adding, her reply could take the form of a development of her view of Samaritanism. In order to rebut the objection that the standard of aid is too minimal, she could reply as follows: Following Carol Gilligan (1982), Samaritanism is a distinct sort of moral perspective that others call caring or love, and it may well be more demanding than the Minimally Decent standard. Samaritanism or caring leads the woman to want *ceteris paribus* to nurture, to give the life-sustaining resources of her body to the fetus (still assuming full status for the sake of argument). Caring leads one to want to care, whether the fetus is seen simply as anyone (as Thomson's Samaritanism example suggests) or already as a particular person. Yet caring, Thomson could say, involves one in multiple responsibilities; one cares for many others (strangers and particular persons) and one legitimately cares for the self. The fetus's life is at stake but important goods relevant for the quality of life of self and others (including the fetus) may also be at risk. Thus to say that the standard should be more than minimal does not decide the question whether to sustain a particular fetus or not. Moreover, Thomson might continue, there is no metaprinciple to decide how one should balance various responsibilities; each woman has to work out which responsibilities to fulfill and which not.

Furthermore, Thomson could add, even if one posits a general *right* to aid and argues for more than a minimal standard, the duty is still not decisive. The thrust of the reply regarding Samaritanism would also apply to duties of justice. In addition to the crucial question of cost to the self, there is the possibility of a web of duties to help others (the near and dear, or the stranger), the performance of which would be compromised if the woman extends lifesaving support to a fetus. Even on the supposition that these duties involve only the quality of life and not life-sustaining aid itself, it cannot be assumed, Thomson could argue, that a set of duties to others would never outweigh the general duty to render lifesaving aid. Thus whether a more demanding standard is assumed on the side of justice or Samaritanism, no conclusion regarding abortion could be reached without some notion of how to deal with multiple duties. I mention these matters again in regard to aiding the starving, but there, too, I will have to leave this issue for another day (cf. Dworkin [1993], 56–60).

The Precedence of the Right Not to Be Killed

I want to maintain a right to aid, in any case, however the question of the standard is settled. Yet what of cases where to save life one would have to take it? Following Foot I want to maintain that the right not to be killed takes precedence over the duty to save; in this sense the negative right is more stringent or "stricter" (Foot 1978, 29).[31] For Foot, the negative duty not to kill overrides any positive duty of justice to save, and it also overrides charity, when the types of considerations conflict. To use Foot's well-known example:

> If we consider killing a man in order to use his body to save [five] others, we are thinking of doing him an injury to bring others aid. (1978, 28)

The precedence of the negative right can be expressed either by saying that it overrides the duty to save or by saying that the duty to save does not obtain when the right not to be killed would have to be violated to fulfill it; the five patients in Foot's example who need new organs have a right to be saved, but that is defined or specified so that the aid owed does not include cutting up a healthy patient; the patients have a right to be saved in a morally permissible way.[32] As I proceed, my aim generally is to qualify the meaning of the rights and duties in question, but in the discussion of precedence ahead it is sometimes clearer to say that one duty or right overrides another.

Why should this precedence obtain? Foot makes a deep moral assumption: our bodies (or at least the fatal use thereof) are not to be considered simply as resources for the good of others; a fence of protection is erected around the individual. We often need and want help but the bodies of others should not be fatally used, without their consent, to provide that help. Thus, whether aid is construed only as an "ought" of charity or as a right, these norms are "limited," as Foot puts it, by the negative right of noninterference.

Some representatives of the natural rights tradition would say that we have a duty to provide aid only at the level of Minimal Samaritanism. Others—for example, Gewirth—would presumably argue that the right to

31. Foot says that the obligation to aid cannot be discharged when the means is not a moral possibility (1983a, 384, 389). On "precedence," see Meilaender (1987, ch. 6) and Quinn (1989a).

32. It is precisely such a decision that Harris's two dying patients who need organs to live, and advocate a lottery to select a donor, would reject (1980b, 150).

be aided would require me to give one of my kidneys to save your life. Aid should be given not only when it costs a little, but when it costs a lot; we should give up to the level of comparable cost to ourselves. For Gewirth, however, I am not required to give my life (to give two kidneys) even if *two* other persons could be saved. I am not required to make this sacrifice even to save others from the same loss.[33] I am not required to sacrifice my life for others, and no one has the right to sacrifice me. If we were to kill some to save a much greater number, then we would have required each of them to suffer in order to save others from a similar loss; this would exceed even Gewirth's standard. If I can live (I am lucky enough to be a healthy person) whereas five others will die unless they have my organs, I do not have to consider myself a resource for others.[34] My negative right takes precedence.

Objections and Replies

What objections to this distinction between rights should we consider? First, consider issues about how harm occurs, and moral responsibility. Suppose someone argued that the right not to be killed takes precedence because only in a positive act do we cause, and hence are morally responsible for, the death in question. Nancy (Ann) Davis argues, however, that there is no conceptual connection "between positive acts and harms or benefits such that we cannot speak of harming or benefiting unless there is a positive act" (1980, 181; cf. 182–83); we can harm someone by "'doing nothing,'" that is, by refraining. If the right to life has precedence over the right to be saved, it cannot be because in failing to save we do not cause harm, but merely permit it.

Consider Davis's examples:

> We are rock climbing. You ask me to drive in another piton so that you, who have a shorter reach than I, can execute a particularly difficult part of the climb. I agree, but in fact do not drive in the

33. Kagan (1987, 650) reads Donagan ("One does not fail to respect another as a rational creature by declining to procure a good for him, if that good can be procured only by relinquishing an equal or greater good for oneself" [1977, 86]) to mean that we are required "to promote the well-being of others—no matter what the cost to ourselves—provided only that the *overall* good outweighs the overall losses." Donagan means, I believe, that one is not required to sacrifice a certain good even to protect that good for many others.
34. See Blumenfeld (1981, 327) on Tooley's (1980) "diabolical machine."

piton. Instead I remain seated in my safe position and watch you tumble down the mountain.

I am ice-fishing, and (since I am rather bored) I am putting a new notch in my harpoon. You skate up to me, not seeing the harpoon, which is angled directly at you. Though I believe that you will not see the harpoon until it is too late (you will either skate into the harpoon, or else fall through the ice in trying to avoid it), I do not move at all. You skate directly into my harpoon. (1980, 181)

Davis argues that even if we refused to say that refraining in cases such as these *causes* harm, we could still say that those who refrain are morally responsible for the harm. (In my terminology the piton case is a case of killing because the one who refrains from driving in the piton intentionally brought about the dangerous situation by agreeing to drive one in; the harpoon case is a case of letting die because the harpoon fixer did not intentionally bring about the dangerous situation.)

But does one cause harm when one refrains from preventing it? O. H. Green argues that letting die is a necessary (though not sufficient) causal condition. It is true, of course, that had causal condition c been absent, no death would have resulted—for example, had Kitty Genovese's attacker not appeared, she would not have died (see Thomson 1984, 184–85). It is also true that had the bystanders (who failed to come to her aid) been absent they would have played no causal role, but in the circumstances the bystanders' failure to aid was also a causal condition. Says Green:

> A's refraining from preventing B's death is not a causally necessary condition for B's death where A is absent or unable to prevent B's death, (but) where it is possible for A to prevent B's death, A's refraining from doing so is a causally necessary condition to B's death. (1980, 202)

By "possible," I take it Green means possible in the circumstances. For Green my not coming to the aid of a drowning swimmer far away is not a necessary causal condition of the swimmer drowning, for I did not know of it and even if I did, I had no way to perform the rescue. For my not saving to be a necessary causal condition, I must at least have the knowledge, ability, and opportunity to prevent the death.[35]

---

35. To counter the objection that if omissions are causes, then the absence of any condition that would have prevented an outcome is a cause, Kuhse makes a distinction between being a cause and being causally responsible (1987, 57 n. 40, 57ff., 67, 69–71). One is "causally responsible" only for refraining, which presupposes ability, opportunity, and awareness (cf. 1987, 43). Another way to reply to the objection is to say that omissions can be causal factors only when the opportunity, ability, and awareness conditions are satisfied.

Yet even if one rejects this notion of causation, one can still agree with Davis (1980, 191) that refraining could permit harm for which one is morally responsible.[36] Thus, any precedence accorded the right to life should not rest on the supposition that one is not responsible for harm unless one causes it.[37]

Second, consider issues about the general distinction between noninterference and aid. Davis raises an important objection to what she calls the "Negative/Positive Duty Doctrine":

> Other things equal, negative duties understood as duties not to perform some positive act which harms are more stringent than positive duties understood as duties to perform some positive act which benefits. (1980, 178)

Does Foot, asks Davis, really want to claim that one may never violate any negative duty in order to fulfill a positive one (1980, 187)? For example, are we forbidden to steal in order to feed starving children? Would it never be permissible to injure someone slightly (without their consent) in order to save the lives of others? Davis notes that even if we assume that the harms in question are equally serious, Foot's thesis still needs to be clarified:

36. Feinberg acknowledges that one could be culpable for an omission even if one denies that allowing harm is to cause it (1984, 166–71ff., esp. 168). However, against Mack's claim that if nonpreventings are causes, then "*any* absence of an action (or event) is a cause of outcome Y if that action (or event) would have prevented Y" (1980, 241), Feinberg claims that "not every earlier causally necessary condition of an outcome is a causal factor in the genesis of that outcome . . ." (1984, 182, 185; see 257–58 n. 34). Feinberg proposes that "prior necessary conditions are not causes when (1) their connection with the outcome exemplifies no generalizations or natural laws . . . or when (2) the connections are so trivial, obvious or remote that it serves no practical purpose" (1984, 182ff.). Compare Brock who distinguishes a "but-for" sense of causality (1986, 126ff.), which embraces both killing and allowing to die: but for having been poisoned or having the respirator turned off, someone wouldn't have died. Brock argues that when one seeks *the* "cause of death" one is selecting among the "but-for" causes on moral and legal grounds: the doctor causes death in a but-for sense when the respirator is removed, but the disease is the "cause of death" if what the doctor did is morally or legally justified. See also Michael Levine (1988) on the moral determination of causality. On these issues, see Harris (1980a; 1982), James (1982), and Kleinig (1976).

37. For arguments against the view that refrainings are causal conditions, see Mack (1988, 63–64; cf. 1976; 1980; 1984; 1985). Also see Audi (1978, 44–45, 50). Note that Mack holds as I do that even if refrainings are not causes, one could be held morally responsible (Mack says for violating the right to life; in my idiom, the right to be saved). On Mack, see Gruzalski (1988), and Levine (1988). Both Gruzalski and Levine make the point that although there could be a set of causal conditions which, were they regarded as the only operative causal conditions, would be sufficient to cause death, the existence of an option to intervene, in Gruzalski's words (1988, 76) "*does* alter the potential causal sufficiency of the *otherwise* independently existing train of events that would have brought about the death."

If Foot's view is that negative duties outweigh positive duties when the negative duties and positive duties correspond, then it will not underwrite refusal to inflict some harm to procure greater benefit. Though we will not be permitted to inflict serious harm on someone in order to prevent serious harm to someone else, we may be permitted to inflict less serious harm on one person to prevent graver injury to another (or others). (1980, 188; cf. 175, 184)

Davis rightly sees that the "Negative/Positive Duty Doctrine" needs clarification. How it is clarified, however, depends on how much of a person's resources are protected by negative rights (to property, limb, life) and what is owed to others.[38] We might indeed be justified in taking some of a person's blood in order to save five others even if we are not justified in killing someone to do so (1980, 175).[39] The consensus view I try to sketch here affirms that the five patients should not *take* the one patient's organs (and hence *life*) without consent, and that the one patient has no duty to *give* at that level of cost; the thesis is that these convictions are the opposite side of the same coin: the protection against the fatal use of one's body.

Third, is failing to save as bad as killing? An affirmative answer to this question (for cases where other morally relevant features are the same) is often intended as an objection to a view attributed to Foot and others: Because in a case of conflict of duties the duty not to kill has precedence over the duty to save, because it is worse in this situation to kill than to fail to save, it is worse generally. The view under attack is that although it is wrong to let the starving die (it is at least a failure of charity), it would be worse to kill them; it is less bad to fail to save even where there is no conflict of duties. To show that it is just as bad to let die *(ceteris paribus)*, the critic adduces parallel instances that seem equally heinous—for instance, Rachels's examples of the greedy uncle who drowns the nephew and the one who fails to save him (1975, 1986).

So far as I can tell, Foot does not hold the view that when there is no

38. A violation of a negative right is not necessarily worse than a violation of a positive duty. Letting someone drown who could have been saved with little cost is worse than stealing a dollar (Belliotti 1978, 582).

39. Rachels (1986, 146–47) tries to disarm Dinello's example by saying that where the organ was still in the patient's body it wasn't "available." (Dinello's [1971, 85–86] example is a case where we would have to kill Smith to get an organ for Jones, but we can get the organ Smith needs by waiting for Jones to die.) But the issue seems indeed to be whether in choosing whom to save in this case it is morally significant that one option involves a fatal extraction of the organ in order to make it available.

conflict of duties, failing to save is not as bad as killing;[40] she insists that there is a distinction between what is owed by way of noninterference and by way of aid, but she never avers that a failure of a positive duty of service or even of charity cannot be judged equally bad as the violation of the negative duty. Foot argues indeed that failing to save can be as bad as killing when there is no conflict of duties—and not only when a special positive duty of justice is involved but also if there is a failure of charity:

> If someone saw a child drowning in a bath it would seem just as bad to let it drown as to push its head under water. (1978, 49)

> Both charity and the special duty of care we owe to children give us a positive obligation to save them, and we have no particular reason to say that it is "less bad" to fail in this than it is to be in dereliction of the negative duty by being the agent of harm. The level of badness, we may suppose the same, but because a different kind of bad action has been done, there is no reason to suppose that the two ways of acting will always give this same result. (1984, 182)

Furthermore, it does not follow from the view that in situations of conflict the duty not to kill overrides the duty to save, that one must hold that when there is no conflict the failure to save is not as morally bad as killing.[41] Underlying the view that there is a duty to save, but that the duty not to kill overrides it, is a moral conviction about the extent of our duty to aid others. If I am sick and cannot aid myself, then you should try out of your resources to aid me at whatever level the standard of aid is fixed, but you are not required to give your life and no one else has the right to take it.[42]

If this is the reasoning expressed in the conviction that the right not to be killed takes precedence—that is, that in the conflict case too much is asked—then it can be the case that in certain instances where there is no

40. Foot, however, may have given the impression that a failure of charity toward the stranger is not as bad as a failure of justice (1978, 26–27).

41. Quinn (1989a, 289) makes the point I emphasize here, namely, that the greater "strength" of one right over another does not entail that its violation is worse. See also Kamm (1992, 364) on the point that one can admit that acts of killing and letting die are equally bad without saying that the distinction has no general moral significance.

42. I assume that one part of the overlapping ethic I discuss here is the conviction that we should undergo a greater cost not to kill than to save (compare Morillo 1977, 35). I have the duty not to kill (the innocent) even though it costs my life; I do not have the duty to save at the cost of my life. I cannot take your life to save mine (or others), and I do not have a duty to give mine to save you (or others). These convictions are the mirror image of each other: neither you nor I have the duty to give up life. See the Conclusion.

conflict not saving is as wrong as killing. If other things such as motivation and circumstances are equal, we can judge James Rachels's "Jack Palance" as Rachels does, namely, just as blameworthy as a murderer:

> Suppose there were a starving child in the room where you are now—hollow eyed, belly bloated, and so on—and you have a sandwich at your elbow that you don't need. Of course you would be horrified; you would stop reading and give her the sandwich, or better, take her to a hospital. And you would not think this an act of supererogation: you would not expect any special praise for it, and you would expect criticism if you did not do it. Imagine what you would think of someone who simply ignored the child and continued reading, allowing her to die of starvation. Let us call the person who would do this Jack Palance, after the very nice man who plays such vile characters in the movies. Jack Palance indifferently watches the starving child die; he cannot be bothered even to hand her the sandwich. There is ample reason for judging him very harshly; without putting too fine a point on it, he shows himself to be a moral monster. (1979, 160)

Of course, if we saw this case as one where no positive duty of service, no requirement, but only "charity" in the optional sense is at stake, then we might think it natural to assess a failure to save as less bad than killing. However, when there is a requirement to save, even at minimal cost and whether the requirement is one of justice or charity, then it would seem *ceteris paribus* we have a basis for judging that failure to save is as bad as killing (see Malm 1989; 1990).

Fourth, consider the objection we can call "the symmetry of reasons." I argue it would be open to someone who holds that it is as bad to let die as to kill when duties do not conflict to hold also that the duty not to kill overrides the duty to save in a conflict situation—that it is worse in this sense to kill than to let die. One argument against the view that there is such a general moral significance attached to acts of killing and letting die, a significance that accounts for the conviction that the duty not to kill has precedence over the duty to save, is that the "bare difference" that one act is killing and another letting die cannot make a moral difference; no general moral significance attaches to the difference in types of action (Rachels 1986, 111). The objection, some authors claim, does not depend on one's having any particular set of moral convictions—for example, a "deontological" or a "teleological" view (Tooley 1983, 235ff.). The point is that simply in itself the bare difference between killing and letting die is not morally significant.

The objection is sometimes put as follows: if a reason (or set of reasons) is morally significant in a case of letting die, it is equally significant in a case of killing. Thus, suppose that in a pair of cases the motive is to end suffering, the result will be the patient's death, and the patient gives permission. According to my interpretation of Rachels (1986), unless there are other morally relevant factors, if not starting or ceasing treatment is legitimate, so is killing. Although particular acts of killing can be worse than particular acts of letting die, and vice versa, there is no general moral distinction between the two species of acts, and hence, even in a situation of conflict, there is no general basis for saying that the one duty overrides the other; at most one could say that in a particular instance of conflict killing would be worse than letting die. Thus, in the case of the five patients who need the one patient's organs, for example, Rachels would presumably say that it is the one patient's failure to consent in this particular case that is significant, not some putative general difference between killing and letting die (1986, 127–28).

Foot would say, I believe, that the conviction she has about the five patients case does express a general moral significance attaching to these acts: the moral distinction is precisely between the duty not to kill without consent and the duty to save; the conviction is that the one generally overrides the other.[43] Whereas Rachels sees only a difference in particular cases, Foot sees a general difference based on her moral framework.[44]

43. Kuhse (1987, 23) argues against the "qualified Sanctity-of-Life-Principle":

It is absolutely prohibited either intentionally to kill a patient or intentionally to let a patient die, and to base decisions relating to the prolongation or shortening of human life on considerations of its quality or kind; it is however, sometimes permissible to refrain from preventing death.

For this principle to be consistent, its advocate, Kuhse says, must assume that refraining is neither intentional or causally efficacious (1987, 23, 53–54); the advocate, she maintains, is mistaken on both counts: "all instances of refraining from preventing death (are) . . . instances of the intentional termination of life" (1987, 24ff.); moreover, to refrain from preventing death is just as much a cause of death as killing is. Thus although there is a "residual difference" between killing and letting die, a difference in "causal role" as distinct from causal efficacy or agency, she does not think this difference makes a moral difference (1987, 79). I agree with Kuhse's basic analysis of the distinction between killing and letting die—a difference in causal role—but I hold that this "residual difference" can be morally significant given a certain pattern of moral beliefs. I am not holding that the difference in causal role is morally relevant in itself, as if the causal difference somehow *produced* the moral difference; the difference in causal role becomes morally significant because of a set of moral beliefs (cf. Kuhse 1987, 79).

44. Cf. Tooley (1983, 187–88), who says that cost to the giver is one of the factors that "generally" (in the sense of typically) can morally distinguish acts of killing from failing to save, but who rejects an explanation in terms of a "distinction between negative and positive

Note that to hold that the duty not to kill takes precedence does not commit the defender of this view to the normative claim that the right not to be killed cannot be waived, that it differs in this fundamental way from the right to be aided or saved. If the right not to be killed could not be waived, in contrast to a right to be aided, for example, medically, then in this additional sense there would be a distinction between killing and letting die: the reasons that make refusal of treatment legitimate, including the patient's consent, would not be sufficient to legitimate lethal injection; the patient may desire such an injection, but cannot consent in the sense of yielding a discretionary right. The notion I defend here, the precedence of the duty not to kill, does not imply this further asymmetry as some critics may have supposed. I assume that the right not to be killed is discretionary, that is, it can be waived as well. Thus the defender need hold only that the precedence of the duty not to kill obtains in a situation of conflict and that this precedence should be described as a type of general moral significance attaching to the two sorts of acts.

Finally, consider an objection to the idea that killing is the only impermissible means: if it is wrong to kill in order to save (as in the case where five patients need organs), isn't it wrong as well to let die in order to do so? Would it not be as wrong to let a beggar die to get fresh organs as it would be to kill the beggar (Foot 1978, 28; Davis 1980, 176)? And if this is so, then isn't there a principle involved that has no special relation to the killing/letting-die distinction? The principle, Judith Lichtenberg (1982) suggests, is that it is at least prima facie wrong to "sacrifice" one person for another, no matter how one does it, by killing or letting die (cf. Audi 1978, 50 n. 6, 53; Brock 1985).

I agree with the thrust of Lichtenberg's view, but it is still the case that a *general* significance attaches to the distinction between killing and letting die in the sense that the one overrides the other in a situation of conflict. Lichtenberg and others make clear that this general significance is, normatively speaking, only part of a larger framework that limits the duty to save by convictions about morally permissible means. As Dan Brock puts it, "when an. evil can be prevented only by doing something unpermissible, then it is wrong to prevent it. But an unpermissible doing might be either . . . killing or allowing to die."[45] Thus, although there is a broader principle

---

duties." The latter is what I mean by a "general difference." Cf. also Brock (1985), Kagan (1988b; 1989), Kamm (1991b), and Malm (1989; 1990).

45. Brock (1985, 863) argues this point against Donagan. See also Tooley (1983, 253ff.) and Glover (1977, 133ff.). See Russell's statement of a principle similar to Lichtenberg's: "To adopt a plan where someone is killed or let die for the sake of others is to treat the relevant person as a means only. To use people in that way is an affront to their worth and dignity in

involved, in the language of the "Pauline" principle, "do not do evil that good may come," it is precisely in virtue of this broader principle that a general significance attaches to the distinction between killing and letting die.

The broader principle, that it is wrong to sacrifice one person for others, whether by killing or letting die, needs to be clarified, however. Does one sacrifice a person in the morally impermissible sense when one turns a trolley onto a side-track killing the one, but saving five others on the main track? I deal with this question in Chapter 4 and argue that while one would wrongly sacrifice or use the one patient killed or the beggar let die, without their consent, in order to save five others, one does not do so in the trolley case.[46]

The Starving: Letting Die and Killing

I argue that the duty to aid is as morally serious as the duty not to kill, and thus I would reject the judgment that letting people starve is wrong, but not as bad as killing them (cf. Davis 1980, 182–83, 186). My thesis, then, is that a violation of a right to lifesaving aid is as morally serious as a violation of the right not to be killed. Failing to save life when one can do so within the limits of sacrifice defined in the duty, and without violating the right not to be killed (or doing something else morally impermissible), is as morally wrong as killing.[47] I would join Rachels and Kuhse (1987,

---

a way that simply letting someone die is not, given there are no means available (short of bringing about the death of another) for saving that person" (1977, 96; see also 1978; 1979). Also see Davis (1980, 189–96) on Foot.

46. Foot (1984, 183–84) responds to the question, "Why . . . is it not morally permissible to allow someone to die deliberately in order to use his body for medical procedure that could save many lives?," by saying that this case involves the "direct," that is, deliberate, "intention of *evil*." I think she means one would intentionally violate the duty (of charity) in one instance in order to fulfill it in another.

47. See Singer (1977a, 25–26ff.) and Rachels (1979, 162–63); but cf. Bennett (1983, 192), Gorr (1985), and Lichtenberg (1982, 25, 32–33). I am indebted here to Wolterstorff (1984, 24–25; 1981, 81–82), who argues that we have a "right to sustenance as well as a right to freedom from assault," and Shue (1980), who also argues for a basic right to sustenance. (Note that both Wolterstorff [1984, 25] and Singer [1977a] cite Aquinas, *Summa Theologica* II–II, Q. 66, Art. 7.) In my terminology one could fail to give lifesaving aid by not rescuing a drowning person or by failing to give sustenance to those who in Shue's terminology have been deprived of the means to sustain themselves. And one can kill, as I note ahead, by drowning or by depriving of the means of sustenance. Whereas Shue and also Wolterstorff (1983) distinguish the good of security and the good of sustenance and three rights that pertain to each (not to be deprived, to be protected, to be aided when deprived), I stay with the twofold rubric of a right not to be killed and a right to be saved. See Chapter 3 on Shue.

71–76) in opposing those who hold the contrary, for instance, O. H. Green. If A refrains from preventing B's death and A did not cause condition c, then, says Green,

> A can claim . . . that had there not been a condition not of his making which was sufficient to bring about B's death unless he prevented it B would not have died. And, all other things being equal, this does diminish A's responsibility. (1980, 201)

To insist that the right to life has precedence in conflict cases, one need not affirm that moral responsibility is diminished in other instances simply because the agent's causal role in letting die is different than in killing.

It is important to note, moreover, that this point holds whether one adopts a minimal standard of aid, such as Thomson's Minimal Samaritanism, or whether one argues for giving up to the level of comparable cost. The former might be specified as a small percentage of disposable income (Singer 1977a; 1977b; 1979). Thus to the objection that whereas one could rescue one person at little cost, the costs to oneself will snowball if there are many who need help, one can reply that one has done one's duty when one expends a certain portion of one's resources (see Beauchamp and Childress 1989, 200ff.). Wherever one sets the standard of aid, failing to save *ceteris paribus* is as wrong as killing.

It is also important to note that the thesis holds no matter how one handles the myriad issues lumped under the *ceteris paribus* clause. A host of issues arises when one tries to think through a view of our duty to the stranger; but on the assumption that some duty to the stranger remains even when difficulties of execution, fairness among givers, or countervailing considerations such as duty to friends or family, are taken into account, one can still hold that to fail in this duty is as morally serious as killing.[48]

48. Feinberg (1984, 168) argues that the "duty to attempt an easy rescue" is as "stringent . . . ceteris paribus, as the corresponding duty not to cause the harm directly by one's own action" (cf. 166–67). He also argues that a duty to aid everyone who needs aid cannot be discharged; it would be "utterly chaotic" if everyone tried to do so independent of any assignment of "shares and special responsibilities" (1984, 169–70). But a duty to rescue a specific individual(s) with minimal cost can be discharged completely (1984, 170–71). It seems to me, however, that aid to strangers could be required if there are channels to distribute it; in the absence of a governmental system of aid all we need is Oxfam or some other agency to save as many as we can up to the level of cost we acknowledge as required (1984, 158). Feinberg seems to recognize this possibility and even suggests contributions could be legally required (1984, 158). But he still says that "coordination" problems could be too great, for some "beggars" would still starve and others would get too much. He even suggests that "love of neighbor" should be construed as responsibility for those in peril in one's own proximity where no one with a special duty to rescue is present (1984, 259–60 n. 50). Feinberg also argues that it would be "unfair" for some people to contribute at a substantial level

I argue, then, that *ceteris paribus* it is as bad to fail to save the starving as it would be to kill them. There are occasions, moreover, when we actually kill the starving by refraining from helping them.[49] I assume here that the action in question is failing to save, but it could be killing by refraining. Onora O'Neill notes that when the affluent do not aid the starving, it is often said that they allow them to die (1977, 153). In the past, argues O'Neill, it may have been the case that the affluent "had often done nothing to bring about" the deaths they failed to prevent. Yet today, due to "economic and technological interdependence" (1977, 154), deaths by starvation are caused by those in affluent countries and thus it is not a right not to be allowed to die but a right not to be killed that is violated (1977, 154–55; see also O'Neill 1986, chap. 2; 1993).

Following out her view that the right not to be killed can be violated even when the agent does not act alone, the death is not immediate, not certain, and not necessarily intended (1977, 154–55), she argues that a company, for example, that operates so as to pay wages that lower survival expectations does not allow to die but kills (1977, 156–59). Thus, O'Neill says that even if we do not act alone, do not kill "instantaneously," do not know which individuals will die, and do not intend "famine deaths," we

---

while others do not do their duty; not only are public agencies more effective, e.g., fire fighters, but the cost is equally split among taxpayers (individuals might not even have to give at a minimal level if everyone did their duty) (1984, 70). In addition to the problems of coordination and fairness Feinberg raises, there are questions about the best method of life-saving aid (direct relief, population control, economic and political development), whether to rank saving life for as many as possible over meeting other basic needs for a fewer number, the use of aid to motivate indigenous population control and saving, the effect of the redistribution of wealth on the incentive to produce, the relation of the duty to aid the stranger to duties to those in special relations such as friends or family, whether we have a greater duty to the starving stranger in our own country than abroad, and the role of our own individual projects and commitments. On these issues, see Bennett (1983), Brock (1991), Gewirth (1982a), Kagan (1991b), O'Neill (1977; 1986; 1993), Rachels (1979; 1986), and Singer (1977a; 1977b). When resources are scarce, moreover, one may have to let some die; in such a case, one fails to save but the choice is presumably just according to some distributive criterion for "who shall live." I do not discuss such a criterion here, but in the next chapter I briefly deal with distributive questions in connection with nothing-is-lost cases. On the distributive issues, see Childress (1978b), Rescher (1978), Kilner (1990), and Kamm (1993). See also Chapter 2, note 21, this volume.

49. On killing the starving, see Kuhse (1987, 51–52). Also see Finnis: "Feeding the hungry is the subject of a grave affirmative responsibility, whose implications for particular individuals depend on their other responsibilities" (1988, 158). And he also says that "failures to feed the hungry can be omissions chosen in order to hasten death," and thus these violate the basic prohibition against *killing* the innocent (1988, 161). In my view, even were one to intend to hasten death, one still *lets die* if one did not intentionally create the antecedent situation in which refraining from aid brings death.

kill and do not merely allow to die. For as a result of our actions in concert with others, some will die who might have survived had we either acted otherwise or had no causal influence. (1977, 161)

O'Neill's analysis of killing and letting die in these cases is, I believe, roughly the same as mine. The company *intentionally* brings about conditions sufficient to cause the famine deaths and then refrains from the action that could prevent death from those conditions, although it does not necessarily intend those deaths themselves either as means or end.[50] We should, however, distinguish clearly situations where under "sufficiency" conditions one kills from those where one lets die. O'Neill argues that in conditions of sufficiency—for example, a well-equipped lifeboat Earth where there is (at least at present) enough for all to survive—*any* distribution of resources such that some die is not allowing to die but killing, for "the acts of those who distribute food and water are the causes of a death that would not have occurred had those agents either had no causal influence or done other acts" (1977, 155). Yet even if refraining from helping through a certain distribution of food and water is a cause of death, we should not equate this causal role with the causing of the famine situation in the first place. In our world, some people kill by refraining (because they bring about the lethal conditions) and some let die (they did not bring about the conditions but fail to save).

There is the additional issue of complicity, moreover. Some of us may not even own shares in the company in O'Neill's example, but what if we *benefit* from its policies? What if we cannot avoid benefitting, for instance, from lower prices of essential goods? Presumably we could adjust our level of giving accordingly (in light of our standard).

In sum, assuming a right to be saved from death in certain circumstances (the cost to the saver is within the bounds specified in the right), and assuming that the right to be saved is as morally weighty as the right not to be killed, then allowing to starve to death is as wrong as killing. When the negative right or some other equally serious consideration does not

50. See Brown (1987), and compare his notion of "structural violence." Note that to object to such "killing by refraining," what Brown calls "overt structural violence," does not require one—any more than an argument for aiding the starving does—to adopt the view that economic inequalities are *never* to be permitted or that private ownership of the means of production is inherently evil. Cf. Singer's classic article (1977a); even his strong standard—forgo luxuries *until* all have necessities—does not commit him to the view that economic inequalities would never be justified.

stand in the way, failure to respect the positive right is just as blameworthy.[51]

Conclusion

In this chapter I sketch a right not to be killed and a right to lifesaving aid. I also show how in a situation of conflict the right not to be killed has precedence over the duty to save, but how in other circumstances the violation of each is equally blameworthy. If this view is eventually accepted, our enjoyment of luxuries while others starve (because we fail to give at the level of Minimal Samaritanism or whatever standard we think is required) will seem as heinous to our progeny as slavery does to us.

Using the framework of the two rights, I now proceed to deal with a series of types of cases—yielding, nothing is lost, pursuers, and double effect—further refining the framework as I go.

51. Cf. Glover (1977, 104ff.) and Kamm (1986, 5–7; also 1982).

2

Yielding and Nothing Is Lost

Yielding

The right to be saved and the right not to be killed can be yielded or waived. For example, consider this case discussed by James Rachels:

> —a patient who is dying of incurable cancer of the throat is in terrible pain, which can no longer be satisfactorily alleviated. He is certain to die within a few days, even if present treatment is continued, but he does not want to go on living for those days since the pain is unbearable. So he asks the doctor for an end to it, and his family joins in the request. (1975, 78; see also 1986, chap. 7)

The competent patient requests that treatment be discontinued. Treatment only prolongs life, and as long as life remains the disease will cause the suffering; thus to end the suffering one must end life; and to end life one ceases treatment.

Rachels, however, says:

> Suppose the doctor agrees to withhold treatment, as the conventional doctrine says he may. The justification for his doing so is that the patient is in terrible agony, and since he is going to die anyway, it would be wrong to prolong his suffering needlessly. But now notice this. If one simply withholds treatment, it may take the patient longer to die, and so he may suffer more than he would if more direct action were taken and a lethal injection given. This fact provides strong reason for thinking that, once the initial decision not to prolong his agony has been made, active euthanasia is actually preferable to passive euthanasia, rather than the reverse. To say otherwise is to endorse the option that leads to more suffering rather than less, and is contrary to the humanitarian impulse that prompts the decision not to prolong his life in the first place. (1975, 78)

Rachels adduces the possibility of greater suffering to convince us that a moral distinction between death by cessation of treatment and death by lethal injection is groundless. If the justification for cessation of treatment is to spare the dying patient suffering, it applies equally well to both situations (1975, 78–79). Let us consider an alternative analysis which nonetheless preserves the moral substance of Rachels's view.

First, let us look at what is involved in deciding to cease treatment. Rachels's case is one in which one ceases treatment in order to end life, for that is the only way to end suffering, in contrast to a case where one ceases the treatment to end the suffering *it* causes, with the result that life is not prolonged. These cases are different, but in both the agent yields the right to life-prolonging aid in order to relieve suffering. The patient who decides to cease treatment (in either sort of case) waives whatever right to help he or she has.[1] Others may have a duty to help, but the right-holder has an option to waive or yield the right. This is so whether one is speaking of a

---

1. Steinbock (1980, 71–73) notes that in ceasing treatment one need not intend that the patient die. She argues that the 1973 AMA statement does not distinguish active intentional termination of life (killing) from passive (letting die), but contrasts any intentional termination with the cessation of extraordinary means, which she interprets as ceasing treatment in order to avoid "painful and pointless treatment" (1980, 74). Boyle also argues that in some cases of terminal suffering, one may cease treatment in order to lessen suffering, with the unintended result that the patient dies (1977a, 445; cf. 442–43, 439–40). In Rachels's throat cancer case, however, the suffering is caused by the disease not the treatment; the treatment is prolonging life, however; withholding treatment speeds up death but a lethal injection would do it sooner.

contractually based duty (for instance, a doctor's) or a general duty. If others want to help us out of benevolence or for some other reason, then a decision to cease treatment would be to insist that, at least when competent, we do not have to accept help unless we choose to.[2]

Consider then these cases: 1) one gives a drug to relieve suffering but on a "pyramid" basis the drug will eventually cause the patient's death; 2) one ceases treatment to relieve the suffering—the bad quality of life—caused by the treatment; but without the treatment, which prolongs life, the patient will die; 3) one ceases treatment in order not to prolong life and hence to relieve suffering; the treatment prolongs life and does not itself cause unacceptable side-effects, but the disease is such that the mere continuance of life entails extreme suffering; the judgment is that quality of life does not warrant prolongation. In case 1, the patient or the proxy (if the patient is incompetent) can presumably authorize the drug even though it hastens death. If refusing treatment (directly or by proxy) is yielding a right, then one can refuse in order to end the suffering caused by the treatment—case 2—or by the disease itself—case 3.

Note that one can yield the right to treatment (in either sort of case) even in curable cases, as opposed to so-called terminal illnesses such as Rachels's case above. Even if the disease is not necessarily fatal and the patient will not shortly die whatever is done, the patient (or the proxy) could still judge that the value of continued life does not outweigh the disvalue of continued suffering.

But note also that the patient who waives a right to treatment could also waive the right not to be killed, and thus request a lethal injection. The patient in case 1 who consents to a program of medication that eventually is lethal has also in effect yielded the right not to be killed.[3] (Administering the drug is the initiation of an independent causal sequence sufficient to cause death, even though death is unintended as end or means; see Chapter 1.) But the right not to be killed and a right to treatment are distinct rights, and to refuse treatment does not entail that the right not to be killed has been waived. The moral decisions are distinct, but both could be made in

2. Brock (1981) treats the right to refuse treatment as an expression of a more general right to self-determination, the right to form, revise, and act on one's own values or plan of the good. See Brock (1992, 14) also on waiving the right not to be killed.

3. The patient who waives the right to treatment and a patient who chooses a pain-killer foreseeing that it will, as a side effect, hasten death both make a cost-benefit judgment about the value of continued life. Since the judgment here pertains only to the good of this agent, I do not treat the case where a pain-killer causes death as a side effect under the rubric of double effect. Here consent is necessary, but in cases where double effect applies consent is not required of the person who dies as a side effect of lifesaving action. See Chapter 4 on double effect. Cf. Quinn (1991, 511–73).

Rachels's case, and for the reason Rachels mentions, namely, the avoidance of suffering. Thus the moral judgment that Rachels makes (that killing can be justifiable) could be sustained without admitting that there is no general moral distinction between "killing" (lethal injection or the pyramid drug) and "letting die" (not starting or stopping treatment). Whether there are objections to a legal policy that permitted lethal injection, it is clear that the moral right not to be killed can be waived.[4] The objection that a legal right to be killed would allow abuse because competent patients would feel pressure not to cause relatives pain and expense (and noncompetent patients would simply have the decision for an early death made for them) cuts equally against a legal right to refuse treatment (directly exercised or by proxy). Although I do not try to argue the case here, it seems to me that if we can guard sufficiently well against abuse as regards refusing treatment, we can do so as regards being killed.

It is worth noting here the contrast between a natural rights ethic and a paradigmatic theological view. The right not to be killed on a certain theological view signifies an interhuman right that expresses God's rightful dominion or sovereignty over human life; to say that humans have the right to life is to say that humans have a duty to respect God's right over life; the duty not to kill and the duty to save are responsibilities assigned by God. As Paul Ramsey put it:

> Thus, every human being is a unique, unrepeatable opportunity to praise God. His life is entirely an ordination, a loan, and a steward-ship. His essence is his existence before God and to God, as it is from Him. His dignity is "an alien dignity," an evaluation that is not of him but placed upon him by the divine decree. . . . Respect

---

4. I support Kuhse's (1987, 203–4, 217–19) point that it is morally justified to use a painless injection when the patient's life is no longer of value to the patient, provided that proper procedures for direct or proxy consent have been followed. See Brock (1992) on abuse, slippery slope, and other public policy concerns that apply both to refusal of treatment and "active voluntary euthanasia." See Cahill's criticism of arguments against killing based on future social consequences (1977, 57ff.). For an analysis of these and other issues related to patient autonomy, see Beauchamp and Childress (1983; 1989; 1994). I do not take up here issues related to proxy judgments for noncompetent adults or children in regard to cessation of treatment or lethal injection. I think that previously competent patients should have their previously expressed views respected, and where no previous views were expressed, that a "reasonable person" standard as to the best interests of the patient should be used (I refer to both of these as types of proxy consent). Infants who are not yet competent but will be if allowed to live constitute a more difficult case. Because the option is forced, I believe a reasonable person/best interest procedure is also in order here. See Brody (1988), Childress (1982b), Santurri and Werpehowski (1982), and Brock and Buchanan (1989) for discussion of these issues.

not of him but placed upon him by the divine decree. . . . Respect
for life does not mean that a man must live and let live from some
iron law of necessity, or even that there is a rational compulsion to
do this, or a decisive rational ground for doing so. . . . Because of
God's decrees and election, a man, in his own case, can and may
live; he should ("must") accept his life as a trust superior to his own
determination. (1971, 13, 15)

Thus it is often said in both Judaic and Christian traditions that humans
do not have the right to take their own lives or have others do it for them
simply to escape suffering.[5] The right not to be killed in this view is not a
"discretionary" right, in Joel Feinberg's phrase, but "mandatory"; it is a
right one has against everyone else, but it is not one that can be waived or
yielded (Feinberg 1980b).

Moreover, a discretionary right to treatment (one that can be waived) is
not something possessed by individuals on the basis of their own capacities
as it is in the natural rights tradition. Whatever discretion one has or doesn't
have is a matter of how much dominion has been delegated. Some strands
of the Judaic and Christian traditions argue, for example, that treatment
should never be stopped except in the actual "throes" of death.[6] In the
words of David Bleich,

It is quite true that man has the power to prolong life far beyond
the point at which it ceases to be either productive or pleasurable.
Not infrequently, the patient, if capable of expressing his desires and
allowed to follow his own inclinations, would opt for termination
of a life which has become a burden both to others and to himself.
Judaism, however, teaches that man does not enjoy the right of self-
determination with regard to questions of life and death. . . . Man
does not possess absolute title to his life or his body. . . . Judaism

5. Cf. Rachels (1986, 69–71) who neatly explains how on a certain theological view of
the right to life it can be forfeited but not waived.
6. As Newman (1990) points out, however, other contemporary interpreters want to
redefine the category of *goses* so that it is not limited to a seventy-two-hour period. If the
goses period is short, then the distinction some interpreters find in classical sources between
actively hastening death and merely removing some preventing factor (the sound of the woodchopper) would be irrelevant not only to many cases of terminal illness but to other cases
where the disease is incurable but death is not imminent (1990, 22–23). See Newman, however,
on varying interpretations regarding which impediments could be removed (the woodchopper
analogy) and under what circumstances (failure to respond to therapy, irreversible coma, any
situation of extreme suffering) (1990, 24, 28). Newman argues that Jewish ethics needs a
revised hermeneutical theory in order to account for the role of the interpreter as well as
constraints of tradition and community.

does recognize situations in which certain forms of medical intervention are not mandatory. . . . Man must use the full range of benefits
made available by science but he is not obliged to experiment with
untried and unproven measures. Nor is he obliged to avail himself
of therapeutic measures which are in themselves hazardous in the
hope of effecting a complete cure. . . . The sole exception to these
principles which halacha recognizes is the case of a *goses*, a mori-
bund patient actually in the midst of death throes. . . . Man is never
called upon to determine whether life is worth living—that is a
question over which God remains sole arbiter. (1976, 16, 17, 20)

Before "death throes" the only treatments which can be stopped are experi-
mental or hazardous ones.[7]

Ramsey, however, once argued that all treatments may be stopped when
it is clear that nothing can stop the "dying process" and medical efforts
will only at best prolong the dying. If such treatment does more harm than
good, then it can cease, for one's duty changes when the status of the
individual changes, namely, when the dying process has begun; the duties
one has as a trustee of God can change if death is imminent, and the
calculus of good shifts away from prolonging life. At that point one's duty
is only to "care." In effect, although Ramsey expresses his point in the
language of duty, the patient has a discretionary right to treatment that
can be waived in certain circumstances (or can be waived by a proxy).

Thus Ramsey wanted to identify the stage at which a patient "has begun
to undergo irreversibly the process of his own particular dying" (1970a,
125). This is apparently different from death throes but also from merely
fatal illness. But what are the criteria for the process of dying? When medicine can only delay death but not cure? But wouldn't this apply to all fatal
illnesses? (cf. 1970a, 133). Is there a quantitative measure for when death
is imminent, as opposed to being merely inevitable?[8] If the criterion is the

7. Views such as Bleich's or Ramsey's can rest on appeals to scriptures or other texts that
contain the divinely mandated constitution for human existence. Ramsey (1971) refers to
Psalm 139 and other passages; Bleich (1976) presents his view as a distillation of talmudic
law. Other theologians appeal to "reason" as the source of their views about the divine-human
relationship. See Grisez and Boyle (1979). For a critique of the model of the sovereign (and
patriarchal) deity on which notions of the delegation of authority or dominion rest, see
Harrison (1983).

8. Cf. Ramsey (1978, 321–27) where he stresses the notion of the imminence of death.
As Meilaender (1991, 141) notes, Ramsey distinguished the "dying" and the "incurably ill."
On Ramsey's distinction between "only caring" for the dying (in order to avoid treatment
that only prolongs the dying process) and "hastening death," see Beauchamp and Childress
(1983, 125); Kuhse (1987, 95) argues that some refrainings to treat intentionally aim at death.
See Meilaender (1991, 142, 147), on Ramsey's (1978, 146ff.) injunction to choose "not against
life" but "against the burden of treatment." See also Werpehowski (1991).

time when medicine can not only not cure but also not delay (1970a, 134), then the cost-benefit judgment between the value of prolongation and the disvalue of suffering is moot. Is the criterion simply the time at which prolongation is too burdensome? If so, then it would seem that patients have a right to refuse treatment generally when they judge that the prolongation of life is not worth the cost. One would have defined the "dying process" simply as the time when one decides it is not worthwhile to continue.

In any case, it is important to note that this theological paradigm, although sometimes expressed only in the vocabulary of duty can nonetheless include a notion of a delegated right, a right, for example, to waive treatment under certain circumstances. Although Bleich's version of Judaic tradition allows in effect no discretion before death throes (except for hazardous or unproven measures), Ramsey's version of Christian tradition allows treatment to be waived in the "dying process." Neither Bleich nor Ramsey contemplate a delegated discretionary right not to be killed, although some reforming theologians have urged this on the grounds that if God has given humans authority (delegated "dominion") not to prolong life in some circumstances, why is it granted in one sort of case and not the other?[9]

Potholing and Proleptic Yielding

If the right not to be killed can be waived, this has important implications for other sorts of cases. Alan Donagan presents his principle of respect for rational creatures as an ethic of duty, but he allows consent to play an important role in one sort of case (see Brock 1981; 1985). Hence he in effect treats the right not to be killed as a discretionary right that can be

---

9. I am grateful to Cadet Eric Rubio, U.S.C.G.A., for reminding me of this point. Meilaender (1991, 144–45) notes that Ramsey once (1970a, 157–64) allowed two exceptions to the imperative to continue care: one could not only let die but also kill those for whom care is "inaccessible" and those who cannot receive care because the pain cannot be alleviated. Evidently he withdrew this view later (1978a), however, because of the objection that we cannot really know when someone is beyond care. Ramsey also evidently feared, says Meilaender (1991, 145ff.), that he would be read to support not only the withdrawal of futile treatment from dying patients (I gather this means futile or useless for a cure, though able to prolong life and hence the dying process), but also the withdrawal of treatment from nondying patients whose lives are judged not worth living. Ramsey (1970a, 136) had earlier suggested that such withdrawal (for the nondying) could perhaps sometimes be justified as removing unduly burdensome treatment for the competent patient, but never for the noncompetent (Meilaender 1991, 141, 147–48ff.).

waived. (I henceforth assume in speaking of rights that they are discretionary.) Here is Donagan's case:

> A rockfall occurs, catching the first of a group of potholers who are making their way out of a cave, in which water is rising rapidly. The man caught in the rocks is not seriously injured and may expect to be rescued in a day or two by search parties. Those behind him, however, will be drowned in a few hours by the rising water unless they make a passage through the fallen rocks. They can do so, but only by blasting the rocks away with the explosive they have with them, which will cause the death of the man caught in the rocks. (1977, 177)

There are several important things to notice about this case. First, in Donagan's version the individual is caught in a rockfall that blocks the way. In Kai Nielsen's version of the case, however, it is the man who blocks the way:[10]

> Consider the story (well known to philosophers) of the fat man stuck in the mouth of a cave on a coast. He was leading a group of people out of the cave when he stuck in the mouth of the cave. In a very short time high tide will be upon them and unless he is promptly unstuck, they all will be drowned except the fat man, whose head is out of the cave. Fortunately or unfortunately, someone has with him a stick of dynamite. The short of the matter is, either they use the dynamite and blast the poor innocent fat man out of the mouth of the cave or everyone else drowns; either one life or many lives. (1973, 69–70; 1990, 132)

Second, notice that the individual is facing out in both versions; this individual would thus live if nothing is done.

Now note Donagan's way of justifying an action to save the trapped potholers, which will also cost the life of the individual in the rocks:

> Human beings are not morally forbidden to risk their lives on suitably serious enterprises . . . of which it is not unthinkable that potholing is one. And, although it is not beyond dispute, it does not appear to be impermissible for a group of human beings embarking on such an enterprise to agree that, if in the course of it, through

---

10. Donagan (1977, 256 n. 13) notes this distinction.

nobody's fault, they should be confronted with a choice between either allowing certain of their number to be killed, or doing something that would, against everybody's will, cause the deaths of fewer of their number, the latter should be chosen. In so agreeing, each member of the group would act in his own probable interest. And so, if the situation contemplated came about, and the agreement were put into effect, it would not be a case of one subgroup, because it was larger, sacrificing the lives of another that was smaller. An agreement of the kind described would have force even if it was tacit: that is, even if, without saying so, all members of the group take it as accepted by all that they should conduct themselves in accordance with it. And perhaps it would have force even if it were virtual: that is, even if all members of the group, were they to think about it, would agree that everybody in the group would think that so to conduct themselves was the only rational course. (1977, 178–79)

I wish to accept Donagan's verdict yet amend his analysis: 1) If it were a rockfall that blocked the way, one could handle the case under the rubric of double effect; since the parties are moral equals in the sense that they have all taken the risk of going potholing, I would argue that those trapped may blast away the rocks in order to save their lives, killing the one of their number trapped in the fall as an unintended effect. Roughly, one may cause certain states of affairs that would be wrong if intended as means or end, provided that these states of affairs occur as the unintended consequences of otherwise permissible actions, and that the overall result is proportionate, that is, assuming certain values, the overall benefits outweigh the costs (see Chapter 4 on double effect). In this case, an action is taken sufficient to cause death (blasting the rocks away), but death or fatal injury is not intended as the means; the overall result satisfies the criterion of proportionality since more lives are saved. In the Nielsen version, however, one must intentionally do a fatal injury to the fat man in order to remove him from the hole (as the case is stated the fat man is not at fault, and hence bears no special responsibility). Thus, here one must appeal to a Donagan type of agreement to yield in order to justify the killing. 2) In the Nielsen version the proleptic agreement is necessary only if the person's head is sticking out; but if the person's head is facing in and thus he or she will die along with everyone else if nothing is done, then the right is suspended and does not have to be yielded, as I argue subsequently. 3) The yielding argument works only if there is an explicit or implicit agreement;[11] if the stuck person has not agreed in one of these ways, then that individual is free to insist on the luck of the draw; an appeal to what Donagan calls a "virtual" agreement (what the parties *should* have agreed to in their own self-interest *before* the emergency occurs) will not work, for the individual now knows he or she is safe. Dan Brock makes this point and also asks if it is not fairer for the one who is stuck to reason as if the facts were not known, and thus yield the right (1981).[12] On the view I suggest here, however, what is fair is what rights establish, and the right not to be killed allows either a self-interested proleptic yielding or a refusal to yield if it is not in one's interest. 4) The one stuck in the cave could yield on the spot even if no proleptic agreement had been made; but at that point the yielding would not be based on a calculation of probable self-interest, but would be an expression of supererogatory sacrifice; note also, however, that for the proleptic agreement to work, it has to be irrevocable; once on the spot, the one stuck cannot decide to back out. 5) Even if the proleptic yielding is in their interest so far as preserving life is concerned, the parties could decide, in order to preserve other values, to leave the natural lottery alone or to toss a coin once in the situation where someone is stuck.

Donagan contrasts the potholer case with another where in his view the blasting would not be justified:

> A sizable group of people are trapped in an excavation by the collapse of the one passage leading out of it. However, there is a shaft for a periscope, which they can ascend by ladder to within six feet of the earth's surface. At this point the periscope goes through to the surface in an airtight steel pipe. Water is rising in the excavation, and they will all be drowned before they are rescued, unless they can rapidly break through the six feet of earth between the top of the periscope shaft and the surface. They can do so only by blasting it with explosives left in the excavation. However, if they do, as they can see through the periscope, they will blow up a small party of

11. One would also have to ask about how to recognize a tacit or implicit agreement, and, more generally, about how to gain in real situations some degree of certainty about each case. I am grateful to Christine Lehmann and Zachary Lesser for these points.

12. Donagan later rules out virtual agreements (1985, 874–75). I am indebted here to Michael Levine and Terrence Reynolds. See Kamm (1993, 119ff.) on the *"ex ante"* self-interest argument that what is morally correct is what one *would* have chosen when ignorant of one's actual position (in contrast to versions of this argument that require actual agreement ahead of time). She notes that it is not necessarily the case that one would choose even in ignorance a maximizing or "number-counting policy" (1993, 120). See Kamm's (1992, 374ff.) criticisms of Thomson's *"ex ante rationality"* account.

picnickers, who are lunching by the periscope's "eye." Signals through the periscope are not understood, and its shaft is too strongly built to be dismantled in time for them to call through its pipe to give warning. (1977, 179)

Donagan's view is that no agreement would exist in this case because there is no common risky endeavor on which the parties embark.

Again, I accept his judgment, but amend the moral analysis: 1) The situation is apparently one of double effect: blast out, killing the picnickers as a side effect. 2) However, Donagan's point about the absence of a common risky endeavor bears on a double effect as well as a proleptic yielding interpretation. It seems correct to limit the situations where double effect applies; if one has taken special risks, one is entitled to take proportionate measures to distribute or remove a threat only if those who would be killed as a result of one's action have also taken those risks. In other words, only if the special risks of potholing were not involved could those trapped blast out, killing the picnickers, provided that more lives were saved (proportionality).

Consider also Bernard Gert's jumbo jet case which he presents in order to counter Donagan's example of the picnickers. Suppose that instead of potholers

we have a captain of a jumbo jet with more than 300 passengers who must make an emergency landing in an open field. He sees the family of picnickers but knows that if he pulls up and does not land on this field the plane will certainly crash in the forest immediately ahead. Should he pull up, thereby saving the picnickers? My intuition on this matter does not indicate that the Pauline principle [do not do evil so that good may come] is to be obeyed without question. (1977, 414–15)

What may underlie Gert's judgment, however, is not the sheer weight of numbers of lives to be saved, but the fact that in our society we do not regard taking a plane as a risk outside the ordinary course of life; taking planes is within the ordinary risk spectrum, which also includes going on picnics. Thus the plane should land, but not merely because of the numbers; it is a double effect situation, where all the parties are within the ordinary spectrum of risk.[13] The pilot lands on the field in order to save the passen-

---

13. Note that one could say that the Roman Catholic teaching on the cancerous uterus makes a similar assumption. See Chapter 4 on double effect.

gers (and hence the greatest number of lives), killing the picnickers as an unintended effect. Those who go potholing in contrast have no right to blast their way out, killing the picnickers; they have taken an extraordinary risk and must be prepared to suffer the consequences if things go badly.

Brigands and Tyrants

The yielding paradigm can be applied to cases of oppression. These are not fanciful examples, but reflect actual events in Jewish history that are treated in talmudic law (Daube 1965; Donagan 1977, 181–83). Here is a type of case as Baruch Brody states it:

> A small village is surrounded by a hostile group of brigands who, desiring (for their own diabolic reasons) to compel the villagers to sacrifice an innocent man, demand that they kill Pietro. If the villagers do not kill Pietro, the brigands threaten to (and the villagers have every reason to believe that they will) kill all of the village leaders (among whom Pietro is not included). The village is cut off from outside help, and acceding to the brigands' demand is the only way to save the village leaders. (1975, 16)

Note that the case is analogous to the case in which the potholer's head is facing out; Pietro will live even if the leaders are killed. If no proleptic agreement has been made, then Pietro can insist on his right. If a proleptic agreement (explicit or tacit) had been made to the effect that should it be necessary, a villager should die for the sake of the village leaders, then Pietro could be killed.

In another sort of case a tyrant doesn't name the victim but asks a third party to select one; but the issue, other things being equal, is whether the individuals in the group make an agreement and proleptically yield. Here is Nielsen's version of the case:

> Suppose we have the good fortune to live in a quite open tyranny . . . and that we are faced with a moral dilemma forced on us by the fiendish local representative of the leader. This beastly man presents one of us, as a representative member of the dwindling intelligentsia, with the following (as far as can be discerned) thoroughly earnest proposal: unless we torture one innocent man, our kleiner Fuehrer will, with even greater torment than he requires of us, tor-

ture five men to death. That is, one member of the intelligentsia is singled out for harassment; unless he tortures one man, five *others* will be tortured and killed [italics mine]. (Nielsen 1973, 74–75; 1990, 137)

One could argue as Donagan does (1977, 208–9) that the officer could not be trusted or that accepting the offer would have "bad results," for example, increase the number of incidents against the populace; thus an agreement per se may not be sufficient to make killing someone right. The parties might believe, therefore, that there are constraints on yielding; they might believe that the decision should not be based entirely on probable self-interest. If we assume that other things are equal, however, and all six accept the agreement, then the third party has not violated the right of the one tortured and killed. (I assume Nielsen meant that the one tortured would also die. If not, we would not have a case of one life for five.) The third party has not fallen into utilitarianism, but assumes a proleptic agreement to yield.

Judicial Punishment of the Innocent

The proleptic yielding paradigm can even be extended to this case:

A magistrate or judge is faced with a very real threat from a large and uncontrollable mob of rioters demanding a culprit for a crime. Unless the criminal is produced, promptly tried and executed, they will take their own bloody revenge on a much smaller and quite vulnerable section of the community (a kind of frenzied pogrom). The judge knows that the real culprit is unknown and that the authorities do not even have a good clue as to whom he may be. But he also knows that there is within easy reach a disreputable, thoroughly disliked and useless man who, though innocent, could easily be framed so that the mob would be quite convinced that he was guilty and would be pacified if he were promptly executed. Recognizing that he can prevent the occurrence of extensive carnage only by framing some innocent person, the magistrate has him framed, goes through the mockery of a trial and has him executed. (Nielsen 1973, 73–74; 1990, 136; cf. Donagan 1977, 203)

1) To apply the argument, one first has to ask whether the "useless man" is a member of the small and vulnerable minority. If so, then the case looks

similar to Brody's brigand case above: either one member or a larger number of the minority community will die at the hands of the mob (parallel to the brigands who threaten the village); in Brody's case the brigands chose Pietro, here the judge chooses a "disreputable" individual. But what if the individual chosen were not a member of the minority group? Would this change the case fundamentally? I don't think so; now it is a choice of one member of the community at large or a larger number. 2) One has to assume in any case that there is an agreement among the parties (whether narrowly construed as the minority group or as the larger community) that if such a situation arises, each of them would be prepared to yield their right not to be falsely accused and executed. 3) It is not the case that if nothing is done all will die; even on the version where the victim is from the minority group the one chosen would presumably not be killed in the pogrom, just as Pietro would live even if the leaders die; but the death of one could save the lives of many. 4) Note again that the notion of virtual agreement will not work on the view I present here. The parties must have agreed explicitly or implicitly; they must agree as individuals; third parties cannot yield their rights for them. Otherwise, third parties could yield the right of the one to be executed despite the victim's manifest unwillingness to be sacrificed for the group. 5) Even if we assume the possibility of an agreement, however, we would still have to consider whether the possibility of damage to institutions that protect rights would influence our choice. As Donagan suggests, perhaps we have to take into account whether our action will uphold justice in a number of other cases as well. If the right is yielded, we must make a judgment based also on proportionality, in the vocabulary of the Catholic tradition, or maximization in another idiom; but the goods or values to be considered could well extend beyond the immediate saving of the greatest number of lives. 6) Also relevant to the question of overall justice would be the criteria for the selection of the victim; even if the judge can assume a proleptic agreement, should the criteria be disreputability, unpopularity, and uselessness? Or should some random method be employed? Note the judge can select, whereas the villagers in Brody's example could choose only whether to go along with the brigands' selection.

These cases differ, then, in some respects; in the potholing case and the brigands case there is no choice as to *whose* life could be sacrificed; there is a choice in the tyrant case and (I assume) in the judicial punishment case. The cases also differ in how the problem arises; in the potholing case, it arises from natural causes; in the brigands, oppressor, and judicial punishment cases some unjust human force is the cause (the brigands, the tyrant, the mob's threat of pogrom). In some of the cases the group as a whole has to make the immediate decision (potholers, villagers), but in others some third party has the choice to make (the member of the intelligentsia, the judge). But in all the cases it is a choice of one life or more, and a proleptic agreement to yield could justify *ceteris paribus* saving the greater number.

Nothing Is Lost

There is another range of cases where if nothing is done all will die, but where by killing one or more, a greater number could be saved. In the proleptic yielding cases, not everyone will die if nothing is done; the choice is between killing one or more who would live if we did nothing, and saving a greater number of others who will die if none are sacrificed. But now, all will die if nothing is done.

First, potholing:

> Consider the story of the fat man stuck in the mouth of a cave on a coast. He was leading a group of people out of the cave when he stuck in the mouth of the cave. In a very short time high tide will be upon them and unless he is promptly unstuck, they will all be drowned [including the fat man, whose head is facing in]. (Adapted from Nielsen 1973, 69–70; 1990, 132)

Compare similar versions of the brigands and tyrant cases:[14]

> A small village is surrounded by a hostile group of brigands who demand that the villagers kill Pietro, an innocent villager whose death the brigands seek. If the villagers do not kill Pietro, the brigands threaten to (and the villagers have every reason to believe that they will) destroy the village and everyone in it (including Pietro). The village is cut off from outside help and acceding to the demands

14. See Davis's discussion of the "intervening agent" and a putative distinction between nothing-is-lost situations brought about by natural in contrast to human causes, e.g., tyrant cases (1980, 202ff.). She concludes that the distinction between natural and human disasters is "artificial and too arbitrary to serve as the ground for differential obligations" (1980, 206). But she still searches for an explanation of why we "object to being used as instruments of another's will" (1980, 207); she thinks the answer lies in our notions of free agency and responsibility (1980, 208–9), not in "moral asymmetry" views like Foot's. Compare her remarks on "using and being used" (1980, 214 n. 34) and Chapter 4 on Thomson.

of the brigands is the only way to save the inhabitants. (Brody 1975, 12)

Jim finds himself in the central square of a small South American town. Tied up against the wall are a row of twenty Indians, most terrified, a few defiant, in front of them several armed men in uniform. A heavy man in a sweat-stained khaki shirt turns out to be the captain in charge and, after a good deal of questioning of Jim which establishes that he got there by accident while on a botanical expedition, explains that the Indians are a random group of the inhabitants who, after recent acts of protest against the government, are just about to be killed to remind other possible protestors of the advantages of not protesting. However, since Jim is an honoured visitor from another land, the captain is happy to offer him a guest's privilege of killing one of the Indians himself. If Jim accepts, then as a special mark of the occasion, the other Indians will be let off. Of course, if Jim refuses, then there is no special occasion, and Pedro here will do what he was about to do when Jim arrived, and kill them *all*. Jim, with some desperate recollection of schoolboy fiction, wonders whether if he got hold of a gun, he could hold the captain, Pedro and the rest of the soldiers to threat, but it is quite clear from the set-up that nothing of that kind is going to work: any attempt at that sort of thing will mean that all the Indians will be killed, and himself. The men against the wall, and the other villagers, understand the situation, and are obviously *begging him to accept*. What should he do? (Italics mine.) (Smart and Williams 1973, 98–99)[15]

And finally judicial punishment:

Recognizing that he can prevent extensive carnage only by framing some innocent person [who would certainly be killed by the mob if nothing is done], the magistrate has him framed, goes through the mockery of a trial and has him executed. (Adapted from Nielsen 1973, 73–74; 1990, 136)

Brody argues that in cases where if nothing is done, all will die, then "nothing is lost" if one or more are killed to save a greater number. That

15. Cf. Donagan (1977, 207–9) who discusses Williams's case in order to point out to consequentialists the difficulty of *knowing* what would happen. See Mack (1985, 23, 23 n. 27) on the two versions of Williams's "Jim" case.

is, no unfairness is done to the one or ones killed, for their lives would have been lost anyway if nothing is done. The conviction that underlies this thesis is that rights exist to protect the well-being or liberty of an individual; when in effect such well-being or liberty would be lost in any case, then the right in question ceases to operate; it has no function to perform. Thus, let us say that when nothing is lost the right is *suspended*.[16] And if the justification for killing is nothing is lost, it is not morally relevant whether the one to be killed proleptically consents; when the right ceases to be functional, it is suspended. Pietro cannot protest that he does not yield. The Indians who beg Jim to kill one of their number rather than allow them all to be killed are not agreeing to yield, but are, on my interpretation, acknowledging that nothing is lost and hence that one of them should be killed.

It is instructive to compare the nothing-is-lost rationale to the "miniride" principle enunciated by Tom Regan and to relate each to a case he discusses:

> Special considerations aside, when we must choose between overriding the rights of many who are innocent or the rights of few who are innocent, and when each affected individual will be harmed in a prima facie comparable way, then we ought to choose to override the rights of the few in preference to overriding the rights of the many. (1983, 305)

Here is the case:

> Fifty-one miners are trapped in a mine cave-in and are certain to die in a very short time if nothing is done. Suppose there is only one way to reach fifty of the trapped men in the allotted time. An explosive charge, deftly placed, will open a parallel shaft through which the trapped men can then escape. But suppose there is this complication: If the explosive is used, the remaining miner, who, as it happens, is trapped in that shaft, is certain to be killed. This one miner could be saved, however, if we placed a similar charge in the shaft

---

16. Brody does not accept the notion of the fetus as a pursuer—or double effect—and thus justifies abortion only when "nothing is lost." Cf. Davis (1980, 197–201) who notes that Foot's treatment of what Brody calls nothing-is-lost cases would require revision of the negative duty not to harm; Foot permits killing the potholer whose head is facing in because "there is no serious conflict of interests" (Davis 1980, 198). I try here to show how the right is suspended in nothing-is-lost situations, thus removing the difficulties Davis finds in Foot. Cf. Devine (1978, 147) who rejects nothing is lost (what he calls extreme necessity) in the village and lynch mob cases.

where the other miners are trapped; but doing this will have the foreseeable consequence of killing all fifty miners in that shaft. (1983, 298)

In these circumstances the "miniride" principle says we should save the fifty miners. Because we respect the rights of all equally we try to preserve the most (1983, 305, 307).

First, note that the mining case as Regan describes it is actually one in which nothing is lost; all fifty-one miners will die if nothing is done. Thus, if nothing is lost obtains, then the right of the one miner is not overridden, rather, it ceases to be operative. More precisely, the rights of all the miners are suspended, since they would have all died if nothing is done. I assume that proportionality would still lead us to save the fifty instead of the one.[17] Thus on my view the miniride principle is not necessary if all would die if nothing is done—the one miner's right is not overridden but suspended. I argue in Chapter 4 that the miniride principle applies only in one restricted sort of case.

Second, the case could be redescribed so that nothing is lost would not apply, but it still would be covered by double effect. Suppose that the one miner is not trapped, and hence would not die anyway if nothing is done, but would be killed as a side effect of the rescue effort to save the fifty. On a double-effect interpretation, one has to blast a shaft free, killing the one miner therein, but proportionately saving fifty. Note, moreover, that double effect even seems to be applicable in principle (formally, as it were) to the case as Regan describes it: one still blasts the shaft free, killing the one miner as a proportionate side effect. The point to see here is that, if nothing is lost applies, then while double effect is in principle applicable, it is, in the language of Richard McCormick, unnecessary (1981a, 443; see also n. 19 in this chapter). It does not actually have to be applied because the miner's right is suspended where nothing is lost.

What difficulties does nothing is lost present? Brody argues it is not

---

17. Taurek (1977) argues that where all will die if nothing is done, one must flip a coin to decide, for example, whether to kill one to save fifty or fifty to save one. He reasons that one cannot sum lives into an aggregate; thus the numbers do not count. Regan grants that each loss is as significant as any other but thinks that harms can be aggregated; there is no one individual who suffers the various harms, but they can be added up. Thus we treat all the miners fairly when we save fifty instead of one (Regan 1983, 297–301). On Taurek, see Kamm (1993). Note that cases of the distribution of scarce resources where some are saved and others let die are parallel to the nothing-is-lost cases where one has to kill in order to save: in both sorts of cases, all will die if nothing is done; in the first, one must let some die to save others, and in the second, one must kill.

necessary that in nothing-is-lost cases all would have died from the *same cause* if nothing is done. Here is Brody's example:

> By a series of accidents for which no one is to blame, the two people in room r2 will be blown up by a bomb within a few minutes. The only way to prevent the ignition of the bomb is to defuse it by destroying the triggering mechanism which is located in room r1, but the single person in room r1 will be destroyed along with the mechanism. However, he is having a massive coronary attack and will certainly die anyway within the same range of time. (1975, 21)

This case shows that for Brody, the fact of distinct causes is not morally relevant. Brody does not accept double effect, so the fact that one destroys the triggering mechanism and the one person dies as an unintended side effect is not significant. The one person must be about to die anyway, but that death need not be caused by the same event that would have killed the greater number, in this case the bomb.

But Brody does argue and I agree that the element of time is significant; if the one we must kill to save the others would live for a "significant length of time" if nothing is done, then

> our taking his life now means that we will have unfairly subjected him to a significant loss. (1975, 21–22)

But what is a significant amount of time? Nielsen's indispensable serum case raises this issue neatly:

> Suppose that several dangerously ill people can be saved only if we kill a certain individual and use his diseased dead body in the preparation of a serum. (1973, 74; 1990, 136)

If we assume that the diseased person would die if nothing is done, then the issue is how long this person would live. But this is not the only question. What if those who could be saved would still have shorter life spans than normal (due to the disease), thus narrowing the gap between the time the diseased man would have if nothing is done and the time those saved would have? The nothing-is-lost rationale seems to depend on a comparative judgment: the one killed must have a relatively short time to live in comparison to the time that would be left to those who are saved.

There is another important element of judgment here. The basic point of nothing is lost is that, as Brody puts it, the one to be killed does not

·"suffer any significant losses . . . in unrealized potential" (1975, 151 n. 18).
The judgment rides on "significant," and hence depends on assumptions
not only about the quantity of life remaining, but also its quality.

Whom to Kill

I noted above that in some proleptic yielding cases there is no choice about
whom to kill. The same is true of some nothing-is-lost cases. There are
cases in which some particular individual(s) must die if some other(s) is
(are) to be saved. For example, in the potholing case, it is the one who is
stuck who must be killed. In the indispensable serum case, a certain diseased
individual must be killed, presumably for medical reasons. In some classic
abortion cases, the threatening fetus will live if the woman is allowed to
die, but in others both will die if nothing is done, and, moreover, the choice
as to who shall live is forced: for example, in one sort of case if nothing is
done both the woman and the unborn would die, and only the woman
could be saved; killing the unborn will save the woman but allowing the
woman to die will not save the unborn.[18]

   In another set of cases there is a choice about who is to be killed. If there
is a choice, what criterion should we use to make it? Let us ask the question
with regard to the nothing-is-lost cases (whatever we decide would be applicable, *mutatis mutandis,* to the yielding cases). In Williams's oppressor case,
Jim must choose which Indian to kill; in the judicial punishment case, one
must choose whom to frame and execute. Consider these cases of Nielsen's:

> There are five shipwrecked people on a liferaft. All are of sound
> health, with people who love and depend on them at home, except
> for one ill old man slowly dying of cancer and whose relatives and
> close friends are all dead. Suppose further that the sea is getting
> rough and that it is as evident as anything can be that (a) they will
> not soon be rescued and (b) unless one man gets out into the freezing
> waters, the raft will be swamped.

> There are two men in a liferaft. One is simply a plain man (a plain

18. When Foot (1978) argues that it does not matter whether you have to crush the fetus's
head or merely kill it as a foreseen result of a hysterectomy, she is presumably assuming that
in both cases the fetus would die if nothing is done. In the hysterectomy/cancerous uterus
case, however, it is not necessarily the case that the fetus would die if nothing is done (see
Nicholson 1978, 21). See Chapter 4.

banker, teacher, car dealer, trolley-car conductor), the other a scientist on the verge of making a major discovery in cancer research which will lead to a breakthrough in the treatment of cancer. (Nielsen 1973, 70, 71; 1990, 133)

These cases are similar to another sort of abortion case where if nothing is done both would die but *either* the woman or the unborn could be saved.[19]

In some cases the immediate situation puts one life against another (abortion, the two persons on a raft), in others the situation requires a choice of taking one life (or conceivably more) out of several (Williams's Indians, the five people on a raft). In all of these one must choose who will die by some distributive criterion. These cases are like lifesaving cases where resources are scarce and one must choose who gets them; they require a decision about just distribution. In the classic cases involving the distribution of kidney machines, for example, some die and some live depending on how the resources are distributed; in the nothing-is-lost cases, one has to choose whom to kill.

Brody insists that in such cases the only fair solution is to cast lots.[20] He

---

19. Here is a sketch of the nothing-is-lost abortion cases: 1) Both would die if nothing is done, but the choice will be *forced:* either it will be possible to save the woman but not the fetus, or vice versa. 2) Both would die if nothing is done, but one must *choose* whom to save. N.B.: In ectopic pregnancies—often covered by double effect in the Catholic tradition—both woman and fetus will die if nothing is done. When nothing is lost obtains, some Roman Catholic moralists say that double effect is otiose; one needs only the notion of lesser evil, or if the goods are incommensurate, some random method of choice (see McCormick 1981a, 443). McCormick suggests that the difference between an abortion case and the framing of an innocent in order to stop a lynch mob is that in the former the deed that kills also saves but in the latter "there is never an inherent connection between killing an innocent person and changing the murderous mind of a lynch mob" (1981a, 444). In my view, if the innocent would die in any case, then nothing is lost would apply to the frame case also. If the innocent would not die anyway, then it is not the lack of an "inherent connection" in itself but the moral fact that the innocent's right against fatal use remains intact. Cf. McCormick's treatment (1981a, 445ff.).

20. Ramsey might have agreed at least on this point. Ramsey, unlike Brody, as I note in the following chapters, uses the notion of material aggressor and double effect to justify some abortions. Ramsey (1971; 1973) makes clear, however, that his justification of abortion in craniotomy applies only where both fetus and woman would die if nothing is done. Thus, if the fetus could be delivered alive, but the woman would die, Ramsey would not allow the craniotomy, for he resists any judgments of the comparative worth of lives *in themselves* or *to others*; a judgment of proportion in favor of the woman is not allowed. But if both would die, then one is not required to lose both lives. Because he seems to be assuming not only that both would die but also that only the woman could be saved, the choice as to whom to save is forced. If either could be saved, presumably he would have agreed with Brody that some method of random choice is necessary, since he insists that one cannot weigh the worth of lives in a conflict of one life with another.

argues, for example, that some random procedure should be used when both the woman and the unborn will die if nothing is done, but *either* could be saved. Nielsen, however, casting his argument in utilitarian terms, argues that the greatest length and quality of life overall should be achieved. In the case of five people on a life raft, for example, we not only want to save the most lives, but we choose who will die on the grounds of the greatest amount of future good overall. His criteria, however, could also be interpreted as criteria of fairness chosen by right-holders for situations where their right not to be killed is suspended: 1) in the case of the "dispensable oldster," the oldster has had a greater share of life in contrast to the young people aboard and has very limited expectations regarding the quantity and quality of life remaining; 2) in the case of the cancer scientist, usefulness to others is a criterion of the fair distribution of a scarce resource. Thus, as opposed to casting the debate here simply as a conflict between the utilitarian who appeals to the greatest good of the greatest number, and the rights advocate, who does not adduce the overall length or quality of life but uses only a random equalizing method for deciding who should live, we can see the criteria Nielsen adduces as criteria rights holders could accept.

In what sense would the people on the rafts accept these criteria? First, they do not make a proleptic agreement to yield (on the basis of a calculation of their self-interest) as in the cases where the one to be sacrificed would live if nothing is done; because the one to be sacrificed would die with the others if nothing is done, the right not to be killed is suspended. The ones who normally have the right must now forge criteria of distribution that do not assume it. Second, if the right is suspended, they still could assume an underlying commitment to the welfare of all. Furthermore, if they assume this underlying commitment, then it seems that the parties find themselves in effect behind a veil of ignorance, where they disregard their own place in the natural and social lottery. Retaining a commitment to the welfare of all, but having their right not to be killed suspended, they would reason without regard to the particulars of their own situation. Not "knowing" whether they will be old or young or sick or well, a plain person or a cancer doctor, it seems to me that they would choose, when the right not to be killed is suspended, and on the assumption that length and quality of life are basic goods, to maximize those goods in the two cases as Nielsen suggests.[21] With no right to "trump utility," no right that constrains maxi-

21. See Reeder (1992) on the famine in Ursula LeGuin's novel *The Dispossessed*. When *all* would die if nothing is done, then one distributes food so as to maximize lives saved. I do not pretend to have dealt adequately with the distributive question of whom to save in a situation of scarce resources. My general sense, however, is that, where the parties have no special claim on the resources, respect for the equality of persons does not require that we

mization, the parties, assuming they retain a commitment to the welfare of all, would reason so as to maximize the "greatest good of the greatest number."

Collaboration with Tyranny

I argue, following Brody, that when all would die, one can take innocent life because "nothing is lost." That all would die, however, is not sufficient in major strands of the theological traditions and it is important to ask why. Here again we see a hard case where the consensus apparently breaks up.

David Daube interprets teachings in Judaic tradition concerning "collaboration with tyranny" (1965; see also Daube 1987).[22] The issue, which reflects the historical experience of the Jewish people, concerns

> what is the proper response of a group if the oppressor puts before it the alternative of handing over a member for killing or perishing in its entirety. (1965, 2)

Stretching over a number of centuries this issue arose in confrontations first between Jews and hostile groups of gentiles and then between communities of Jews and non-Jewish governments.[23] I do not attempt to report, much less treat as a historian, Daube's account of the development of Rabbinic doctrine, but rather I attempt only to raise some interpretive questions about the teachings he discusses.

Daube summarizes the ruling on which subsequent teaching was apparently based:

> If a company of Jews . . . walking in the road is threatened by heathen who say, "Give us one of you that we may kill him, otherwise we shall kill you all," they must rather all be killed. However, if the demand is for a named individual like Sheba son of Bichri, then, in order to avoid wholesale slaughter, he should be surrendered. (1965, 18–19)

---

use a randomizing method. In any case, whatever we do, we will justifiably let some die (fail to save). See Chapter 1, note 48.

22. Cf. Donagan's treatment of Daube's cases and rulings (1977, 181–83).

23. Daube dates most of the texts between ca. 100 C.E. and ca. 500 C.E.

We should note first that the fact all will be killed if nothing is done is not a sufficient condition of the rightness of handing someone over; one may not hand someone over to heathen thugs even if all would otherwise die. It is also necessary that someone be named, and the someone should be in some, but not necessarily all, respects like Sheba, son of Bichri, who was a rebel against King David (2 Sam. 20). David's general said to the city where Sheba had taken refuge, give me Sheba and I will leave the city alone; Sheba's head was cut off and was thrown out to the general. (A "wise woman" arranged all of this.) The teaching apparently is as follows: someone who is in trouble with the ruling authority, even if the demand is unjust (it was just in Sheba's case), and even where the ruler is not a legitimate Jewish monarch (like David), may be given up to be killed (in Sheba's case the community does the killing) (1965, 21–23). The first part of the teaching refers to groups of heathen or gentile oppressors, the second to a ruling power. The teaching as a whole lays down the conditions that it must be a government that demands, and the demand must be for a particular individual (1965, 25); an individual may not be given up even on the demand of the government if someone is not named. The teaching refers to handing over for death, but following Daube, as I note subsequently, the community would apparently be equally accountable whether it does the killing as in Sheba's case or merely hands the individual over to the authorities.

Daube gives an example of what is not allowed:

> The mayor of a village may be uncertain where his duty lies if told by the commander of occupying troops that acts of sabotage have taken place in the region; that three villagers are to pay with their lives; and that unless that number is forthcoming by 12 noon, a detachment will be sent in to put every human being to the sword. (1965, 20–21)

"Jewish law is unambiguous"; only a named individual may be surrendered. The demand of the authorities is at least not arbitrary: "the [named] man had done something to draw such wrath on himself" (1965, 76).[24] Thus, the government must make the demand and the demand cannot be simply for some member(s) of the community to act as a scapegoat; it must be for whoever has explicitly offended the ruling power (for instance, by committing acts of sabotage).

---

24. Daube presents the mayor's case as a moral dilemma: "the mayor would be fatefully wrong whichever decision he makes" (1965, 21). But if Jewish law is clear, then the mayor does no wrong in letting the village die. See Chapter 5.

Thus, the fact that all would die if nothing is done is not a sufficient condition, as it arguably would be in an ethic where rights exist for the sake of finite human capacities. If Bleich's theological ethic is in continuity with the ancient Rabbis, then life is God's; one does not have title to one's own life in virtue of one's own capacities for temporal liberty and well-being or in light of any other rationale for the protection and promotion of these capacities alone; one has one's title from God, and temporal possibilities do not exhaust the field of moral considerations (for this point, see Newman [1990]). It is not sufficient that all will die if nothing is done precisely because one's title to life is not suspended for that reason alone. Since God values human life and wants people to live (individually and as a community), it is significant that if nothing is done all will die and that the one(s) to be killed would have perished in any case. God would rather have some of the community survive than none. But the fact that the one(s) to be killed would have died anyway does not in itself permit the community to save itself. There must be some reason for handing over that pertains to the individual's relation to the government. Such a reason—along with the threat to the entire community—is enough, for it seems to reflect the divine will for the conduct of the community during its unfortunate sojourn under foreign rule: the authority of government to lay hands on an offender must be respected even when that government is gentile and possibly unjust.

Thus, when we properly understand the religious significance of the fact that all will die if nothing is done, we can see why it does not warrant the moral conclusion drawn when "nothing is lost" is sufficient. The fact that all will die if nothing is done does not alone warrant taking life in the Judaic sources because the duty not to kill rests on different premises.

The additional conditions that the demand must be for a named individual and that it must proceed from the government are also reflected in a talmudic teaching about women:

> "And thus, women to whom heathens say, Give us one of you that we may defile her, otherwise we shall defile you all, let them defile them all, but they shall not surrender a single soul from Israel." (1965, 69)

Daube takes this passage to say that

> the demand here would always be put by gangsters, would not be directed against a political offender who had become intolerable to the government. That would be so even if a certain woman were

singled out. There may be a glimmer of justice in the killing of a person, there cannot be in defilement. (1965, 76–77)

It is not that the "guilt of selection" itself must be avoided (1965, 78), but the fact that even if named by the mob there is no justifiable reason here for a woman to be harmed (1965, 77–78, 81–82).[25] The request does not come from a ruling power.

However, two sorts of women could be handed over: one already unclean and a slave woman (1965, 78). According to Daube the first signifies "an immoral woman, an adulteress, a harlot," and the second a Jewish slave; the latter "were commonly misused and, above all, they had a reputation for being free with their favors" (1965, 79). Daube says these two sorts of women have already broken sexual laws; thus, defilement is not to them "the greatest of evils" (1965, 79). Yet in what sense is defilement an evil? Daube's interpretation seems to rest on the assumption that the evil is uncleanness. If a woman is already unclean because of adultery, for example, then rape changes nothing or at most only adds to her impurity; but even if a woman has not broken sexual laws, rape no less than adultery can apparently render her impure. Apparently the immoral woman and the slave woman are both already unclean; to neither is rape the greatest of evils.[26]

The only exceptions, then, to the requirement that an individual be named by the government are the cases of the unclean women.[27] Daube also notes that it is not permitted to kill a named individual to save one's own life (1965, 26–27). He refers to the famous teaching that the precepts of the Torah can be transgressed to save one's life except in three cases:

A man bidden to commit a sin on pain of death may do so, with three exceptions—idolatry, gross sexual crimes, and murder. The murder envisaged would in general be of someone specifically desig-

25. In the cases dealing with men, one would also not hand over to thugs even if they select. The individual must be named, and thus the community does not have to select a scapegoat; but naming alone is not enough: the naming must proceed from a government (cf. Daube 1965, 22). On these points I learned from a paper by Barry Bloch. I have also profited from comments by Louis Newman on these issues and other features of my interpretation here.

26. Does this teaching suggest that no further significant harm can be done through rape if uncleanness is already present? That in effect nothing is lost because the relevant sort of damage has already been done? I am not competent to address these questions historically, but on conceptions of women in the classic Judaic sources, see Adler (1978) and Wegner (1988).

27. In the Middle Ages Daube says the notion of a named individual was extended to the defilement case (1965, 80–83). However, he takes this as contrary to the original teaching in the Mishnah and the Jerusalemite Talmud.

nated by the oppressor. We hear of a case that occurred in the first half of the fourth century A.D.: the governor of a place (whether a heathen or a Jewish stooge must be left open) ordered a man to put another man to death; if he refused, he would be killed himself. The man so ordered consulted a prominent Rabbi (Raba or Rabbah) who decided in accordance with the principle just mentioned, adding the argument: "Is your blood redder than his?" It is an impressive contrast: a community threatened should hand over the man wanted (though even a community must perish rather than yield to an unspecified demand for just some man), an individual must let himself be killed rather than become a murderer. (1965, 26–27)

Daube adds the comment that "the main rationale of this structure is the enormous difference between the extinction of a group and the loss of an individual" (1965, 27). The difference between the two cases, Daube suggests, makes sense only if we assume that God wills the preservation of the community, but does not permit individuals to preserve their lives at the cost of killing another demanded by the oppressor.

Of course, if in this case the one whom the authority wants killed would be *spared* if the one asked to kill refuses (and is killed instead), then the cases of the two individuals and the group would be fundamentally dissimilar. "Is your blood redder than his" might indicate that it is indeed a case of whether the one asked to kill should choose his life *over* the other's. The ruler seems to want *someone* dead and gives the one individual the choice of whom. The ruler is not saying, kill the offender or I will kill you both; the ruler (on this interpretation) says kill the offender and I will let you live; if you don't, I will kill you and let the offender live. On this reading the difference between the cases has nothing to do with a contrast between preserving a community and preserving an individual, but with the fact that in the case of the two individuals the nothing is lost condition does not obtain.

However, if it is assumed that both individuals will be killed if the one does not execute the other, then the situation is at least parallel to the case of the group where all will die if nothing is done. That the texts make a distinction between the two cases could be explained perhaps by the fact that the group only hands over for execution while the individual is asked to be the executioner. But those individuals who hand over would seem to be equally responsible (Daube 1965, 23). It does not seem to me that the distinction between handing over and doing the killing oneself is significant in this case or in the cases involving the community. In the biblical Sheba case, we remember, the community did its own killing.

What could explain the difference (assuming that both individuals would die) could also be perhaps that it is not simply the fact that all would die which is at work here, for that applies (by hypothesis) to both the case of the two individuals and the group. Rather one could argue that the order to kill in the case of the two is arbitrary; the one to be killed is not a political or criminal offender, and hence there is no "glimmer of justice" here even though the ruler makes the demand.[28] The interpreter would need to argue that in the case of the two individuals, even though the ruler names an offender, the selection is arbitrary, and hence the ruler does not deserve the respect generally owed to the authority of government.

Alternatively, one might argue that the order does satisfy the "named by the government" condition but that this case makes clear that a community must be threatened with death if the nothing-is-lost condition is to have any weight; perhaps nothing is lost simply in itself has no weight at all (much less sufficient weight) when only individuals are concerned, and applies only when a *community* is threatened with extinction (this seems to be Daube's interpretation). For nothing is lost to have any weight, it must pertain to a community organized around a set of social and religious practices; on this view it would not have weight when applied merely to a collection of individuals. Thus, although the named-by-the-government condition does obtain here—so the interpretation goes—the idea that all will die is not relevant because it is not the life of an organized community that is at stake.

Another possible interpretation, still assuming both individuals will die if nothing is done, is that the difference between the rulings in the case of the two individuals and the Sheba case might have to do with the community's *relation* to the ruling power. When the community is involved, then the ruler's demand can be respected and the community saved; the case of the two individuals does not raise perhaps the issue of respect for the government as the case involving the community does. On this interpretation, nothing is lost would be relevant both in the case of the community and the case of the individuals, but only in the former does the factor of respect for the ruling power come into play: only when the community is involved does the named-by-the-government condition obtain. Thus, even if in the case of the individuals the demand is from a ruler and not a mob,

---

28. In Genesis Rabba a legend about King Jehoiakim who rebelled against Nebuchadnezzar has the former appealing to the teaching "one does not push away a soul (life) for a soul (life)" (Daube 1965, 57). Jehoiakim, of course, is not innocent but conforms in part to the Sheba paradigm (1965, 56, 62). Daube seems to say that in the paradigm case the charge could be unjust, but still, since the individual has committed the offense, there is a "glimmer of justice."

and even if it can be assumed that there is a "glimmer of justice" in the demand, the community as such is not involved and hence the named-by-the-government condition does not come into play. Even though a ruler makes the demand in the case of the individuals, the named-by-the-government condition does not obtain because the relation of a community to a ruling power is not involved.

In any case, the Sheba ruling that a named individual could be handed over to a foreign power was affirmed in later teachings according to Daube (1965, chap. 1). A Rabbi named Joshua ben Levi took the view that the named individual should be surrendered, and he delivered over a certain Ulla:

> It happened that one Ulla bar Qosheb, wanted by the—non-Jewish —government, fled to the Rabbi, who gave him asylum in his house. It is clear that Ulla was not a common criminal; his offence was political, or perhaps of a personal nature against the ruler; and to be caught meant certain death. In the eyes of most Jews, we may safely suppose, he was deserving of protection, a hero, though for some he may have been a liability, a troublemaker. The authorities, in turn, from their point of view, were not, it appears, without a reasonable case against him. They sent troops and threatened to destroy Lydda unless he was handed over. (1965, 5)

In one version of this story the prophet Elijah, who had been a regular visitor to Joshua but subsequently stays away, says that a true saint should not have approved the handing over at all, even if it was legally permitted (1965, 12); thus one could read this story as teaching a distinction between what is legally permissible according to Jewish law and what is morally approved. (On law and supererogation, see Newman 1989.) However, in another version, according to Daube, the objection is softened; now Elijah only objects to Joshua (as Rabbi) having handed over Ulla, not to its having been done (1965, 14).

Daube notes, however, that opposition to the idea that a named individual should be surrendered to a non-Jewish government appears in other sources. In certain sources a Rabbi affirmed: "Since he would be slain and they would be slain, give him to them and you should not all be slain." To this R. Simeon ben Johai retorted: "Anyone rebelling against the kingship of the house of David is deserving of death" (1965, 2).[29] Daube interprets

---

29. A tradition from Tosephta and Genesis Rabbah, but not in the Jerusalemite Talmud (Daube 1965, 28).

the first Rabbi to be saying, hand over a named individual to the non-Jewish government when the threat to the community is real (1965, 30–33); this is the standard Sheba ruling. But Simeon is saying do not hand over to the gentile government even a named individual because the situation is not sufficiently like the case of a rebel against a Jewish king (1965, 38).

Later in the third century a view develops that is similar to Simeon's but not as radical; Resh Laqish says the individual must be "deserving of death." Resh Laqish in effect accepts the standard ruling but qualifies it (Daube 1965, 41–42); the ruler does not have to be Jewish, but the individual must deserve death.

Yet what does "deserving of death" mean? Daube says it does not mean deserving of death according to the law or practice of the foreign government, nor in a strict sense according to Jewish law. Rather, says Daube:

> Resh Laqish, we argued, though drawing on Simeon, does admit some relevance in the case of Sheba and must be employing "deserving of death" in a sense which leaves his utterance with a minimum of real substance. Probably, in his mouth, the phrase denotes guilty of a deed for which by the general standards of Jewish doctrine, and taking account of what is due to Caesar, death is the adequate retribution. (1965, 45)

In any case, no formal court sentence is required (1965, 47).[30]

What these ancient debates may reveal, I believe, is that in the moral universe of the Talmud the nothing-is-lost justification is not sufficient, at least in the tyrant cases. For it to have weight at all, as Daube apparently argued, the community may have to be at stake. I suggest, however, that perhaps the community had to be involved, not for nothing is lost, but for named by the government to come into play. The tradition in any case does not grant permission to hand someone over for death unless the individual has crossed the ruling power. The spectrum of offense varies from the broadest understanding, which would evidently include any sort of political difficulty (any named individual), to Resh Laqish's attempt to narrow the category. This is Daube's hypothesis:

> In the second century, during the Hadrianic persecution, sophisticated argumentation was needed to find a basis for warding off wholesale slaughter; and the case of Sheba was adduced as indicating

---

30. Daube suggests that perhaps conformity to the Noachide commandments could be a guide (1965, 45–46).

that a community bidden to hand over a man wanted by the authorities or else all would be killed must go on living. By the third century, the worst being over, equally sophisticated reasoning is employed the other way; emphasis is now placed on such features of the case of Sheba as will rule out a handing over in any but the most exceptional circumstances. (1965, 43; cf. 76)

My sense is that the underlying moral doctrine is that God is lord of life; God has concern for communities, but it is better that all die rather than one be killed who has not crossed the government. That all would die if nothing is done is a necessary but not sufficient condition of the rightness of handing over a member of the community. The early view Daube distinguishes suggests, perhaps, a grudging acceptance of the authority of the state and even legal positivism (according to the Babylonian Talmud "the laws of the state are laws"); but the view of Resh Laqish seems to introduce a standard for judging the ruler's judgment (1965, 43–44). Not every action the rulers say morally and legally deserves death really does.

In sum, then, the theological tradition and the view Brody develops overlap but their assessments apparently do not coincide. Brody's case where all would die would not be accepted by the Rabbis—"Pietro" is named, but only by "brigands."[31] At other points in the tradition, however, nothing is lost may have been taken as sufficient. There is a classic teaching in the Talmud that when the woman's life is in danger one may perform embryotomy if the unborn is still in the womb, but one may not do so if the "greater part," or the "head" in one reading, is sticking out (Feldman 1974; cf. Daube 1965, 58). (The assumption, apparently, is that full moral status is achieved when the head or greater part emerges.) But there is another ruling where it is said that even when the head is out, one may perform embryotomy if otherwise *both* the woman and the baby would die (Feldman 1974, 283–84). In the tyrant cases, however, nothing is lost does not appear to be sufficient; the role of government in the divine plan must also be taken into account.[32]

31. Brody says that nothing is lost is "essentially, the opinion of R. Yochanan in (*Jerusalem Talmud, Trumah,* Chapter 8) his discussion of the biblical case of Sheva ben Bichri" (1975, 150–51 n. 13; cf. Brody 1975, 13, 18).

32. One could speculate that there is a reason for this difference. In the abortion case, it is perhaps assumed that only the woman can be saved; there is no choice about whom to save. In contrast, in the cases where the life of the community is at stake, and nothing is lost obtains, the tradition insists on a certain sort of selection, that is, named by the government.

3

The Pursuer

So if someone has been forced to attack or cannot control their actions they also forfeit their right to life?

Some people hold that the right to life of the "innocent" <u>may never be</u> <u>overridden</u>; that is, those who have not voluntarily attacked others may not be killed even to save the lives of many others. Chapter 2 describes two sorts of cases in which this principle would not allow killing. I justify killing in cases of yielding and nothing is lost, and hence amend the principle. I argue in this chapter that in addition to voluntary attackers who seek to take life, nonvoluntary and involuntary "pursuers," in the vocabulary of the Talmud, may be fatally repelled. Strictly speaking, one *forfeits* the right to life only when one voluntarily brings lethal force against others. Yet what about nonvoluntary and involuntary attacks? Here I argue that the attacker should not be said to forfeit the right—the attacker does not voluntarily fail to respect the rights of others—but nonetheless the attacker loses the right. Whether through a nonvoluntary action or involuntary behavior, something befalls the attacker that gives the victim or third par-

Agreed

[handwritten annotation at top: + you know that the attack is nonvoluntary or involuntary then [the] use of deadly force is unethical. If [aware] of it you are willing [reason] to protect yourself.]

ties the right to repel the attack even to the point of killing the pursuer if necessary.[1]

These conditions can be expressed as part of the concept of the right to life, as circumstances under which it is overridden, or as exceptions to it. How the conviction is expressed varies with the context, but we make the point in all these ways. I try here to write conditions into the concept of the right. I try to show, however, that there are a limited number of conditions that should be written into the right. I answer the question why some killings are unjust, and some not, by appealing to the coherence of the overall account, not by appealing to an already determined notion of the right to life.

Judith Jarvis Thomson (1976, 7) objects, however, to the view she held previously that the right not to be killed is a right not to be killed unjustly ("moral specification"), because one still needs to explain why certain killings are unjust. The method of "factual specification" (the conditions under which the right is void are written into the concept of the right) is also flawed because there are too many cases to include (1976, 8–9).[2] In my view, however, we can uncover at least some of the convictions that underlie our agreements and still defer the larger task of justification (see the Introduction). As for the variety of cases, the tradition (of overlapping traditions) I am explicating and developing here finds a coherent and limited set of circumstances in which we kill or let die, but not unjustly.

Aiding and Protecting

To carry forward the argument, let me say more about the basic rights delineated in the previous chapters. Henry Shue (1980) posits basic rights

---

1. Murphy (1973, 546–47) argues that those who use their freedom to "invade the rights of others" forfeit their rights to noninterference and justify counterinterference by others. However, I cannot save someone by interfering with an innocent person (a perfect duty overrides an imperfect duty). He rests his absolutism not on a "proof" but on the desire not to abandon the principle that persons do not belong to others to be used in their projects (549–50). Note that, as stated, the thesis is too strong; some rights of noninterference can perhaps be overridden to prevent a great evil; note also that if the only condition under which one loses the right to life is when one voluntarily interferes with others, then nonvoluntary and involuntary attackers may not be repelled.

2. Thomson has another objection that cuts across moral and factual specification. On her view, in some cases we must assume that someone has a right—even when it is morally permissible to infringe it—in order to explain why compensation is owed (1976, 10–11); if the circumstances were such that I don't really have the right in question, then why should I be compensated? I discuss these points in Chapter 5.

to security, subsistence, and liberty, each of which breaks down into three more specific sorts of rights: a right to avoid deprivation of the good in question, a right to be protected from deprivation, and a right to assistance once deprived. Shue argues that since the right to protection already includes the duty of others to act on our behalf, we should not think of rights as exhaustively divided into "negative" rights of noninjury or noninterference, and "positive" rights of aid. In my view we can say with equal justification that if protection is a positive duty, then it is *part* of aid; and thus we would have again the traditional distinction (discussed in Chapter 1) between not hurting and helping. The person on the road to Jericho had already been injured when the priest and the Levite failed to come to his aid (in Shue's sense); if the robbers had been about to attack, or the robbery were in progress, then it would have been a case of protection. But whether the attack is over or not, the question is whether others should act to enable the person to maintain the goods in question: if the victim is already deprived, then one tries to restore the goods lost (heal the injuries); if the victim is threatened or in the process of being harmed, one seeks to protect by preventing or interrupting the attack. In both cases, one is not merely fulfilling a duty not to injure, but one takes steps to secure goods for others. Thus, I include protection under the category of aid; the police or the soldier who prevents or stops harm is also providing a form of aid.[3] The threats that have already done harm, or that one tries to prevent or at least interrupt, can be either humanly caused or occur through some force of nature. One helps when one protects from deprivation or assists the already deprived.

The broad view I assume, then, in this chapter is that we have the right to protect ourselves, or to be protected when we cannot protect ourselves. More precisely, we have a "right" to defend ourselves at least in the weak sense that we are morally *permitted* to do so; whether we also have a duty to protect ourselves will depend on the broader moral views of parties to the consensus I outline here. For example, seeing one's life as a gift of God or oneself as a trustee could lead one to believe in a duty to preserve one's life. In any case, the consensus insists we have a right to the protection of

3. The inclusion of protection as a "positive" duty rests for Shue on the assumption that "social guarantees," including enforcement, are "analytic" in the very concept of basic rights (Shue 1980, 16ff., 32–33, 38–39, 60). One can build in such a meaning, but it seems clearly possible to define rights to security or subsistence only in terms of avoiding and aiding (in Shue's sense); what society should enforce about each could be treated as a separate question (cf. 1980, 55). However, if the notion of aid is broadened to include protection, and it seems reasonable to do so if our aim is to *maintain* a certain range of goods for all, then it becomes clearer why enforcement is necessary.

others in a stronger sense as well: not only are they morally permitted to help us, but they have a duty to do so; we have a right that is "correlated" to their duty, that is, we can demand their protection as a duty of justice. In theory, then, an onlooker would have been permitted, and I believe required, to use deadly force to repel Kitty Genovese's pursuer. As a second-order restriction we may decide to delegate this sort of aid to police or soldiers, but in principle the duty belongs to us all.

My central contention is that we are justified in protecting ourselves or being protected not only against the voluntary attacker, but against the nonvoluntary and the involuntary as well. My argument in short is as follows: if I do not protect myself or if I am not protected by others, I am in effect helping the nonvoluntary or involuntary attacker (the pursuer) at a cost beyond my duty to aid. The pursuer has not yet lost anything, nor is the pursuer under attack; but if I or others allow the burden of the nonvoluntary or involuntary pursuit to fall on me, then it is as if I were assisting the attacker. Not to be protected is to lose the good in question so that the attacker can continue to enjoy a similar good; it is in effect a choice, as I argue, to aid the attacker at a supererogatory cost.

Voluntary Aggression

It is commonly said that one has the right to repel an attacker who voluntarily and unjustly attempts to injure or kill; the voluntary attacker may be violently repulsed.[4] If necessary, in the words of Alan Gewirth, one may inflict "basic harms as severe as those the assailant threatens to inflict" (1978, 213–17; also see Donagan 1977, 84–85; Fried 1978, 43–44; David Richards 1971, 180–81). This doctrine—if necessary, inflict harms only as severe as those threatened—may not be correct, however. Suppose a rapist threatens a woman not with death but with cuts on the face unless she submits; should she not have the right to *kill* the rapist to avoid the cuts?[5]

---

4. Mack (1985, 13) says that "the right to self-defense is a second-order right to thwart by injurious force attacks upon one's life, limbs, and liberties. . . . Its appropriate exercise is governed by a conceptually prior specification of the rights to be defended"; cf. Kadish (1976; 1977) and Wasserman (1987).

5. If the behavior is not life-threatening, but injurious to some lesser degree, then, some have argued, the victim is entitled to cause harms up to and including the level of the harm threatened (depending on what is necessary), but no more. For example, the victim, in order to repel a threat that would cost a limb if not opposed, is entitled to harm the threatening party, if necessary, up to the level of the cost of a limb but not of life. I define "pursuer" here as life-threatening, so we would need some other term for an attack that is less dangerous to the victim. On whether the aggressor can be killed (whether at fault or not) if the cost to you would be less than life (limb or property), see Thomson (1991, 285–86). Thomson argues

If not the cuts, does not the threat of rape, even assuming that rape is not as severe a loss as death, justify killing the assailant?[6]

In any case, I begin by assuming that it is justified to kill if necessary in order to repel a lethal attack on oneself or others. In order to disarm the attacker, one may shoot at the attacker's weapon, killing the attacker in the process, or, if necessary, intend the death of the attacker as the means— shoot to kill. (See my concluding remarks on Ramsey in this chapter and the discussion of double effect in the next chapter.) The voluntary aggressor or pursuer attempts a lethal attack, and can in this sense "forfeit" the right to life. The justification for the right (whatever that may be) specifies that one's possession of the right is conditional on respecting the rights of others (cf. Thomson 1976, 15). However, the pursuer does not forfeit the right merely by the attack. The attack must continue; if it ceases, we must believe that it will resume so shortly that a counterattack is still necessary. In the case of Thomson's (1976) tank that stalls, for example, a counterattack would still be legitimate if the victim believes that the tank will restart immediately. Moreover, it is often said that the aggressor only forfeits the right if there is no way to stop or escape the aggression short of a lethal counterattack. The counterattack is a last resort.[7] Furthermore, we can assume that other standard conditions must be met if the counterattack is to be legitimate: one must have a "reasonable hope of success"; one's response must be "proportionate" (one would not be permitted to repel the attacker if one's response would as a side effect kill more than one would save); and one should intend to rectify the injustice, as opposed to using the occasion to express one's dislike or resentment. And of course, one's means of defense must not violate comparable rights of others; for example, one may not terror bomb noncombatants in order to restrain an aggressor.

Thus, one has a right to protect oneself against a lethal attack; others also have a duty to protect as part of their duty to aid.* I will not distin-

---

you may kill in order to avoid grave bodily harm, but not to avoid minor loss of property. See also Feinberg (1993, 216–18).

6. On taking the life of a rapist, see Finnis, Boyle, and Grisez (1987, 313).

7. See Ryan (1983, 511–12) who asks what is different about what the aggressors do when in one case the victim can escape and in the other cannot. The justification of self-defense in the case of "feigned" attack seems to me parasitic on the real case; we *excuse* someone who believed the attack was real.

*In fighting an aggressor, the soldier is most often presumably both exercising a right of *self*-defense and is simultaneously fulfilling a duty to aid (protect) *others*. The duty to others could be interpreted both as an expression of a general duty to aid (delegated for various reasons to the soldier) and as a special obligation to protect a particular political community. In some circumstances, the soldier could also be fulfilling a duty to help the community fulfill its duty to other communities.

guish what we are permitted to do to the attacker in our defense from what others can do on our behalf; the conditions for resorting to violence are the same. Some traditions do, however, draw a radical distinction; it is said in some versions of Christian ethics that we should not use lethal force to defend ourselves, but that we should use such force if necessary to protect other innocent parties; we are not, in other words, even *permitted* to defend ourselves by the use of lethal force, but we have a duty to defend others (see Outka 1992). For the purposes of the consensus I develop here, though, I assume that lethal force is appropriate either for self-defense or the defense of others.

There are differences between self-defense and the defense of others, of course, that pertain to the costs the defenders undergo. If one is defending oneself, one is presumably prepared to suffer grave loss if necessary, since one's own life is at stake. If others are the defenders, there will be different views as to the required cost to the defenders, ranging from "minimal" to "up to comparable cost" (see Chapter 1). What should they risk in order to defend you? In some cases, a defender could use lethal force with little risk to himself or herself (the defender can fire from behind a barrier), while in other instances the defender would undergo, or at least risk, grave injury. The cost required in any case presumably also depends on whether the defenders are acting as private persons or in certain roles, such as police or soldiers who have assumed additional obligations.

Another important difference between self-defense and defense of others is that in *self*-defense (the defense of oneself alone) one may not cause, even as a side effect, the death of an innocent bystander(s) (fatally injuring the bystander as a *means* is ruled out either in self-defense or defense of others; see Chapter 4 on double effect). I assume throughout that in self-defense one may not cause even the death of one innocent bystander, but that, for example, in defense of others the deaths of innocents as a side effect are permitted so long as the criterion of proportionality is satisfied. The underlying principle here is apparently broader: Either in self-defense or in defending *one* other, we may not take as a side effect another innocent life; as Paul Ramsey would put it, one may not weigh one life against another (see the conclusion of this chapter). The principle of proportionality—roughly, achieve the greatest good or least evil—would not be satisfied when one life is exchanged for another. However, to save more lives, which could include one's own, one may take—providing the means are permissible—a lesser number.

Are there objections to saying that the voluntary attacker "forfeits" the right not to be killed, thus justifying either self-defense or the protection of others? George P. Fletcher (1980) argues against the idea that the aggressor "forfeits" the right to life. In a standard range of legal cases where one forfeits rights, the "intentions of a putative violator are irrelevant" to the rights being forfeited (1980, 142–45). If I have legally forfeited my right to a copyright, and you publish my book, your conduct is justified whether or not you knew of or appealed to my loss of the right. But a jealous lover who fatally attacks someone in bed with his or her beloved is not justified because it turns out that the beloved was in fact being raped (on the assumption that a fatal attack would be justified if the lover had believed a rape was in process). Since the lover who acts out of jealousy did not have the right reason, the conduct was not morally justified. Thus, argues Fletcher, we should not think of the right to life being morally *forfeited*. The rapist's right to life is intact against the jealous lover.

Fletcher is correct in saying that the legal notion of forfeiture is only partially similar to the defense case, but the analogy is appropriate because the offending agent voluntarily does something that contributes to a change in his or her moral status. We extend the narrow legal use of the concept of forfeiture to a broader use if we include the various conditions noted above. For example, a standard condition is that the defender have as a reason the rectification of injustice; this is a matter not only of the goodness of the agent, but the rightness or legitimacy of the action. The change in moral relations that the aggressor's voluntary action brings about justifies the victim's or the third party's response provided the other conditions are satisfied; in this sense, the aggressor forfeits the right not to be killed.[8]

I argue in the last section of the chapter that moral relations are also analogously changed in the case of the nonvoluntary and involuntary aggressor. In an important sense, aggressors all deprive the victim of a good they had no right to take. It is important nonetheless to use the language of forfeiture to identify the voluntary aggressor. The standard doctrine of defense against a deadly threat (that I assume so far) specifies that a lethal counterattack is justified *when necessary,* and this is often interpreted to mean: use lethal force only if no less injurious means will disarm the attacker. I argue subsequently, however, that where voluntary aggression occurs, it may well be justified to use lethal force, even when a lesser injury—a nonlethal wound—would disarm the "guilty" attacker. If the *defender* would suffer a wound as a consequence of refraining from the use of deadly force, merely injuring the attacker instead, it may be justified to use deadly

---

8. Childress (1982a, 71–72, 75) takes the view that in a just war *(jus ad bellum),* the prima facie duty not to injure or kill is overridden by some other duty (not forfeited, but outweighed). On self-defense and the notion of forfeiture, see Thomson (1976; 1991), Parent (1980), Montague (1981), Wasserman (1987), and Stout (1990).

force anyway. Thus, I will amend the traditional doctrine as follows: Whereas against the nonvoluntary/involuntary pursuer one may use lethal force *only* when necessary, against the voluntary and guilty aggressor one may also use lethal force in cases when deadly force is not required to disarm but will protect the defender from injury. To say that the guilty aggressor *forfeits* the right to life therefore points to an important difference between this aggressor and the nonvoluntary/involuntary attacker.

My effort, then, in this chapter is to preserve two commonly occurring convictions: on the one hand, the voluntary pursuer breaks moral bonds, however various traditions explain these, and this fact is significant for our view of what can be done to repel such a pursuer; on the other hand, as I argue in the last section of the chapter, the fact of the "material" aggression of the nonvoluntary and involuntary pursuer is morally significant; such a pursuer also threatens life and this justifies our use of lethal force when necessary.

Are Soldiers Voluntary Aggressors?

The "domestic" situation and the war context are not strictly parallel. For example, in the domestic context one should try to avoid, say, an armed robber simply by fleeing; the job of protecting property and restraining the violent should be left to the police. But in the international context, where at least until recently there has been no police power, nations have had no recourse but to defend themselves or others. (I assume here that nations will sometimes be obligated to defend others; whether groups such as nations have a general duty to aid as individuals do I will not attempt to argue.)

There are also important differences between an aggressor who threatens one's life for some private purpose in a domestic context, and the aggressor in war whose threat is part of an attack by another political entity. Assuming, as Michael Walzer (1977) argues, that we are entitled to repel attacks on political sovereignty and territorial integrity on behalf of ourselves and others, are there other sorts of aggression we may legitimately repulse?[9]

---

9. See Hauerwas (1992, 137–38, 156 n. 5, 187–88, 203–4 n. 26) who, following Ramsey (1961), refers to the difference between interpreting war as self-defense or as defense of the innocent. Hauerwas argues that in just war theory these themes can be combined; the state defending itself is defending its people. Forms of Christian pacifism, of course, do not endorse violence even to defend others, but see Johnson (1991a, 9–10) on Ambrose's teaching that love requires one to protect the neighbor from unjust harm. On these issues, and the underlying questions about the tension between "natural justice" and love of enemies, see Ramsey and Hauerwas (1988), Miller (1991), and Cahill (1994). On *jus ad bellum,* see Johnson (1973; 1984).

Although we would continue to rule out wars of conquest in the name of national self-interest, would we acknowledge that there are forms of "economic aggression"? Are there economic resources vital to military defense? Are there resources necessary to prevent economic collapse (not just our current style of life) for ourselves or for many other states? And on what occasions should nations (unilaterally or acting under U.N. auspices) intervene in secessions, civil wars, or situations of domestic oppression? In regard to the latter in particular, should intervention be limited to situations in which, as Walzer argues, there is massacre or enslavement? Or should political torture or exclusion from political participation be sufficient *ceteris paribus* to intervene? Walzer, for example, seems to extend the notion of enslavement to cover cases of political and economic exclusion—for example, under apartheid (1985).

I do not pursue here these difficult issues regarding the doctrine of *jus ad bellum* and responsibility for international police actions. I will focus briefly, but with no pretense of offering an adequate account, on the question of the guilt of the aggressor in war.[10] Is there a difference in the domestic and international contexts? If the attacker in the domestic context is a voluntary or responsible agent, and hence "guilty" for the unjust attack, this guilt is part of the explanation why those who do not respect the rights of others "forfeit" their own right to immunity from attack. (I assume that voluntariness signifies both freedom and knowledge.) Walzer, however, does not think that soldiers even in an unjust cause are ever *guilty* attackers (Walzer 1977, 25–29, 34–37).[11] According to Walzer, combatants lose their

---

10. I assume here that combatants are participants in an organized attempt to make war; they may be combat soldiers, supporting soldiers, governmental leaders, or civilian workers who support soldiers. I incline to the view that those who support soldiers qua human beings (for example, with food, clothing) as well as those who make weapons are also legitimate objects of attack (cf. Nagel 1972; Murphy 1973, 532, 546–47; Walzer 1977, 133–37, 144–46ff.). Perhaps we need to distinguish military logistical support from the economic infrastructure of the enemy—for example, farms and farmers. In any case, civilians who merely approve the war are not combatants. See Mavrodes's attempt to interpret noncombatant immunity as a convention that is justified only if it would produce greater justice and less loss of life in the long run (1975, 129–30). Mavrodes objects to defining guilt in terms of degrees of participation; other factors such as approval of the war effort are relevant. Fullinwider (1975) in contrast bases the distinction between combatant and noncombatant on the principle of self-defense. Alexander extends Fullinwider by stating a principle of self-defense that not only makes moral guilt irrelevant, but also would allow one to kill some noncombatants who are a "necessary or sufficient cause of danger" (1976, 411–12, 415). Some theorists would see Alexander's "noncombatant supplier . . . driving a truck full of munitions" as a combatant (1976, 414).

11. Walzer agrees with Ramsey (1971) therefore that it is not the guilt of the attackers that justifies defense.

Agreed

immunity when they violate the rights of others to life and liberty by attacking the territorial integrity or sovereignty of a political community.[12] But for Walzer, at least under modern political conditions where nation states wage war, individual soldiers are not guilty. Whether a volunteer or a conscript, and whether or not the government has been freely elected, the soldier is not free, hence not a voluntary or responsible agent, and hence not guilty. For Walzer, only high officials of government are responsible and hence blameworthy for the initiation of an unjust war.[13] The generals, much less ordinary soldiers, are not blameworthy for going to war, no matter what the character of the regime that orders them into battle or the nature of its purposes. This doctrine makes "obedience to superior orders" a sufficient excuse for going to war. I believe Walzer intends it only as an *excuse:* members of the German Army or the U.S. Army in Vietnam were wrong (unjustified) in fighting their respective wars, but because they were un-free—they did not themselves make the decision to wage war and they would have preferred *ceteris paribus* not to—they were not fully voluntary agents and hence not responsible or blameworthy.

These soldiers are still liable to a lesser degree but still possess autonomy.

Is Walzer's thesis convincing? He seems to assume that because the decision is made in the first instance by the government, not the individual, and because the individual would presumably prefer not to be going to war, the soldier's participation is not free and hence not voluntary. These reasons do not seem intuitively sufficient, however, to classify the soldier's decision to participate as unfree. We do things freely even if we would prefer not to do them, and even if the government makes a decision, we still could decide not to cooperate.

But what if the soldier is threatened with death or imprisonment if he or she does not go to war? Would we say that this individual was unfree, and hence excused, not morally responsible? Consider the story of Franz Jägerstätter, an Austrian farmer and a Roman Catholic who refused to fight in the German Army on the grounds that the war was not being fought for a just cause. He was eventually beheaded (Donagan 1977, 15–16). Because of the threat of death, would we *excuse* Jägerstätter if he had fought?

According to Gewirth (1978, 31–37), choices can be unfree when forced (among other reasons). For Gewirth, a choice is forced when a person is "compelled to choose between two undesirable alternatives that someone else has set for him with the intention of causing him to choose one alterna-

---

12. See Walzer (1977, 80ff., 138ff.) on preemptive strikes.
13. See Walzer (1977) for a discussion of these matters, including the possibility of appeasement. He also holds lower-level officials responsible unless they work against immoral policies or resign when they can no longer be effective; the "best and the brightest" outside the government are also blameworthy if they do not personally protest. See also Dubik (1982).

one alternative by threatening that, in case of noncompliance, he will undergo the other, even worse alternative" (1978, 32). Thus, forced choice exhibits "compulsiveness" (the alternatives are strictly limited), "undesirableness" (neither alternative is the course of action the agent would choose for his or her own "informed reasons"), "threat" (some external power threatens the worse alternative), and "intrusion" (the threat makes the alternatives even worse than they would have been under normal conditions) (1978, 32–34).

Gewirth himself (1978, 33) seems to acknowledge that we can be held responsible even under the conditions of forced choice. He gives as an example a situation where a gunman threatens to kill an innocent bystander unless you surrender your money. The gunman apparently threatens you with the worse alternative of the death of a bystander unless you hand over your money. But, says Gewirth, there is a "moral precept" that says that you "ought to surrender" the money, even under these conditions of forced choice. Yet if you really have a *duty* to surrender your money, then are you not being held responsible, and if responsible, are you not assumed to be free? Gewirth's considered view seems to be that even forced choice is partially voluntary. Since "some aspects of the direct forced-choice situation are not under the person's control" the action is not fully voluntary, but it is sufficiently so that the agent can be held responsible (1978, 33). Thus the person accosted by the gunman who says "Hand over your money or I will kill a bystander" is still responsible.

Yet if Gewirth grants that one can be responsible even when the action is not fully voluntary, then one could hold that we are responsible when the government wants *us* to kill the innocent ourselves, that is, fight in an unjust war, or otherwise suffer death or imprisonment.[14] Now in this situation it seems that the government believes it is presenting the prospective soldier with a forced choice: fight in this war or suffer the "worst alternative" of prison or death. Of course, the prospective soldier might reject this description; perhaps the soldier believes it would be "worse" to serve in an unjust war than to suffer the penalty; thus the attempt at forced choice fails from the outset.* But even if the prospective soldier believes the choice

---

14. Walzer holds soldiers generally responsible for the conduct of war (*jus in bello*), but excuses even those who intentionally kill noncombatants if there is a gun to their head; he is not inclined, however, to excuse civilian massacres on the grounds of lack of knowledge (1977, 312–15). See Davis (against Walzer) on being responsible for obeying unjust orders even under the threat of death (1992, 87–88).

*One could expand the concept of forced choice to include cases where the agent is simply presented with a severe threat to his or her own well-being, even if this is not regarded as the "worst alternative." But would not the choice still be partially voluntary?

is forced, on Gewirth's analysis the choice is still partially voluntary, and if there is a duty not to fight in an unjust war, we can still hold the agent responsible.

And if we have an obligation not to fight an unjust war, then this obligation would seem to apply both to the grunt and to the general, no matter how dire the penalties for noncompliance. Even under threat of death, neither one is excused from the obligation. As noted in Chapter 2, according to the Talmud one may not take the life of another even to save one's own, a teaching that seems to assume that the individual is free and responsible for the decision even under threat of death (*Talmud Sanhedrin* 74a; see Gendler 1978, 207; Konvitz 1978, 247 and passim; see also Greenberg 1978). On this Jägerstätter and the Talmud would seem to agree: the individual is responsible and has a duty not to kill, even at the cost of his or her life. As Leslie Griffin (1989, 49) notes in a discussion of the Roman Catholic category of "cooperation," it might be morally permissible to perform some actions under coercion even if they harm others, for instance, helping in a burglary when the burglar holds a gun to your head. Nonetheless on the Jägerstätter paradigm one is not excused, and the duty not to kill stands, even when one is threatened with the loss of one's own life. There is an obligation not to murder, and we are not excused even under threat of death.

Soldiers are sometimes said not to be voluntary agents and hence not held responsible because they do not have the requisite knowledge to make a moral decision about going to war. Jägerstätter believed he did know enough, but it seems likely than many of the members of the U.S. Army in Vietnam, for example, may not have had the requisite understanding of the nature of that conflict. It is not only difficult, however, to make a judgment about how much knowledge is enough, but it is also difficult to draw a line between factual knowledge and differing moral interpretations of the facts. Many soldiers and civilians were equally well informed about basic facts pertaining to Vietnam, but they interpreted the moral situation very differently. The debate in large part was about which moral-legal descriptions apply—for instance, did "North" Vietnam "invade"? Were the Viet Cong "insurgents" in a "civil war"? I do not refer here to moral disagreements about which categories to apply but to disagreements about how to apply agreed-on categories.

Thus, can an eighteen year old or even a career soldier be expected to decide, for instance, whether North Vietnam had really invaded the South or not?[15] My sense is that here we must hold a high standard and excuse, if

15. For a revealing study of these questions of moral-legal description and the depths of American self-deception, see Sheehan (1988).

at all, only in individual cases. To take up arms should require an individual judgment as to the moral and nonmoral facts. We should not endorse paternalistic delegation of the determination of *jus ad bellum* to state authority on the grounds that soldiers are too ignorant. (Nor, I believe, would there be a serious argument today that one's duty to obey the state overrides all other considerations.) We can excuse particular soldiers on the grounds of ignorance. We can even excuse high-ranking officers whose mind set reveals an ignorance for which we would not judge them culpable. But we need not offer a *blanket* excuse to officers who arguably knew that the cause was not just and yet persisted because they had been ordered to do so by the state. I agree with Walzer that judgments about the conduct of war—*jus in bello*—are more likely to be within the capacity of many soldiers than judgments about going to war—*jus ad bellum*—but we should not offer a blanket excuse on the grounds of ignorance.

I agree reluctantly

Nonvoluntary and Involuntary Pursuit

I argue, then, that we should not offer soldiers a blanket excuse for going to war. Even if I reject a blanket excuse, however, I acknowledge that some soldiers are not voluntary, and hence guilty, aggressors. What, then, justifies us in repelling the aggressor who is not guilty? Judith Thomson rightly objects to the idea that a schizophrenic tank driver whose hallucination turns innocents into enemies should be confused with a voluntary aggressor who "forfeits" the right to life (1976; see Parent 1980, 412). I think she is right, but I also want to show why we have a right to repel the hallucinating aggressor.[16] I argue, on the basis of our views about aiding others, that we may repel nonvoluntary and involuntary pursuers.[17] I interpret, in other

16. See Thomson on forfeiting even without fault (1991, 302). She argues that someone can be about to violate your right even without fault or agency. One can resist because someone will otherwise violate your *right* not to be killed, not simply kill you (1991, 302). (See also her remarks [1991, 303 n. 14] on Anscombe's views.) She claims (1991, 289–91), however, that not only is "using" a person to save one's life wrong, but also "substituting" another victim (by deflecting a trolley, for example), or "riding-roughshod" over a bystander.

17. Against Reynolds (1985), Donagan (1985, 884ff.) argues that material aggression by an agent not capable of voluntary action may be repelled as well as aggression from a guilty party. Cf. O'Neill who links "aggression" with intentional threats, in contrast to "innocent threats" (1977, 150–51). But she argues for a right of self-defense as a corollary of the right not to be killed (1977, 150–51); thus, one has the right to repel innocent threats as well as voluntary aggressors. Cf. Taylor (1986, 265, 268).

words, the common conviction that the nonvoluntary/involuntary pursuer is rightly repelled in terms of what we owe and do not owe to others. Let us begin with the abortion case.

Baruch Brody raises the question, Who is the "pursuer" (aggressor) whom we have a right to repel? Even if one grants the fetus a right to life, is the case of the fetus whose movements endanger the woman similar or dissimilar to the case of attacker versus attacked, or, in the language of the Talmud, pursuer and pursued? Brody has in mind, and I principally discuss here, those cases (now rare) where the fetus's movements endanger the woman, and which some years ago required a craniotomy to save the woman's life.* In this instance (granting for the sake of argument that the fetus is a moral person), the question is whether we have a case of justified *self*-defense. I assume that if self-defense is justified against nonvoluntary or involuntary aggressors, then *mutatis mutandis* it is also justified for us to defend others. Where the case is one of self-defense, the question often posed is why we are justified in taking one innocent life (the aggressor's) to save another (our own). Where the case is one of defense of others, a similar question would arise: Why is it justified to take one or more innocent lives to save even a greater number? The answer I propose applies in both scenarios: roughly, the misfortune of becoming a nonvoluntary or involuntary aggressor should not be transferred to the victim or victims (cf. Otuska 1994, and n. 37 in this chapter).

Brody says there are three conditions associated with a standard case of pursuit (1975, 8, 10):

1.   The continued existence of B poses a threat to the life of A, a threat that can be met only by the taking of B's life . . .
2[a].   B is unjustly attempting to take A's life . . .
2[b].   B is doing some action that will lead to A's death, and that action is such that if B were a responsible person who did it voluntarily knowing that this result would come about, B would be responsible for the loss of A's life . . .
3.   B is responsible for his attempt to take A's life. . . .

According to Brody, condition 1 is not sufficient by itself to have a true case of pursuer-pursued. For instance, if C owns some medicine A needs to live and will only let A have it if A kills B, then the "continued existence" of B is a threat to A. Since it would clearly be wrong for A to kill B, then

*Craniotomy generally signifies crushing the fetus's head in contrast to embryotomy, which suggests dismembering the fetus.

"threat" itself does not turn B into A's pursuer, that is, A cannot say he or she has the right to kill B in self-defense (1975, 7–8).[18] Condition 3 is not required, because as the Talmud says, a minor can be a pursuer in sense 2a, but not technically accountable for his or her deeds in a legal sense.[19] I think Brody extends his point to moral accountability as well: children or psychopaths (including the hallucinating aggressor) can be pursuers, although we would not hold them morally accountable (1975, 8–9).

In addition to condition 1, Brody insists on either 2a or 2b. But the fetus, he says, fits into neither of these categories. It is not intentionally trying to kill the woman, that is, attempting to do so. Moreover, the fetus is not doing something else which, were it voluntarily (knowingly and freely) to do it, would be wrong, for instance, pressing a button to turn on a light, which will also cause an explosion and do great harm. Indeed the fetus is not acting at all;[20] its movement is not the product of purposive agency.[21] Brody argues, therefore, that a woman cannot kill a fetus on the grounds that it is a pursuer (1975, 9–11). Only where both would die if nothing is done can the fetus be killed, and only then under certain conditions (1975, 12ff.).[22]

First, a comment on the thrust of Brody's doctrine. Condition 2b identifies a case where the agent nonvoluntarily kills others, for example, the light switch case; there is action, but it is nonvoluntary, shall we say, in

18. In an earlier article (1973), Brody uses another example to make his point: there is only enough medicine to keep A or B alive; B owns the medicine and will not give it to A; B's continued existence is a threat to A.

19. Regan (1983, 293–95) calls a child assailant an "innocent threat" and believes that we are justified in harming him or her if necessary to defend ourselves.

20. See Mack's (1985, 13, 15–17) distinction between "self-defense" (a defense of one's rights against injurious attacks by agents) and being threatened by the "forces of nature." See also Feinberg (1993, 219), who, like Brody, says the fetus is not only innocent but not an aggressor in the sense of one who intends or purposes to harm you. See his remarks on the relation of "nonaggressive innocents" and "innocent bystanders" (220). Cf. Otsuka (1994).

21. In the earlier essay Brody noted that even if we endow the fetus with beliefs and intentions so that it is capable of action, what it is doing does not fall under 2b (1973, 108). The fetus would only be "trying to grow to maturity and be born mortally": it would not "be to blame" for the mother's death. But even if the fetus by hypothesis was only cognizant of trying to turn its own "light" on, would it not be responsible if it knew that doing so would cause the death of the woman?

22. Brody distinguishes the nothing-is-lost cases (both will die if nothing is done) in which one does not have a choice as to who may be saved—for example, only by killing the fetus can the woman be saved but the fetus cannot be saved—from those cases where either may be saved; in the latter he argues for a random method of choice (1975, 18, 23). Cf. Brody's position with views in the Catholic tradition; see also Connery (1977, 274ff.). See Nicholson (1978, 67–69) for an analysis and restatement of Brody's view. See Chapter 2, this volume, on the nothing-is-lost cases.

contrast to the movements of the fetus, which do not constitute action and therefore are involuntary. In the light switch case, the agent does not know that turning on the light will kill others. Thus, whereas the agent may be responsible for the action in 2a or not, 2b is by definition nonvoluntary and the agent is not responsible.

Second, an objection that does challenge Brody's doctrine. Brody allows nonvoluntary threats to be repelled but not involuntary ones, for instance, the threatening movements of the unborn. His conception of the pursuer seems unduly restrictive, however. Imagine a case where through no fault of his or her own, a skier begins to skid out of control down a steep slope (cf. Fried's example VII [1978, 49], and Nancy Davis's mountain climbing case [1984a, 190–91]). In the path of the skier is an individual who will be pushed over the precipice if hit by the skier, but the skier will be deflected and saved. The individual, however, can move out of the way or push the skier in such a way that the skier would go over the cliff but the individual would not.

Now how should we analyze this case? It does not fit under Brody's condition 2b. In the case where B presses a button that turns on a light but also explodes a bomb that will destroy A, there is an action. However, the skier is not doing anything; there is no action of any sort. The skier's descent is involuntary.

I believe, however, that we should add another condition to Brody's list in order to take account of the threat posed by the skier.[23] Brody argues that threat was not a sufficient condition for a case of pursuit because of the intuitive wrongness of taking B's life in the medicine case. The wrongness here consists in the fact that C is unjustly using his or her leverage over A to take B's life; B's life is no threat to A, were it not for C's unjust intention. Note that B's continued existence is a "threat" only in the sense

23. Compare my skier case to Thomson's falling fat man (1991, 287ff., 302). Thomson's general thesis is that the "Villainous Aggressor," that is, the guilty pursuer, the "Innocent Aggressor," that is, the one who attempts, in Brody's language, to take your life but is not guilty, and the "Innocent Threat," that is, the falling fat man who is not acting at all, are all about to violate your right not to be killed and hence you may use lethal force to repel all three (1991, 308). See Alexander (1993, 57–58), who criticizes Thomson's (1991) *ex ante* rationality distinction between "trolley" and "surgeon." Alexander argues that the "difference rests not on the right not to be killed but on the right not to be involuntarily appropriated as a resource for others." This suggestion is obviously congenial to me, but here I try to make the right to life itself depend on the idea of not being involuntarily appropriated. Alexander also argues that neither the Innocent Aggressor nor the Innocent Threat (Thomson 1991) are "appropriating you" (Alexander 1993, 61). I would reply that if you do not take countermeasures, these threats will live at your expense; see my reply to objection 3, in this chapter. Alexander asks as well whether it makes a difference if there are multiple Innocent Aggressors or Threats. I would still argue that the burden should be shifted to the threat.

that C wants B dead and will not give the medicine to A unless B dies; no threatening force issues from B. Thus, we need to take account of a skier-type case where there is no attempt (condition 2a) and no action for which the agent would be responsible if done voluntarily (condition 2b); indeed in this sort of case there is no action at all:

2c. B's involuntary behavior brings life-threatening force against A (cf. Brody 1975, 8)

Let us understand this case, then, as "involuntary pursuit," that is, life-threatening nonaction or behavior.

With involuntary pursuit understood in this way, we can now ask whether we are justified in moving out of the way or if necessary pushing the skier off. I think we are justified because these actions are consistent with Brody's insistence that we not take life unfairly. Let us assume a duty to help others who are the victims of various sorts of natural or human accidents. Helping others at a comparable cost (or above whatever standard is adopted), however, is supererogatory, beyond what is required (Gewirth 1978, 217ff.). If those whose lives were endangered by involuntary pursuit were asked to bear the burden of this sort of accident by remaining passive, then they would be in the position of aiding others at a supererogatory level. Although the initial accident of involuntary pursuit happens to B, the involuntary pursuer, the victim A would be bearing the burden of the accident, rather than shifting the cost back to B. If the one faced with life-threatening behavior does not move out of the way or repel it, then he or she has chosen to sacrifice his or her life, rather than to cause the death of the involuntary pursuer. The one endangered (A in Brody's terminology) is thus entitled to meet involuntary pursuit with whatever force is necessary, even as I shall argue to the point of killing the pursuer, because to remain passive in the face of the threat would be in effect to aid the pursuer at the cost of one's own life. To sacrifice one's life to save life is not required even for those who adopt an up to comparable cost standard, and, *a fortiori,* it is not required for those who set the standard at a lower level.

The victim then is not obligated to remain passive, but may repel the pursuer, even kill it. It might seem that those who are pursued have no right to be saved if it causes the death of another, since it would seem that they have suffered the misfortune. Since it is actually the attacker to whom the accident has happened, however, it is congruent with the notion of aid I assume to have the attacker bear whatever cost is necessary to protect the life of the victim. Thus, just as agents are not obligated to aid others at a comparable loss to themselves, the burden of involuntary pursuit should fall to the extent necessary on the pursuer. It is not unfair that the contingency of becoming an involuntary pursuer should impose a burden on the pursuer: who shall survive should depend on who happens to become a pursuer, not on who happens to be pursued.

I am morally permitted not only to move out of the way but also to push the skier off if necessary. The involuntary pursuer whom I must push off makes an unjust demand on my life just as a drowning swimmer would who grasps my shoulders in order to save his or her life, but at the expense of mine. If I must push off the swimmer to save my life, I let the swimmer die, but not unjustly; I refrain from *continuing* to offer life support. Just as I am permitted in order to stop helping either to move away from the swimmer or to push the swimmer away from me, so I am permitted either to move myself out of the way or to push the skier away; in both modes of action I am no longer allowing myself to be used as the saving resource. To hold that one may push off the swimmer who voluntarily acts so as to make an unjust demand for aid, but that one may not push off the involuntary pursuer, would be to fail to recognize that the demand is unjust however it arises. Although the involuntary pursuer is not responsible, I am being asked to give more aid than the pursuer has a right to.

Thus, when I push off the skier, I let the skier die because I refrain from providing aid. As I argue in Chapter 1, letting die includes both the cases where one does not begin to provide aid (not starting the respirator, not going to the swimmer's aid, not interposing myself in order to deflect the skier) and cases where one ceases aid one is already providing, or, as in the skier case, ceasing to be positioned so as to provide aid (stopping the respirator, disengaging oneself from the swimmer, not remaining passive in the path of the skier). In the second sort of case—which Green referred to as refraining from *continuing* to provide aid—one can either remove the resource from the person or remove the person from the resource (for example, take the respirator away, or take the person away); either way, taking oneself away or pushing the skier away, one refrains from *continuing* to save (continuing to be in a position to save) and lets die.

It could be, moreover, that I would have to *kill* an involuntary pursuer. Compare the drowning case again. The drowning swimmer grasps my shoulders, endangering my life. But I am unable to pull away from or push off the swimmer. To break the hold, I may have to choke the swimmer; I do so, the hold is broken, the swimmer dies from strangulation. I have moved from letting die to killing because I do not merely refrain from continuing to help and allow the swimmer to die: I introduce a new causal condition sufficient to cause death. I strangle the swimmer so that he or she loses consciousness and relaxes the lethal grip on me. Similarly in the skier case perhaps the facts are such that I have no opportunity to move or push away; my only hope is to draw a gun I happen to have and shoot and thereby deflect the skier. I do not shoot lethally unless necessary; but if necessary I may do so lest I suffer a comparable loss.

This sort of case, moreover, is parallel to the craniotomy: the woman, unless we assume she has made a special commitment to provide life support whatever the cost, is entitled to repel the pursuer. She can't move away or merely push away but must take steps to halt the fetus's involuntary aggression.[24] She does not necessarily intend the death itself of the fetus, but in the craniotomy—on the assumption that forceps crush the head so that the fetus can be removed—she through her agent does intentionally bring about a condition sufficient to cause death. According to the definitions in Chapter 1, she kills. Even if we were to say that in the craniotomy and related cases death in itself *is* intended as the means, however, the killings would still be justified on the doctrine of involuntary pursuit I am arguing; I am entitled to kill if I am asked to give lifesaving aid at a comparable cost to myself (or, more broadly, beyond whatever level of aid one believes is required). When condition 2c obtains, therefore, I may let die or kill.

Here is a diagram of the cases as I see them:

Killing	Letting Die		
lethal injection	not starting respirator	stopping respirator	removing respirator
			removing patient
strangle swimmer	not going to swimmer's aid	stopping the rescue	moving away from swimmer
			pushing swimmer away
shoot skier	not interposing oneself to deflect skier	ceasing to be interposed	moving away
			pushing skier away

24. Kuhse (1987, 116–17) argues, however, that the woman (her pelvic structure) could equally well be considered the aggressor. Cf. Connery (1977, 242).

Killing		Letting Die	
craniotomy	not letting one's body be used initially	cease life support	⟨ remove woman* / remove fetus ⟩

But what sorts of cases does condition 2c cover? The paradigm case is one where B's behavior is the result of natural causes, as in the skier example. But we would still be dealing with involuntary pursuit if B's behavior were the result of an unknowing and hence nonvoluntary action, as in the case where B or a third party unwittingly puts a drug into B's pre-skiing drink (cf. Fried 1978, 48). The behavior in 2c, however, cannot be the result of someone else's voluntary attempt—for instance, the attempt to push B down the slope with the intention of knocking A off. B can be asked to bear the burden of unfortunate accidents that cause him or her to behave so as to threaten others, but B should not be asked to bear the burden of someone's unjust attempt to use him or her to threaten others. Where A is the intended victim of the third party, the tool of the third party (B) should not be asked to bear the brunt of the threat meant for A. In that sort of admittedly improbable case, if A knows the facts, A should not push B off but allow himself or herself to be killed. Otherwise B is used to save A in the sense that B pays an unwarranted cost.

The principle here is as follows: where involuntary pursuit is concerned, we generally ask the ones whose behavior is threatening to bear the brunt of the misfortune; but where a third party voluntarily causes the threatening behavior, the moral situation changes. Now B is being used by a third party to get at A. Although A could justly repel B's involuntary pursuit in the standard case—A does not have to help B—it would seem that if A repels B in the present case, B is being required to sacrifice his or her life for A. If A cannot defend himself or herself without killing B, then it is as if B has been forced to save A from the third party's threat. B has become a tool in the moral interactions between A and the third party. Even though the immediate misfortune has happened to B, it is not due to the natural lottery, but to an unjust human intervention. When A repels B, A is forcing B to pay a cost that would be B's duty to pay only if aid at a comparable level of cost were required. Granted that the third party initiated the events that put B in this situation, it is still up to A to decide whether or not B is

*In the abortion case, one might not want to say that we can physically distinguish removing the woman's life support from the fetus and removing the fetus from its life support, but one can draw the moral parallel with the other cases. And in regard to not letting one's body be used initially—not starting to help—we can imagine today a case where an embryo conceived in vitro was allowed to die.

to be sacrificed. On the view I assume, such a sacrifice is not required, but supererogatory.[25]

A sophisticated twist of this situation would occur if a third party attempted to push B down the slope with the intention, not of knocking A off, but of having A in self-defense knock B off. If A does not knock B off, it will be at the cost of A's life, but if A knocks B off, then it seems that A is cooperating with the unjust plan of the third party. I would not hold A responsible as an accessory, however. A does not owe it to B to protect B's life; the one for whom the aggression is intended should bear it.

I define involuntary pursuit, then, as life-threatening behavior that is neither attempt nor even action; the justification for repelling it is based on an application of the principle of aid. The one who happens to become the life-threatening force should *ceteris paribus* bear the burden.

This moral judgment should also be applied, *mutatis mutandis,* to Brody's 2b (the nonvoluntary "action" condition). The mere fact of doing something that would be unjust if one did it voluntarily is a kind of misfortune, the burden of which one ought not to ask others to bear. In the context of Brody's argument, it is unclear why it is justified to defend oneself against the button pusher and not against the fetus, since the harm is not voluntary in either case.[26] The button pusher acts according to a purpose but does not purpose harm; under one description (turning on a light) the action is voluntary (knowing); under another description (setting off a bomb that will injure others) it is not (since it is unknowing). Thus, if I am unwittingly about to turn on a light that will cause an explosion harming others, I am acting, even though the causing of the explosion

25. Condition 2c would also not extend to the case where B voluntarily caused his or her own involuntary pursuit; B would be morally responsible and we would consider B a guilty aggressor, although the involuntary aggression itself is not an unjust attempt or even an action. I am uncertain what to say about the case of negligence: a third party negligently causes B to lose control on the slope. It would seem here that since someone else caused B to go out of control, we do not want to assign the burden to B; on the other hand, the third party was not trying to get A through B, so we are reluctant to ask A to forgo self-defense; if A repels, the burden of the third party's negligence falls on B. Perhaps a random method?

26. I owe this point to Dan Brock. Note that Brody states condition 2b as an action which if done *voluntarily* would be blameworthy. It would be better, however, to say that it is an action which *if intentional* would be unjust. This would make condition 2b parallel to the "attempt" of 2a without introducing the voluntariness and responsibility condition into the idea of why the pursuit is wrong and may be repelled: hitting the switch intentionally to explode the bomb would be unjust, even if the agent were not responsible. The action of the button-pusher in the case as Brody describes it, however, is nonvoluntary in any case: the button-pusher unknowingly and hence nonvoluntarily *intends* only to turn on the light. The question, therefore, still remains why one can defend oneself against this nonvoluntary action but not against the involuntary behavior of the fetus; neither threat is voluntary.

is nonvoluntary. I may be repelled, moreover, because the misfortune is mine initially.

However, if a third party causes me not to know that my turning on the light will cause an explosion, in order to use me and my action to harm others, the case is different. I have been turned, as it were, into a weapon to accomplish the unjust purposes of another. In this case, then, it would seem that the objects of the intended harm (assuming they know I am being used) have no right to sacrifice my life to save theirs. Condition 2b then, like 2c, should be understood to exclude cases where a person is being used unjustly; 2c and 2b signify not merely the fact of threatening behavior or nonvoluntary action, but the occurrence of these threats as a type of misfortune neither the pursuer nor others voluntarily caused.[27]

Thus Brody's own 2b would seem to rest on the same sort of moral judgment with which I tried to justify taking 2c as pursuit. Moreover, where 2a (the "attempt" condition) is nonvoluntary—for instance, the case of a minor—then the same sort of justification would also seem to be necessary: if we have to justify taking the innocent button pusher's life, we have to justify taking the innocent attempter's; neither is a guilty aggressor. The child or psychopath who is not a voluntary agent and hence is not guilty but attempts, that is, intentionally tries, to kill us nonetheless, suffers a sort of misfortune we can ask the attacker to bear, because not doing so would exceed the victim's duty to aid.

In sum, Brody's own 2b—and 2a when nonvoluntary—require the moral judgment that the burden should be shifted to the one who nonvoluntarily threatens others; this same moral judgment, understood as an application of a notion of aid, as I have argued, applies to involuntary aggression as well. The category of the pursuer should include both nonvoluntary and involuntary aggression as well as the paradigm case of voluntary attempt.[28] The voluntary pursuer forfeits the right to immunity because of a violation of the rights of others; the pursuers who are not voluntary, the nonvoluntary and the involuntary, lose their immunity because of a judgment based on convictions about aiding others. Brody, in contrast, morally assimilated

27. If I voluntarily cause myself not to know that my turning on the light will injure others, then I would be responsible, a guilty pursuer.

28. Following Susan Levine, the concept of "material aggression" could be used to cover not only behavior (nonaction) but nonvoluntary action that threatens others—Brody's 2b, or 2a where nonvoluntary (1984, 69). Donagan, for example, includes in the category of material aggression, along with the fetus and the berserk assailant, a hunter who mistakes a person for an animal (1977, 162). I prefer to retain the category of pursuer with three subcategories: voluntary attempt, nonvoluntary action that includes both nonvoluntary attempt and unknowing action, and involuntary behavior.

the nonvoluntary attacker (both the nonvoluntary attempter and the button pusher) to the voluntary because both are actors. An involuntary pursuer is not in the realm of human agents and their interactions, but becomes like a threat from the nonhuman natural world—for example, a lion or a rock slide. What is not clear is why the fact of action in itself should be sufficient to assimilate the voluntary and the nonvoluntary cases. Yet even if Brody were correct on this score, he would still need the principle of aid for the case of the involuntary pursuer who by definition does not act.

The notion of involuntary pursuit and the right to repel it, therefore, rests on how we think about aid. Let us consider three objections to this thesis: first, the counterthesis that since both attacker and attacked are innocent, the attacker's pursuit is not morally relevant; second, the claim that even if we appeal to the principle of aid, it would still not be justified to repel the pursuer; and third, the thesis that the justification for repelling the skier is not transferable to other sorts of cases of involuntary pursuit.

1. Susan Levine (1984) argues that in cases of involuntary pursuit both parties are equally innocent. Aggressor's aggression is morally irrelevant, and the only moral way to choose between them is to cast lots or some other fair randomizing procedure. However, if this is impossible in a particular case, then the victim, who has the option of choosing, is justified in preferring his or her own life. Similarly, Nancy Davis argues against the idea of attackers who are "morally innocent, but technically guilty." She remarks:

> A person can pose a threat to another person's life and be deemed technically guilty without having done anything at all. How then could the mere fact of posing a threat to another person's life be thought to be of any moral significance whatever? (1984a, 189)

Since the voluntary aggressor is culpably hostile and the psychotic is dangerous to others in addition to the victim, there is a "moral asymmetry" between attacker and victim in these cases and self-defense is justified (1984a, 189–90). However, when the threat is "passive" (no agency), when "mere movements qua physical object or mere presence" constitute a threat, then there is no right to repel that can be defended from a "morally neutral point of view" (1984a, 190–92). We are morally permitted to prefer to preserve our own life if we are the victims; she calls this "agent-relative" permission.[29]

---

29. Davis also argues that third parties are not permitted to aid victims when the permission is agent-relative (1984a, 193–97ff.).

I have no quarrel with the argument that both parties are innocent (that is, not guilty), nor with the thesis that if there were no morally justified way of choosing, or no way that is possible in a particular case, then the only basis for saving the victim's life would be agent-relative. My thesis is that there is a relevant moral consideration based on the duty of aid. The view that when the fetus moves against the woman there is no pursuit reflects the insight that there is no culpability for aggression, and that if taking the life of the involuntary attacker is justified it needs to be distinguished from (but also related to) paradigm cases of defense against voluntary aggressors.[30] On my view, however, it is not necessary to go to lots or much less fall back on agent-relative permission. The common judgment that it is justified to repel the attacker in cases of involuntary threat rests on the moral conviction that since the contingency has happened in the first instance to the attacker, the cost of this accident of the natural lottery should not fall on the attacked, at least not at the level of comparable cost.[31] This moral judgment rests, as I argue, on a view about how misfortunes should be distributed, which is expressed in our convictions about aid.

Does this view, which justifies a lethal defense (if necessary) against the involuntary and nonvoluntary pursuer as well as the voluntary aggressor, allot no special penalty for guilt?[32] Consider a case where life is at stake, but a lethal defense is not necessary; I can save life by wounding the assailant, but if I forgo a lethal response and only wound, I will be wounded myself. It seems to me that it would be plausible to suggest that if the assailant is a nonvoluntary or an involuntary pursuer, one could be required to incur the wound because both you and the assailant are innocent. The intuition here is that, against a guilty attacker who threatens life, the defender should not have to sustain *any* loss; against the nonvoluntary or involuntary attacker, however, the defender can use lethal means if neces-

---

30. Cf. the talmudic view that the fetus emerging from the woman's body should not be considered a pursuer. According to Feldman (1974, 275–76ff.), the category of pursuer is unnecessary before the fetus emerges because it does not yet have full moral status and "her life takes precedence"; Maimonides, however, applied the notion of pursuer to the fetus before it emerges, thus occasioning much comment in later centuries. Brody notes the talmudic teaching (1973, 109 n. 8), and relates it to the idea that even if endowed with intentions, the fetus is doing nothing wrong. From Feldman's analysis the basic thrust seems to be the equal innocence of fetus and woman; neither is at fault.

31. Kamm (1992, 47ff.) argues that although an innocent threat should redirect herself (or be redirected by a third party) even at the cost of a broken leg rather than kill someone, the threat is not required to sustain the loss of her own life rather than someone else's. In contrast, a guilty aggressor can be legitimately killed if necessary.

32. See Thomson (1991) on the irrelevance of fault.

sary, but must be prepared to accept some loss if a nonlethal means could disarm the attacker.

If I am defending myself, I would presumably be willing to risk everything if necessary. But if I am defending myself against a voluntary—that is, a guilty—attacker, may I use more force than is strictly necessary to disarm the lethal threat? Suppose I could avoid any injury to myself by using more force than is necessary to disarm; if I use lethal force, for example, against the attacker I will not be wounded at all, but if I use only the force necessary to disarm—merely wound the attacker—I will myself be wounded. My intuition is that if the attacker is guilty, I may use the force (including lethal force) necessary not only to disarm the attacker, but to protect me entirely from loss. But what if the attacker is nonvoluntry or involuntary? Here my intuition is different: One can use lethal force if it is necessary to disarm, but if less than lethal force will disarm, one must accept a cost to oneself up to the level of cost specified by the duty of aid. If my level is high, then perhaps I would accept a serious wound rather than kill my nonvoluntary or involuntary assailant; if my level is low, I would incur some minimal cost rather than kill, but I would kill to avoid a wound.

But what if I am defending others from a lethal attack? *Mutatis mutandis*, I think the same judgments apply. If the attacker is voluntary, then I may use the force, including lethal force, necessary not only to disarm, but to protect myself and those under attack from *any* harm. If one is confronted by a nonvoluntary or involuntary attacker, however, one can use lethal force where that is necessary to disarm, but in cases where less than lethal force would do the job, one must accept whatever level of cost to oneself one's duty of aid specifies. And, I would also assume, those being defended must also, if necessary, accept such a cost, if the attacker can be disarmed with less than lethal force.

It is said in discussions of just war doctrine, however, that one should use only "necessary force." I think this should mean at least that one should not inflict extraneous injuries on the enemy out of hatred or revenge. It should not require necessarily that one forgo killing an enemy if that is necessary to avoid being wounded. Thus, in the context of just war doctrine where the aggressor is judged to be guilty, "necessary force" would be revised to mean not the minimum force necessary to disarm but the minimal force necessary to disarm and to avoid being wounded oneself. And conversely, despite the difficulty of putting this into practice, if the aggressor were not guilty, then presumably the defender would be required to suffer a degree of injury if the attacker can be disarmed by some means short of a lethal counterattack. This judgment seems counterintuitive, but if correct it would seem *ceteris paribus* that those like Walzer who do not hold combatants guilty would have to accept severe restraints on the conduct of war *(jus in bello)* regarding what can be done to combatants.

2. Levine also raises objections that have to do with the principle of aid itself. She argues first that the aggressor is not literally in need of aid (in cases such as the skier), for one does not need to bring aid to the aggressor to help it survive, one need only remain passive. Thus, Levine's notion of aid requires an intervening act ("X can save P by putting up his hands to deflect P over to a pile of leaves"), in contrast to the sort of case where there is involuntary pursuit and no intervention is necessary to protect the pursuer ("P will live unless X performs some act to save his/her own life at P's expense") (1984, 75–76).

My assumption is that one would be aiding the skier by remaining passive. No additional act of intervention is necessary because one's body is already interposed; but by not remaining passive one lets the skier die. O. H. Green, we remember, construes the case where one removes a respirator as an instance of refraining from *continuing* to intervene against a disease; to remove the respirator is to let the patient die. Similarly, if one does not remain passive in the face of the skier's threat, one does not continue to allow one's body to intervene. One removes the respirator/ moves out of the way, or one removes the patient/pushes the skier away. Admittedly, one does not, in the skier case as I describe it, interpose oneself as one intervenes to turn on the respirator. But one's body is already interposed and one's choice is whether to continue that interposition or not. One has to decide whether to continue or whether to refrain from continuing. To *refrain* from continuing is to let the skier die.

Thus, Levine correctly catches the thrust of my argument when she says:

> If one accepts that one does not have to aid another person if doing so involves a comparable loss to oneself, then one is committed to accept that one does not have to refrain from killing a person [for instance, the skier] if not killing that person involves a comparable loss to one's self (one's own death). (1984, 76)

One has to add, of course, that the case must be one in which the person is a nonvoluntary or involuntary pursuer; one may not kill someone, for example, to gain access to food in order to save oneself from starving. And whether the case is one of killing or letting die, the moral judgment is the same: to save the skier exceeds the standard of aid owed.

But Levine next asks why, if the victim could save the life of the skier only at a comparable cost, there is no obligation to do so; she constructs a case where to save a person who falls from a railing one can deflect and save the faller but be killed oneself, or destroy the faller in order to avoid being crushed oneself. My reply is that most of us do not assume a principle of aid that calls for sacrifice at the level of comparable cost; to help the starving I do not have to starve myself.

Levine also argues that one might be obligated to help the faller if the cost were less than comparable. She constructs another case:

> Suppose P is falling, and if X deflects P, P will die. However, if X does not deflect P, P will be unhurt and X will be permanently paralyzed from the neck down. Reeder's defense of killing a material aggressor on the basis of the principle of mutual aid would not allow a defender of the material aggressor principle to maintain the permissibility of X deflecting P. (1984, 76)

Levine takes me to say that if the cost is less than comparable, one would be obligated to help by not deflecting. I agree that if the principle of aid specifies the standard of up to comparable cost, then X in the case above would be required not to deflect P even at the high cost of paralysis. If I can still preserve my life by not deflecting P, then on the standard of up-to-comparable cost I would be required to accept the injury of paralysis.

If a lesser standard were assumed, however, then in the case of P falling the involuntary pursuer could be repelled even if remaining passive would not cost the pursued what the pursuer stands to lose; P can be lethally deflected to save X from paralysis, or even lesser costs depending on where the standard is set. This case suggests that a doctrine of aid, as I remark in Chapter 1, might apply the up-to-comparable-cost standard where property is concerned, but adopt a lesser cost where bodily resources would be needed to save life.

3. Last, an objection to the analogy between the skier case and other instances of involuntary pursuit. Does the rationale I use for the skier case work only for that particular sort of situation where the passive intervention of the victim saves the pursuer? In the skier case, the body of the victim deflects the falling skier, but what about other cases where the involuntary threat of the pursuer is simply a danger to the victim, and the injury to the victim does not seem to benefit the pursuer? The threatening fetus (in the craniotomy case) of course needs the woman's womb, but the injury the fetus is doing to the woman does not itself aid the fetus in its struggle to survive.

It seems to me that the rationale does apply beyond the skier to a broader range of cases. The basic thesis is that the accident has happened to the pursuer, and for the pursued to allow the pursuer to live (assuming lethal force is necessary to repel the threat) would be, in effect, for the pursued to sacrifice his or her life so that the pursuer would live: the fetus, at least in some cases, would be born alive, but the woman will die. Let us imagine that in another case the skier, who is in no danger, who does not need to be deflected by the victim's body, will bump the victim over a cliff on the way down the slope but would end up unharmed at the bottom of the mountain in a soft pile of snow. In these cases as well, then, not to repel the threat is in effect to sacrifice the life of the pursued for the life of the pursuer.

Conclusion

I therefore argue here that the way to understand the moral justification of defense against involuntary pursuers is through an account of convictions about aiding others. I argue that even if we posit a general right to aid, and even if we increase the standard of aid to up to comparable cost, it is justified, for example, to repel the fetus that threatens the woman's life because not to do so would still go beyond what we owe others. Unless we assume that the woman has created a special obligation, in virtue of a promise or commitment that extends even to self-sacrifice, not saving herself amounts to supererogation. Thus, even if one were to accept a standard of aid above Thomson's Minimal Samaritanism, even a standard that *ceteris paribus* would require pregnancy, one could still clearly hold that the woman does not owe it to the threatening fetus to sacrifice her life.[33]

I thus defend the thesis that one may use lethal force to resist even the involuntary pursuer. I do not do so, however, by using the doctrine of double effect, as Paul Ramsey (1971) attempts to do. Ramsey tries, as I interpret him, to extend the logic of double effect from the cancerous uterus case to the craniotomy.[34] As classic Catholic teaching has evolved, it is generally accepted that the intended means in the cancerous uterus case is

33. Boyle (1977b, 313) says that, in effect, Thomson has identified certain abortions as indirect, but in his view the proportionality criterion is not satisfied. For Thomson the issue in abortion is not whether the death is indirect but whether the woman has a responsibility of any sort or degree to aid the fetus. It is a question of what she has a responsibility to do with her body, not, as in the trolley cases, of what she has a responsibility to do with a certain external evil (or good), the distribution of which may indirectly kill the innocent. See Chapter 4 on the trolley cases.

34. In my interpretation, Ramsey extends double effect to the craniotomy; one intends as a means only the "incapacitation" of a materially aggressive fatal force (1971, 22). Yet he resists this interpretation. He notes that some would say that his view is an application of the traditional notion of the "'indirectly *voluntary*,'" i.e., the death of the fetus is not intended

the removal of the diseased uterus (hysterectomy), an action that not only saves the woman's life, but "indirectly" results in the death of the fetus. In the craniotomy, however, the teaching goes, one must "directly" kill the fetus in order to remove it, and hence save the woman. The Catholic tradition has held, therefore, that since the means is permissible in the cancerous uterus case it is legitimate to act to save the woman. However, since the means in the craniotomy is a "direct" attack on the life of the innocent, it can never be licit, even where both will die if nothing is done. (On Catholic teaching and debate, see Connery 1977, chaps. 12–15; Jung and Shannon 1988.)

Ramsey argues, however, that in the craniotomy one intended as a means not the death of the fetus but only to incapacitate its material aggression or threatening force; death is an incidental or secondary effect, along with the intended end or effect of saving the woman, no less in the craniotomy than in the cancerous uterus. Thus, he argues that what had hitherto been regarded as a "direct" killing was indeed justifiable, at least where both would die if nothing is done, but one (the woman) could be saved.

In the next chapter I argue for a different version of double effect. I argue that in cases such as the craniotomy, even if, as Ramsey argues, the death of the fetus is not in itself one's means, one has to inflict a fatal injury on the fetus to incapacitate it. Thus, in the language of the tradition, the attack on the fetus as involuntary pursuer is "direct." To justify such an attack, I have appealed here to convictions about aiding others.

The approach I take, which builds on Thomson's question whether the fetus is owed life support, argues that the fetus asks too much—barring special commitments—if it demands to be born at the cost of the woman's life. What the fetus requires not only goes beyond Minimal Samaritanism, but beyond even more robust standards of aid. Thus, the justification for repelling the involuntary pursuer applies even in the case where the fetus would live if nothing is done; but the judgment does not rest on valuing one life over another in the sense of its intrinsic value or its usefulness to others. It rests on the idea that the misfortune of becoming an involuntary pursuer should rest on the pursuer, not the pursued.

I agree with Ramsey nonetheless that if his double effect interpretation of involuntary aggression were used to justify craniotomy in cases where

---

as the means (he cites McCormick 1968). Nonetheless, Ramsey says that ". . . there may be some point in still calling this (in the meaning of the action's physical force or target) *direct* justifiable abortion" (1971, 23; 1970b; 1973). Curran (1974, 63–64) insists that, for Ramsey, life can be taken directly in some abortion cases and, hence, Ramsey abandons the traditional condition of double effect that the evil effect cannot be the means in the "order of physical causality."

the fetus would live and the woman would die if nothing were done, then to save the fetus would be to weigh one life over another. On the assumption that weighing one life over another is an illegitimate judgment of proportionality because it violates the equal status of lives before God, then for Ramsey only where both would die if nothing is done can the proportionality condition of double effect be satisfied (better to save one than lose two).[35] The view I present, however, does not suggest that one values the woman over the threatening fetus; the judgment that the fetus can be repelled, even if it would live if nothing is done, is grounded in convictions about what we owe others in the face of misfortune.[36]

I depart, then, from Ramsey on how to understand the fetus as involuntary pursuer and, indeed, on how to understand defense against the aggressor in war. Ramsey also argues (1971), as I read him, that even in the case of defense against the aggressor, one's means is the incapacitation of a threatening force; the death of the aggressor (the combatant) is really indirect. I argue, in contrast, that under certain circumstances one may intend as a means the death of the aggressor. In the next chapter I discuss how, on my view of double effect, the deaths of noncombatants can be regarded as an indirect and proportionate side effect of a legitimate military action.[37]

35. Ramsey may also intend to limit the use of double effect in cancerous uterus cases to instances in which "she alone can be saved" (1971, 18); that is, only where the fetus would die anyway can a "medical action" be taken which causes the death of the fetus as a side effect. In any case, he clearly restricts the application of double effect in craniotomy cases to instances where both would die if nothing is done. (On the Catholic debate, see Connery 1977, 295ff.) Ramsey could not permit double effect to work in the case where the threatening fetus would live if nothing is done because to use the craniotomy to save the woman in that case would be to weigh one life over another (see Connery 1977, 214ff., 262ff.). To so weigh would disregard the inherent equality of creatures of God. Therefore, only where both would die if nothing is done is a proportionality (greater good or lesser evil) argument legitimate. Cf. Ramsey on the war cases where the indirect deaths of some can be measured against the saving of *many* others (1961, chap. 8, especially p. 188). See also Lammers (1990, 578) on the judgment of proportionality in *jus in bello*.

36. Ramsey argues (1961, 186) that contrary to the craniotomy in which both would die if nothing is done, noncombatants who are to be the object of "direct" attack would not die anyway and it is not certain that their deaths would "save life." Nor, on Ramsey's doctrine, would it appear that noncombatants are the bearers of threatening force. Thus Ramsey affirms for war the view of Bouscaren that he had rejected for the craniotomy where both will die: the death of one "in violation of the moral law is not a lesser evil than the death of two, or of many more, without dereliction of duty in their defense" (1961, 189; 183–84). On the shape and development of Ramsey's doctrine of the just war, see Johnson (1991) and Lammers (1990).

37. Otsuka (1994) attacks the view that an innocent threat, whose presence or mere bodily movements endanger your life, violates your right to life or "causes" your right to be violated as an innocent bystander does not; he criticizes Thomson (1991) and Kamm (1992). He argues that an innocent threat, because of a lack of agency, is in effect a bystander to the threat his or her body or movements make (84–85). Thus if one opposes taking the life of an innocent

bystander to save oneself, one must refrain from attacking the innocent threat. I try to offer here a rationale for taking action against innocent threats, but I agree that where it is only a case of saving oneself, one may not use a bystander (see Otsuka 1994, 78) or take some defensive action that kills the bystander as a side effect (see Thomson 1991). Otsuka (1994, 76 n. 7, 77) argues that to save one's life one may duck out of the way of a threat even though one foresees it will instead kill an innocent bystander, whereas one may not, say, drop a bomb to destroy the force, foreseeing it will kill the bystander. I do not see how these cases are morally different; the crucial point in all the "bystander" cases seems to be that to save oneself one sacrifices someone who is not a threat. See Otsuka (1994, 79 n. 16) on the case where you and someone else are both innocent threats to one another; here I would favor a random method if possible. Otsuka (1994, 90–91) also criticizes the view that it is justified to kill an innocent aggressor in self-defense (such an aggressor intends to kill you, but is not "responsible for her behavior because, rather than proceeding from her character, it is explained by other factors completely beyond her control" [1991, 74]). Roughly, if it is not justified to repel the innocent threat, neither is it justified to repel the innocent aggressor; neither is "morally responsible." One may, however, repel someone who remains "morally responsible" but is not to "blame," e.g., someone who falsely believes you to be an aggressor (90–91). I am not sure why this individual should not also be considered innocent in Otsuka's sense. Nevertheless, note that Otsuka clearly distinguishes the cases he discusses here of "one life versus one life" from war cases where one would be justified even in killing innocent aggressors in his sense in order to save a greater number of innocent lives (1994, 91 n. 29). On self-defense and related questions about double effect, see also Suzanne Uniacke's *Permissible Killing: The Self-Defence Justification of Homicide* (Cambridge: Cambridge University Press, 1994), which unfortunately came to my attention too late to be treated here.

4

Double Effect

Alan Donagan (1977) finds a fundamental fault in the theory of action implicit in the principle of double effect. I want to reformulate his point as a morally normative critique of a traditional theological interpretation. To avoid his version of absolutism, however, which I argue would not permit indirect noncombatant deaths in a just war, I present a notion of double effect based on a distinction made by Judith Jarvis Thomson.[1]

Thomson (1975) takes up Philippa Foot's trolley example and makes a

1. For formative debates in the Catholic tradition, see McCormick (1978a; 1978b) and the authors he discusses; for critical analyses, see DiIanni (1977), Carney (1978), Allen (1979), and Langan (1979). McCormick has argued that if an action is intrinsically wrong, it is because in certain circumstances it would always be disproportionate (1978b, 232; 1981b, 371). He argues that one cannot intend an evil as a means unless it is causally necessary to the greater good, but if it is causally necessary one may intend it without approving it (1978b, 261ff.). McCormick, however, interprets the means as not necessary when the greater evil

distinction between doing something to a person to distribute a threat and doing something to a person by distributing a threat. If one accepts the moral significance of the distinction, then one can distinguish certain situations in which lifesaving action violates the duty not to kill from others where it does not. Thus, Foot's emphasis on the priority of the duty not to kill should not be seen as an alternative to Thomson's trolley doctrine: Foot stresses the point that this prohibition should not be violated even in order to save life; using Thomson I try to show that the prohibition is in fact not violated in the trolley case.[2] Thomson's doctrine, however, limits us to the distribution of a preexisting threat; I develop her idea here into a full-fledged conception of double effect. Thomson later changed her view of why it is permissible to turn the trolley to save five people even at the cost of killing one, whereas it is not permissible to cut up one healthy patient to get organs to save five. Thus, to distinguish her views I refer to her 1975 doctrine as *fatal use* (doing something to a person to distribute a threat), the theme on which I base a doctrine of double effect.

I believe that the fatal-use theme has resonances in Judaic and Christian teachings that are not merely modern Kantian accretions but rather reflect early and deep strands in the traditions. For example, Lisa Cahill (1981, 627–29 and passim) interprets Richard McCormick and others as nonutilitarian teleologists who provide for moral absolutes; in this Aristotelian-Thomistic tradition, the *telos* or good includes justice and respect for persons; in particular, the *telos* includes the idea that "no *person* . . . can be treated as a *bonum utile,* a means or object to be subordinated to the purposes of others. Every individual is a *bonum honestum,* an 'end in

---

one is trying to deflect depends on a free response of others—for example, the mob in the judicial punishment case. He imposes the condition that a sacrifice of value not undermine that value or an associated basic value on which it depends. For example, terror bombing is not necessary in the required sense, for it is a form of extortion that denies freedom; moreover, the good of life depends on freedom, and thus terror bombing (universalized and generalized as an acceptable action) undermines the good of life, the very good one was trying to defend (1978b, 236). A difficulty with this argument is that actions directed at military targets could also be said to be extortion, for they are intended not only to destroy but also to coerce the enemy; thus they undermine freedom and hence life as well. (See Levy 1985, 276, for this point.) Here I specify the prohibited actions as fatal use, but I do not address the question of whether this is best understood (along with the traditional weighing of good and bad effects) as a judgment of value, of "proportionate reason." On the development of McCormick's thought and the "proportionalism" debate, see Tubbs (1990) and Walter (1990).

2. Foot (1978) tried to do without double effect. She argued that a proper doctrine of what we owe in the way of noninterference and aid makes double effect superfluous. Quinn (1989a, 290) noted that Foot (1984; 1985) no longer claims that the distinction between noninterference and aid can do all the work of double effect.

itself' in Kant's sense." This view, if I understand it correctly, would affirm Donagan's assertion that respect for persons is not introduced by the Enlightenment but rather is anchored deep within Christian tradition.[3] No matter how one resolves the theoretical debate between Aristotelians and Kantians, Cahill's interpretation of the Thomistic tradition aligns it normatively with the fatal-use interpretation of double effect I develop here.[4]

Donagan's Critique of Double Effect

Donagan adopts Gury's formulation of double effect: one may use a morally good or indifferent means to seek a good end, even if the means also produces an evil effect, provided that the good end proportionately outweighs the evil effect and the evil effect is not the means to the good (1977, 158). The principle is typically stated as follows: 1) the means to one's intended end is either morally good or indifferent; 2) the evil effect is not the intended end of one's action; 3) the evil effect must be equally immediate causally (that is, as a result) with the good effect, for otherwise it would be a means to the good effect (the evil effect must not be causally intermediate between the morally good or indifferent means and the good effect); and 4) the intended end is worth the cost of the evil effect.[5] In traditional statements of the doctrine, "evil" signifies what some call non-

3. See Cahill (1981, 606 n. 12) on Donagan's view of Kant. McCormick (1984, 118) makes clear that he is not a teleologist in the sense of one who counts only "later-on" effects or consequences as determinative of moral rightness/wrongness. Rather he (and others he says) mean by "'consequence'" the "immediate intersubjective implications of an action." Thus a "physical" killing could be described morally in various ways depending on the reason for it (1984, 119). Furthermore, to act "means intentionally to bring into being certain effects, or to refrain from doing so" (1984, 119); in this sense, I gather, we always act to bring about effects (our reason for acting). Thus, McCormick argues that he and others have not been abandoning "morality *ex objecto*" in favor of "extrinsicism"; rather they are trying to move away from a morality that defines actions in only physicalist terms and ignores the question of the intersubjective meaning that renders actions right or wrong (1984, 118–20).
4. See Cahill (1981, 618–19ff.) on the notion of "counterproductive" means, that is, ones that undercut the very values aimed at it; this is apparently a way of expressing the idea that certain acts can be inherently disproportionate (at least when understood to include certain motives and circumstances) even without reference to further consequences.
5. A defender of double effect agrees with Frey (1983, 123ff.) that the agent has "control responsibility" for both the intended and the unintended outcomes; the bad effect has to be justified by a judgment of proportion.

moral badness or disvalue.[6] Certain actions involving certain sorts of non-moral disvalue are morally prohibited and hence morally evil when intended as means or end. This is what the "Pauline principle" means when it says "do not do evil that good may come"; as unintended effects, how-ever, the disvalues are not morally prohibited if they are outweighed by a greater good (proportion). The means must be permissible before the ques-tion of proportion can be addressed;[7] but one can be blamed for a failure of either sort.[8]

According to Donagan, Aquinas's view of self-defense illustrates the prin-ciple. Defending oneself against aggression, one intends one's own survival and the means is "incapacitating him [the attacker] from aggression" (1977, 159). The death of the attacker (if it is necessary in a particular case) is an incidental consequence of the means (1977, 159). By way of example, Donagan reviews the traditional distinction between a craniotomy and a hysterectomy to remove a cancerous uterus. In the former case, the survival

6. See Cahill (1981, 614) and McCormick (1984, 110ff.) on the nonmoral evil/moral evil distinction. See also DiIanni (1977), who argues that direct killing attacks both dignity and welfare whereas indirect killing, when there is a "proportionate reason," attacks welfare alone. As Walter (1990) interprets double effect, the tradition sees the effect of some actions not only as a "premoral" (nonmoral) evil but also as a "moral wrong"; on this reading what can be permitted in some cases as an effect would be "intrinsically" ("*in se*") and "absolutely" wrong if intended as end or means (1990, 130). As far as I can see, whether one thinks of the bad effect as only premoral or also as a "moral wrong" (for example, the death of an innocent noncombatant), the basic issue at stake in the "proportionalism" debate is the same: whether to construe a certain range of actions intrinsically and absolutely wrong because they are against nature or violate a right in relation to God, or to extend the category of proportion-ate reason to refashion the notion of intrinsic moral evil (127–29,. Although here I interpret double effect on the basis of a postulated right not to be used in a certain way, I leave open the question whether or not the moral significance I attribute to fatal use is ultimately to be *justified* in terms of proportionality. (I use the terms "proportion" and "proportionality" for the criterion often referred to in theological ethics as "proportionate reason." I usually use the criterion in a very rough sense: achieving the greatest good or lesser evil [see note 40]). In my version of double effect, I keep the issue of the means distinct from the question of the number of lives saved or rights to life preserved, but I do not address the question of justifica-tion, namely, whether the conviction that in some cases we should not do evil that good may come is ultimately itself to be cast also as a complicated judgment about the goods or values involved, or whether there is some independent type of moral consideration that accounts for our views. Cf., for example, Ramsey (1978b) and McCormick (1978b).

7. For other statements of the doctrine see Brody (1975, 14) and Walzer (1977, 153). I agree with Brody (1975, 15) that double effect is "too weak" for the Pietro nothing-is-lost case (see Chapter 2): "when, in that case, the villagers take Pietro's life, that is precisely what they intend to do as a means of saving their own lives. . . ." But I defend here a version of double effect for a range of other cases. See also Brody (1978).

8. See Kuhse (1987, 156–57). See n. 5.

of the woman is "brought about by means of the bad effect; namely, by the removal of the child from her body, a necessary condition of which was crushing or dissecting its head, thereby killing it" (1977, 159). In the latter case, parallel to self-defense, the means (the medical procedure of removing the uterus) is morally permissible, but the unborn dies as a consequence of having its life support removed.

According to Donagan, the central point of the doctrine of double effect is this: where the bad effect is not your intended means or end, your agency does not encompass it; the prohibition against a particular action is not violated, because you did not do that action, it was merely a consequence of what you did. But according to Donagan's theory of action, killing one's aggressor is as true a description of one's action as self-defense is (1977, 160). One kills a fetus by removing a cancerous uterus just as one does by crushing its head in order to remove it from its mother's body (1977, 159–60). Gury's error was "to take the making of certain bodily movements to be a distinct action from the causing of whatever consequences follow from making them, and the causing of one consequence that follows from them to be a distinct action from the causing of another. On the contrary, . . . an action is identical with the causing of each and every consequence to which the doer's agency in doing it extends" (1977, 160).

Thus, Donagan finds double effect inadequate because it incorporates a faulty theory of action (1977, 161). The traditional view, Donagan argues, claimed that what is not intended as means or end does not "belong" to one's action (1977, 164). In contrast, Donagan claims, with Germain Grisez, that in the hysterectomy no less than the craniotomy you do kill the fetus. But you kill it as a matter of "performance," not as an intended means (1977, 162).[9] Donagan apparently accepts Grisez's argument that if an act is "indivisible" in terms of performance—the act that can save the woman will necessarily kill the fetus—and if one intends only the good end, then the bad effect is not the means to the end, no matter how the two are temporally or causally related. According to Grisez:

> My conclusion is that a good effect which in the order of nature is preceded in the performance by an evil effect need not be regarded

9. Some authors, such as Hart (1968, 120, 122–25) and Frey (1975, 263–64), argue that degrees of the causal likelihood of effects are relevant to the question of whether one intends a particular upshot. Donagan draws a distinction between what one intends and what one foresees (1977, 124–25); he also claims that one does, and hence can be held morally responsible for, more than one intends. Frey also discusses this point (1975, 264ff.); also see Kenny (1966, 647–49; 1975, 59ff.). On the problem of distinguishing acts and consequences, see Glover (1977, 88ff.).

as a good end achieved by an evil means, provided that the act is a unity and only the good is within the scope of intention. Means and end in the order of human action do not necessarily correspond to cause and effect in the order of nature, because a means must be an integral human act. If the unity of action is preserved and the intention specifying the action is good, whether the good or evil effect is prior in the order of nature is morally irrelevant. From the ethical point of view, all of the events in the indivisible performance of a unitary human act are equally immediate to the agent; none is prior (a means) to another. (1970, 89–90)

Thus Donagan finds Grisez's revision of double effect superior to the traditional doctrine. In Donagan's words,

it is lawful to perform a unitary intentional action which has two effects, one good and one bad, provided that the intention with which it is done is to bring about the good effect and provided that the good effect is a proportionately serious reason for permitting the bad effect. (1977, 161)

Grisez's principle would not only clarify the traditional justification of killing in self-defense and in the hysterectomy case, but it would also justify craniotomy as well. As long as the evil is necessary in the order of performance (the good end and the evil event are not "divisible"), then temporal or causal order is morally irrelevant; the death of the fetus in the craniotomy case is not the means in an intentional sense.[10] The death of the fetus

---

10. Ramsey (1973) questions Grisez's criterion of an indivisible action. Sometimes, says Ramsey, a separate action is needed to remove the obstacle, such as the fetus in the cases of a misplaced appendix or aneurysm of the aorta, and another action then intervenes to produce the good effect (saving the woman's life). Ramsey reads Grisez to say, however, not merely that there must be no other way the good effect could have been procured without the bad effect, but also to insist that there must be no other action required to save in addition to the act that produces the bad effect. (Presumably, if some other action is needed, then the first action is the means to the second saving action.) Ramsey judges, therefore, that on Grisez's criterion it would not be justified to kill in the appendix or aneurysm cases. Ramsey insists that it is what the fetus is doing—such as threatening or preventing medical care—that matters. The target is the fetus's "fatal function," not its life. Note, however, that Ramsey's theme of incapacitation does not really seem to cover the misplaced appendix/aneurysm cases; here the fetus does not threaten the woman with its own force, but is merely an obstacle in the way of treating her disease. I have been helped by an unpublished paper on Grisez by Edmund Santurri. For Grisez's later views, see Finnis, Boyle, and Grisez (1987). See also McCormick (1981a, 439ff.) on Grisez and Ramsey.

may precede the saving of the woman but since the act of crushing and removing is indivisible—it both kills *and* saves, thus no other separate saving act is required—the death is not intended as the means.[11]

Donagan, however, finds even this revised version of double effect otiose. Given that one's agency extends to killing in self-defense, hysterectomy, and craniotomy, the only issue for Donagan is whether one is entitled to kill in any of these cases. For him, only if there is material or guilty aggression (or some other factor, such as proleptic consent) is killing licit. Once this is understood, then the principle of double effect is "superfluous" (1977, 163).

Thus Grisez's point is not crucial for Donagan.[12] Donagan's basic point is that one does the evil thing even if it is not one's means. If one does the untoward thing, then the only question is whether one violates a duty. For Grisez, in contrast, it is crucial that what is temporally prior in the "order of nature" is not necessarily a means in the "order of human action." He needs a revised notion of the "means" in order to refashion the doctrine of double effect. For Donagan, however, the issue is whether the death of

11. Cf. Boyle who says (1977b, 310) that in a craniotomy (as a type of embryotomy) "the contents of the skull are removed and this kills the fetus; *then* the skull is crushed and thereby the labour is permitted to continue" (see Boyle 1977b, 316 n. 6; see also Boyle 1991a, 480). His conclusion is that "the evil effect is temporally prior but is not properly causally prior." That is, the death occurs before the crushing, which is what allows causally speaking the removal that saves the woman. Thus the issue is causal not temporal priority (1977b, 310). Boyle's point would hold, I believe, even if the crushing itself killed the fetus; the death is temporally prior to the removal, but death is not the instrument. Boyle (1977b, 311) gives another example: "The just warrior might know in a given case that certain non-combatants would be killed *before* his military aim could be destroyed." Thus for Boyle the intended means in the craniotomy is "changing the dimensions of the skull" just as in self-defense it is "thwarting an attack" (1977b, 314). Boyle also argues (1977b, 315) that in a trolley case where one throws the fat man onto the track, death is not the intended means. However, here Boyle says the fat man had a right not to be thrown from the bridge. Would this move, though, not threaten this defense of craniotomy? The fetus has a right not to have its skull emptied?

12. Susan Nicholson (1978, 44) argues that "two conditions related as cause and effect are also related as means and end, provided that an agent brings about the first in order that the second obtain." (See also Kenny 1975, 55–56; 1985, 49.) Thus Grisez is wrong, she claims, to argue that if the act is proportionate and "indivisible" then the bad effect is not the means to one's end, no matter how the two are causally related (Grisez 1970a; 1970b; Nicholson 1978, 42–44). On Ramsey's reading (1973), however, Grisez would not deny that if the fetus's death was the intended causal instrument, then it would be a means; what Grisez insists on, says Ramsey, is that temporal order—whether the evil effect occurs after or before the good effect—is morally irrelevant. Thus, one cannot use the fetus's death causally to save the woman, but it is not necessary that the fetus's death follow or appear simultaneously with the saving effect (see note 11 above). In any case, the broad assumption I make subsequently is that if X is the cause of Y, and one purposively brings about X in order to achieve Y, then X is the means, or as it is sometimes put, intended as the means.

the unborn, for example, violates one's duty. If one does the bad thing, whether as a means or an unintended effect, then the question is whether one fails to respect a rational creature.

I believe that Donagan, however, may not have correctly read the traditional principle. Although there are, in fact, differing interpretations of double effect in the Roman Catholic tradition, the doctrine, as I understand it, does not hold that you do not do the action and hence the prohibition is not violated. The doctrine holds that what is prohibited is the doing of the action as means or end. What is permitted (or perhaps obligatory) under certain conditions, is precisely the doing of X where X is not one's means or end but a proportionate consequence.[13] The traditional doctrine is a sharpening, a restricting, a clarifying of the prohibition against killing. What you do not do in the hysterectomy case, for example, is a forbidden killing of the fetus, although you clearly do kill it (Ramsey 1973). Thus, the moral difference between the traditional view and Donagan's does not lie in whether the evil effect belongs to one's action—both hold it does—but rather in the normative understanding of which killings are permissible. The traditional view holds that it makes a difference whether the killing is a means or not; Donagan holds that what is morally significant is not the causal or the intentional order in which the evil effect occurs but whether there are other circumstances such that it is not wrong to kill. Thus, the traditional interpretation would rule out craniotomy but allow hysterectomy; Donagan in contrast allows craniotomy because he accepts a doctrine of involuntary pursuit, but as Terrence Reynolds argues (1985), he would apparently have to disallow hysterectomy since no aggression is involved. Moreover, he would also apparently have to rule out the unintended deaths of noncombatants even in a just war.

A Moral Critique

Donagan's critique must be reformulated, therefore. For Donagan, unless there is aggression (guilty or material), or some other factor that suspends

13. Rachels (1986, 92–96) takes intention (means or end) as something separate from an act; therefore an act cannot be made right or wrong by the nature of the intention. See also Kuhse (1987, 148, 163) on the action/agency distinction. I agree, however, with Anscombe (1982), Boyle (1980), and Kenny (1966; 1975) that intention is part of the description of some actions, at least for the sake of moral assessment. As Anscombe says nonetheless, one cannot simply choose a description under which an action is intentional and call it the intention (1982, 23): "For an act does not merely have many descriptions, under some of which it is indeed not intentional: it has several under which it is intentional. So you cannot choose just one of these, and claim to have excluded others by that. Nor can you simply bring it about that you intend this and not that by an inner act of 'directing your intention.' Circumstances,

the duty not to harm, then killing would be prohibited either as intended means or end or as unintended effect. The dispute between Donagan and defenders of the traditional doctrine of double effect is not about whether one does the killing, but about its moral appraisal. I argue that Donagan's normative view needs some version of the traditional distinction between direct and indirect killing.[14]

One has to inquire, therefore, into the normative justification of the traditional doctrine. In a theological context, the doctrine can be understood as a clarification of what the duty to preserve life means. God who as creator has sovereignty over human life does not give to human creatures the right to take life directly as a means except under very special conditions. The deity delegates more broadly to human beings, however, the authority or dominion to take life in some circumstances as an unintended effect. This way of distributing responsibility, the believer affirms, is both beneficent and just.

For example, Joseph V. Sullivan interprets killing when necessary for self-defense in terms of double effect and contrasts it with "direct" killing:

> If a criminal attacks a man, the man may not aim at the criminal's death, but he may place whatever acts are necessary for protecting his own life, even if in doing this the criminal's death would follow as a concomitant effect. . . . Direct killing [in contrast] means an action or omission that has no other immediate end than the death of a person. The death is intended as an end in itself or as a means to an end. (1975, 12–13)

Over against direct there is the "indirect" killing of double effect:

---

and the immediate facts about the means you are choosing to your ends, dictate what descriptions of your intention you must admit. *Nota bene* that here 'intention' relates to the intentionalness of the action you are performing as means."

14. Boyle's (1991a, 479) summary statement is as follows: "One intends one's ends, the states of affairs one aims to achieve in action, and one also intends one's means, that is, the precise steps one takes to achieve one's ends. Features of one's voluntary actions which are not one's ends or means are side-effects. Side-effects are consequences or other aspects of one's actions which are neither the goals one seeks in acting nor the precise states of affairs one is committed to realizing for the sake of these goals." In the craniotomy, one crushes to remove, and "it is the removing and the crushing, not the death or the causing of death which are intended" (1991a, 480; see also 1984). My operative assumption is that the *morally normative* standpoint I try to sketch here could be sustained even if some different theory of action and intention were provided. See my similar remarks in Chapter 1 on concepts of killing and letting die. For the thesis that the significant issues concerning double effect are normative, see Boyle (1991a).

Direct killing must be understood in contradistinction to indirect killing, which may be defined as an action or omission having some other immediate effect in addition to the death of a person. Such a death, even when foreseen to follow an act, need not be intended in itself, but can be merely permitted. (1975, 13)[15]

As far as I can tell, Sullivan's view is that human beings outside of the context of governmental authority are not entitled under any circumstances to take the life of a person directly: "It is never lawful for man on his own authority to kill the innocent directly" (1975, 12). One does not have "dominion" over life, only the "use" of it. Quoting Molina and DeLugo, Sullivan argues that "according to the natural law man does not have direct dominion over human life—either his own life or the life of another man" (1975, 14–16). Sullivan seems to assume that natural reason, which understands human life in relation to its creator, can know that unless acting under the aegis of government (as the agents of divine authority) we are not authorized to kill directly, but that we are entrusted with responsibility for decisions of proportion when death is indirect.[16]

For some traditional theologians, then, God has a right of sovereign authority over the lives of creatures. If God wishes to delegate generally only indirect killing to human agents, then this is both beneficent, for God always aims at human good, and just, for in the believer's eyes it is just that God have this authority.[17] What is more, even if believers are not able always to protect the innocent—they may not "do evil that good may come"—they nonetheless trust that wrongs will be righted ultimately by God. What makes intentional structure—whether something is a means or

---

15. Kagan (1988a, 301) correctly notes that the "doing harm and merely allowing harm" and the "intending harm as a means and merely foreseeing harm as a side effect" distinctions can overlap: one can intend harm as a means by merely allowing it to continue. Note that Sullivan defines the forbidden "direct killing" either as an "action" or an "omission." The discussion of double effect usually assumes that the forbidden means and the side effect at issue are both instances of killing. In fact, though, the means or the side effect could be a letting die. For example, it would be wrong as Lichtenberg argues (see Chapter 1) to let the beggar die as a means even to get organs to save others. But it could be right to do something else to a good end, even if letting die is a side effect. Cf. Boyle (1991a, 489–90).

16. See Ford who denies that Aquinas taught double effect (1970, 27 n. 11); Ford says Aquinas taught only that death could not be intended as an end. For a contrary view of *Summa Theologica*, II–II, q. 64, a. 7, see Mangan (1949). Cf. Montaldi (1986), who argues that Aquinas does not use double effect to justify noncombatant deaths. See Stout (1990, 23–24, 33 n. 55) on the view that only those in authority, e.g., soldiers, may intend to kill the attacker in self-defense.

17. See Cahill (1981, 610) and Schüller (1979, 187–88) on the issue of delegation of divine dominion. For a critique of the model of the sovereign deity, see Harrison (1983).

not—morally relevant is the background assumption that God has delegated responsibility in a morally justified way (see Frey 1975, 279ff.).

Now a reforming Roman Catholic theologian might challenge Sullivan's
view: How does one know that God has not more generally delegated
direct dominion? Perhaps God delegates to human beings in a broader
range of cases, even outside the governmental context, the authority to kill
directly as well as indirectly; when the deity delegates, the reformer might
say, the ultimate authority over life is still God's.

For Donagan, in contrast, the duty not to kill is not an expression of
God's authority over human life, however delegated. His challenge to the
traditional view would be normative. For him the duty not to harm or kill
rests on a neo-Kantian doctrine of respect for rational creatures. The duty
to respect life is not derived from God's right over the lives of creatures,
but belongs inherently to rational creatures and can be justified to both
believers and unbelievers alike. For Donagan, this duty can be violated
whether the killing is a means or an unintended effect. The theologian
holds that God allows persons to exercise judgment in cases where the
killing is indirect and proportionate. For Donagan, however, who seems to
understand human duty in entirely different terms, the distinction between
direct and indirect is not morally relevant. Furthermore, he would seem to
be committed to the following criticism of the normative position that
undergirds the interpretation I have given of the traditional doctrine: if a
rational creature should not be harmed or killed, then the fact that God—
or human parents—brought it into existence does not yield the dominion
over life that the doctrine claims. It would be wrong on Donagan's view
for the deity to fail to respect rational creatures, even its own.

Thus, over against this interpretation of the moral-theological background of double effect, Donagan would say that our understanding of the
wrongness of killing should not rest on the view that we are God's and
that we have been given one sort of responsibility or another; our duty is
grounded intrinsically, inherently, in our natures. The theologian might
object at this point, however, that the interpretation I give of the traditional
background is wrong. The justification of double effect is not a matter of
what sort of dominion is delegated. In forbidding direct killing God is
forbidding injustice. It is not that God simply does not entrust to humans
outside of government a certain type of decision; rather the direct killing
God forbids is somehow inherently unjust within the sphere of temporal
good, and hence God does not allow it.

Thus the distance now between Donagan and the theologian is consider-
ably narrowed, but the normative gap perhaps remains. It is not at all clear
that the theologian's justice amounts to Donagan's respect. Even if we

assume a substantive overlap, Donagan on his view of respect finds no reason to draw the direct/indirect distinction. The theologian who believes that the direct/indirect distinction rests on a notion of justice applied within the realm of temporal good would have to show that Donagan needs a version of the distinction himself. Indeed, I believe Donagan does need such a distinction if he is to retain a crucial judgment about noncombatants; in what follows, I show why he needs it, and what sort of distinction he might adopt. In so doing, I in effect suggest a notion that both Donagan and certain theologians might accept.

Thomson's Trolley Doctrine

A moralist like Donagan, who thinks it can be as wrong to take the life of an innocent human person as an unintended effect as it would as a means, has to face some difficult cases. There is the hysterectomy case, for example. If the indirect death of a person is an unjustified killing, and the fetus is a person with the right to life, then it would seem, as Reynolds argues, that the woman must bring the fetus to viability even if it results in her eventual death from cancer.[18] In this case, however, Donagan might argue (along Thomson's lines) that to remove uterine life support violates neither the woman's specific commitment nor any general duty of aid, and hence to let the fetus die is not unjust.[19]

18. I once suggested that the notion of an agreement to yield the right to life might cover the cancerous uterus case (Reeder 1979, 101). I suggested this because Donagan uses the idea of a proleptic agreement in his potholing case. To make this argument work, however, one would have to argue that the fetus (assumed to have full moral status but incompetent) can be said to yield its right proleptically by proxy consent. Although I am not persuaded that this move is incoherent, especially if an illegitimate notion of substituted judgment is avoided, it seems to me now (see Chapter 1) that the proper way to understand the case is in terms of the special moral relation between the woman and the fetus. See Reynolds (1985) for a critique of the appeal to proleptic agreement and Santurri and Werpehowski (1982) on substituted judgment. I also made the error of saying that in such cases the fetus would die in any case; this apparently is contrary to fact. See Nicholson (1978, 21) and Reynolds (1985). When Foot (1978) had argued that it does not matter whether you have to crush the fetus's head as a means or merely kill it as a foreseen result of a hysterectomy, she also apparently assumed that in both cases the fetus would die if nothing is done.

19. Reynolds (1985) is concerned to show that since the fetus in the cancerous uterus case cannot be killed on the grounds that it would die anyway, yields its right to life in a proleptic agreement, or is a pursuer, Donagan needs another justification. He argues that one could say either that the woman has pledged to bring the child to term at any cost or that she promised on the condition that her support of the fetus would not cost her life; Reynolds's view is that neither option is "compellingly stronger." My view is that Donagan's theory should be modified along Thomson's (1984) lines. Neither on the basis of some general duty to help others nor on the basis of an explicit promise does the woman owe it to the fetus to provide life

The case of the indirect deaths of noncombatants in a just war is more difficult. Suppose that one's nation has been exposed to an unjust attack and, subject to the fulfillment of other traditional conditions, one has begun justly to defend one's country. For Donagan, one might think it is wrong not only to kill noncombatants directly—he affirms the traditional injunction that one may not do evil that good may come—but also to take their lives indirectly as a result of military actions, even to save more lives in the long run. Donagan in fact does not draw this last conclusion, but says that "the deaths of noncombatants who are killed in direct attacks on military installations are to be deemed accidental, on the ground that it is the enemy's fault that noncombatants are there" (1977, 87).

It is hard to see, however, how the enemy's exposure of noncombatants relieves one of responsibility for their deaths. The same might be said in a case where one is tempted to kill noncombatants directly: the enemy has created a situation where killing them (for example, through terror bombing) is the only way you can save more lives. The fact, however, that the enemy has created the situation would not make it right to do a moral evil to prevent other moral evils; why should the enemy's action be relevant only when the death of the noncombatants would be indirect?[20]

Donagan's view, then, would seem to render morally meaningless any purported distinction between direct and indirect killing in war. To cause noncombatant deaths in the course of a military attack would be to do evil that good may come, to help some (the duty of beneficence) by violating duties to others (1977, 85, 154–55).

Thomson's approach (1975) to the trolley case (originally suggested by Philippa Foot) provides a way, however, in which one can reformulate the distinction between direct and indirect and apply it to the case of noncombatants. I attempt to use the distinction Thomson (1975) makes between permitted and forbidden ways of distributing goods and evils to modify Donagan's prohibition against killing (1977, 82–83). Just as Donagan himself has a doctrine of aggression that permits killing, and just as he allows individuals to be killed when they yield their right to life (for example,

---

support at the cost of her own life. Donagan (1985, 883–84) adopts the notion of the fetus as a squatter in the hysterectomy case; it has no right to its location. In regard to the craniotomy case, Reynolds rejects the notion of "involuntary pursuit" but I defend the notion in Chapter 3 and link it to convictions about aiding others.

20. In the case of collaboration with tyranny, Donagan holds Williams's captain responsible for the many Jim fails to save. Nevertheless, if the enemy creating the situation is responsible for direct as well as indirect deaths of noncombatants, then the captain could be blamed for the one death Jim could cause in order to save the many. See Chapter 2 on the Williams case.

certain potholing cases), so I believe he would also provide for the rightness of taking life in certain lifesaving situations including ones in which noncombatants are killed as a result of military attacks intended to repel unjust aggression. Donagan needs, in other words, a version of double effect and Thomson's (1975) trolley doctrine (suitably modified) can provide it.

In a 1975 essay, Thomson first stated her thesis (that it is permissible to turn a runaway trolley to save five, although one other will be killed as a result) and later refined it. My effort is to affirm and modify her original interpretation that turns on the difference between distributing a threat by "doing something to it" or by "doing something to a person."[21] I refer to this interpretation of the intuition that the trolley can be turned, but the patient not cut up, as the fatal-use doctrine.

The versions of the trolley case on which she built her case are as follows:

> Edward is the driver of a trolley, whose brakes have just failed. On the track ahead of him are five people; the banks are so steep that they will not be able to get off the track in time. The track has a spur leading off to the right and Edward can turn the trolley onto it. Unfortunately there is one person on the right-hand track. Edward can turn the trolley, killing the one; or he can refrain from turning the trolley, killing the five. (1975, 206)

> Frank is a passenger on a trolley whose driver has just shouted that the trolley's brakes have failed, and who then died of the shock. On the track ahead are five people; the banks are so steep that they will not be able to get off the track in time. The track has a spur leading off to the right, and Frank can turn the trolley onto it. Unfortunately there is one person on the right-hand track. Frank can turn the trolley, killing the one; or he can refrain from turning the trolley, letting the five die. (207)

21. Thomson (1991, 294ff.) argues that fault in general and intention specifically are irrelevant to whether an action is morally permissible. Thus, she thinks the doctrine of double effect "collapses" (1991, 295). She would reject my attempt to use the trolley to develop a doctrine of double effect, for she remarks that a "focus on the means" cannot say why one may not deflect a trolley on a bystander to save one person ("Substitution-of-a-Bystander") but one may deflect it to save five (1991, 310) even though a bystander is killed. Thomson is correct that a focus only on the means does not explain this difference, but double effect requires not only "discrimination" (a morally permitted means) but also proportionality. Unless one is prepared, as Ramsey and others are not, to weigh one life over another, then proportionality is not satisfied in the substitution case (cf. Thomson 1991, 290). See Mack (1985, 8 n. 5) on Thomson and her early rejection of double effect.

Thomson argues that Edward, the driver of the trolley, would "kill" five unless he turned the trolley off (1975, 206; cf. Blumenfeld 1981, 324–25). If Frank, a passenger, does nothing, "he does not kill them, but only lets them die" (1975, 207; cf. Thomson 1986, 97–98). On Foot's principles, says Thomson, Edward may turn but Frank may not. For Edward the negative duty not to kill five overrides the negative duty not to kill one, but for Frank, to turn would be to kill, thus he must let five die because killing is worse than letting die. However, says Thomson, our intuition is that if Edward may turn so may Frank. Thus, the distinction between killing and letting die does not provide a basis for distinguishing between the two trolley cases. Moreover, Thomson argues, one needs a way of explaining why both Edward and Frank may turn the trolley, but one cannot cut up one healthy patient to obtain organs needed to save five others.

In my view, in both versions of the case not turning the trolley would be to let the five die.[22] Edward (the official driver) no less than Frank (the passenger) is not responsible for the brakes failing; the runaway trolley is a condition neither brought about. Edward or anyone who takes over the trolley "drives" it only in the sense that the trolley can be allowed to continue on the main track or it can be steered off onto the spur (cf. O. H. Green 1980, 198). Both Edward and Frank, therefore, would let the five die if they don't turn the trolley; both kill one if they do.[23]

But Thomson's moral difficulty remains; now we have to explain why both turnings seem different from cutting up the patient (cf. 1986, 100). If turning the trolley is interpreted not only as a killing, but as a violation of

---

22. Cf. Quinn's view of the distinction: "Harmful positive agency is that in which an agent's most direct contribution to the harm is an action, whether his own or that of some object. Harmful negative agency is that in which the most direct contribution is an action, a failure to prevent the harm" (1989a, 301–2). The driver who lets the train continue on the main track performs a "passive" but nonetheless positive action, because such a driver "intends that the train continue forward past the switch, and this leads to the death of the five" (1989a, 305). The driver thus has a choice of two positive actions. See also Quinn (1991, 514 n. 1) on the trolley.

23. Davis (1980, 192ff.) says that in Foot's original trolley example one would allow more to die if one did not turn the trolley to the spur and thereby kill only one. Although Foot says that the case is a conflict of instances of the negative duty not to harm, in reality, Davis claims, it is an instance of allowing over against doing, and thus on the principle that the negative duty outweighs the positive duty, the trolley should not be turned. Davis also takes aim at the moral relevance of the doing/allowing distinction. If there were a junction, and the driver had to switch the trolley in one way or the other (it could not merely be allowed to continue on the main track), then surely we would say switch it so as to save the most lives. Since this case seems no different from the first, Davis says that the doing/allowing distinction in itself (more specifically the killing/allowing-to-die distinction) is not morally relevant. On the trolley as "letting more die or killing fewer," see also Kamm (1991a, 574).

the right not to be killed, then Edward and Frank violate the negative duty in order to save five; what they do is assimilated to cutting up a healthy patient to save five. Something must explain why we do not want to assimilate these killings and Thomson tries to provide a principle to account for our conviction. In effect, she sharpens our notion of what the forbidden killing is.[24]

Thomson's basic point seems to be this: where an evil (or a good) is to be distributed, in regard to which no one has a prior claim or right, we do not unjustly kill someone as a result of our attempt to save the most lives; thus the person on the spur is not unjustly killed.[25] In contrast, Thomson argues, it would be unjust to kill persons in the course of using their bodies, bodily parts, or simply their dismemberment to save other lives. It would be unjust to shove a fat man off a bridge onto the track in order to stop the trolley from killing five; it would be unjust to cut up a healthy person to use the patient's organs or to start a chain of events that will save five others (1975, 207–8, 214).

The difference between the trolley case, assuming that no one has some special claim or right to be saved, and the cases where killing is unjust is that one has a certain title to one's body:

> One doesn't come to own one's parts in the way in which one comes to own a pebble, or a car, or one's grandfather's desk, but a man's parts are his all the same. (Thomson 1975, 213)

In this 1975 article, I take Thomson to say that we have a right not to have our bodies fatally used without our consent (although as I argue in Chapter 2, we can yield or waive this right). Individuals have a right not to have their bodies used where use would lead to death, for example, blocking the track with the fat man. Thus,

---

24. Anscombe notes that the mere fact that a death is not intended as means or end does not signify it is not "murder," such as the arsonist who burns down a house with people in it (1982, 20–22). One needs a principle to show when an unintended causing of death is not permitted, and she suggests the relative certainty of causing death; the death would be wrongful, for example, if one operated on a patient to get an organ for someone else when the patient would surely die as a result (1982, 23–24). It seems to me, however, that arson could be treated, at least legally, as murder because the means (arson) is already prohibited; the death of the people may be unintended but they die because of a criminal act.

25. I disagree with Montmarquet (1982, 447) that we should think of the person on the spur as already "threatened with death"; this individual is not an object of the trolley's threat unless the trolley is turned onto the spur. See also Kamm (1989, 228) on Montmarquet. Kamm argues (1989, 229), as I do here, that the one(s) sacrificed need not die from the same threat.

> what matters in these cases in which a threat is to be distributed is whether the agent distributes it by doing something to it, or whether he distributes it by doing something to a person. (1975, 216; cf. 215)

The distinction is morally relevant because of the importance of how death occurs.[26] Thomson assumes, I believe, that our title to our bodies does not stand in the way of an impartial maximization of good (or some other favored distribution) where it is a matter of the allocation of an evil or good external to us as embodied persons; our title is decisive, however, where others can be saved from some threat or receive some good only by the fatal use of our bodies, bodily parts, dismemberment, or, as we need to add, our very dying, our death itself. We can redistribute the natural lottery even with fatal consequences where evils (or goods) external to us are concerned, but we do not redistribute through the fatal use of persons.

One possible objection to Thomson's view, which she herself subsequently raises (1986), is that the notion of using persons fatally does not adequately explain why the healthy patient may not be cut up for transplants, but a bystander at a switch (parallel *ceteris paribus* to the Edward/Frank cases) may turn the trolley.* She produces another sort of trolley case to make her point (1986, 102). Suppose the spur loops back around to connect to the main track; thus if unimpeded the trolley on the main track would go around to the spur and vice versa (Fig. 1). Also suppose that if the trolley hits the five on the main track it will kill them but not proceed around to kill the one; and if the trolley is turned onto the spur, it will kill the one but not go around to kill five (1986, 101–2).** In this

---

26. Thomson's "doing something to a person" is too broad to convey her meaning, just as "using as means" is. See Audi (1978, 51–52) and Davis (1980). In the 1975 essay Thomson has in mind what Duff calls a "direct, intentional, and inevitably fatal assault on an innocent victim" (1976, 69; cf. 78); cf. Hanink (1975, 149).

*I assume that the conviction that permits and indeed obligates a driver or passenger to steer the trolley onto the spur rather than allow it to continue on the main track also justifies a bystander throwing a switch to turn it. But what if I were one of the five on the main track and I could somehow switch the trolley onto the spur? My sense is that I would indeed be permitted and obligated to do so. I am not saving myself alone from the threat, so I do not exchange, that is, simply substitute, the life of the one on the spur for mine; rather I act to save myself *and* I act to save the other four, so my action is proportionate. Cf. Davis (1980, 1988) and Thomson (1986; 1990; 1991).

**In the loopback, note that if one body on the side track would stop the trolley, then why, as Stan Calhoun pointed out to me, wouldn't the *first* of the five bodies on the main track also stop it, leaving the other four safe? The case needs to be described so that the trolley will kill all five on the main track.

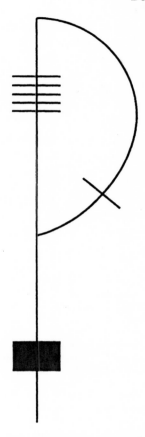

Fig. 1. (For the idea of figures for trolley cases, I am indebted to Davis [1980]).

case it also seems right to turn the trolley, says Thomson, but the body of the one is used fatally to save the five.

Thus Thomson attempts—this is one strand of her argument—to refine her analysis of the right that is not violated in the trolley case but is violated in the transplant example. It is presumably not the right against fatal use, for the body of the one is so used in the loopback case. In the case of the fat man on the bridge, however, she argues that it is wrong to shove and topple the fat man onto the track to stop the trolley because the fat man has a right not to be shoved or toppled (without consent) (1986, 106–9; cf. Boyle 1977b, 315):

> The means by which the agent in Fat Man gets the trolley to threaten one instead of five include toppling the fat man off the footbridge;

and doing that is itself an infringement of a right of the fat man's. By contrast, the means by which the agent in Bystander at the Switch gets the trolley to threaten one instead of five include no more than getting the trolley off the straight track onto the right-hand track [the spur]; and doing that is not itself an infringement of a right of anybody's. (1986, 110–11)

Thus in the fat man case and the transplant case an important right is violated, namely, a right not to be shoved or cut without consent, a right to dominion over one's body. This right is not violated, in contrast, when the trolley is simply turned onto the spur in the bystander or loopback cases.

In my view, this argument does not adequately replace Thomson's earlier interpretation (1975).[27] The fat man's right is stated now not as the right not to have his body fatally used but as the right not to be shoved or toppled (without consent). The right is stated in terms of the individual's

27. Thomson in 1990 rejects her own 1986 explication of the difference between trolley and transplant, namely, that the surgeon infringes more than one claim—that is, the claim not to be cut up as well as not to be killed—in contrast to the one on the spur who does not have a claim that the trolley not be turned (1990, 179 n. 2). She keeps her intuitive thesis, however, that one may deflect the trolley but not cut up the patient. Thomson now (1990, 181ff.) argues, roughly, that in the trolley case, assuming that a group of workmen are randomly assigned positions on the main or spur tracks at the outset of the workday, it is permissible for the trolley to be turned because that increases the probability of their individual survival. Note that Thomson does not suggest that the workmen actually or tacitly consent, nor even that they hypothetically consent: "What I think we should care about is not that such and such people would consent if they were asked, but rather whatever it is about them in virtue of which they would" (1990, 187). Thus, what makes it permissible to turn the trolley late in the day is that it is to the advantage of all at the outset of the day that the trolley be turned later, even if it is not to the advantage at that later time of the one who happens to be on the spur (1990, 193–95); at the outset each has a five in six chance of surviving (1990, 181, 197). It is the fact of advantage that "does the moral work of justifying," not that in light of such an advantage, and given certain conditions (such as being clearheaded), people would agree (1990, 188–89 n. 5); see also Thomson (1991, 310 n. 18). In the transplant case however, the conditions are not the same, at least in the world as it is, and it would not be permissible to cut up one to save five. The probability of the survival of all is not increased (since being healthy is "not a mere matter of chance" but of "how one lives," a policy of cutting up one to save five might "increase the number of those who are in need of parts and thus increase the risk the healthy are subjected to"). Moreover, people would not want to be "suddenly grabbed" to have their organs used and would regard their being cut up to save others with "distaste" (1990, 183–86, 195). I am not convinced, however, that the medical case is so radically different from the trolley. As for the argument that some would get slack on preventive care if they knew there was a five in six chance they would get organs in emergencies, it seems to me this could also cut against the trolley: Would workmen get slack? Would we find dying under the surgeon's knife more distasteful than being run down by a trolley for the sake of others? See chapter 2 on Donagan. On Thomson's recent views, see Thomson (1993a; 1993b), Mack (1993), Russell (1993), Gert (1993), and Harman (1993).

dominion or sovereign control over his or her body. The moral question still remains, however, whether the nonfatal or fatal infringement of this control is ever justified. Must not Thomson's argument assume that the right not to be shoved off is not to be overridden if the result is fatal, whereas it could be overridden if the result were less costly? Surely Thomson does not mean that the right not to be shoved off is somehow in itself not to be overridden, for I think she should want to permit the fat man to be toppled if doing so could save five lives without serious cost to him. Thus what makes the fat man and the transplant cases similar is still the fatal use of their bodies, in contrast to the original case where one turns the trolley onto the spur, thereby killing as a consequence the individual on it.

As for the loopback case, it is important to remember that in the original trolley cases the trolley was turned simply to get it off the main track and onto the spur, but in the loopback version the trolley would be turned onto the spur in order to hit the body of the one there. If the one person were not on the spur, the trolley would come back around killing the five from the opposite direction (cf. 1986, 110). As Thomson herself notes, the body of the one is fatally used to save the five. In the Edward/Frank and bystander-at-a-switch case, it was only causally necessary and hence intended as the means to turn the trolley off the main track; but in the loopback case, where, to be sure, one initially only turns a trolley rather than topple a person, one nonetheless turns the trolley onto the spur in order to hit the person and stop the trolley. The means is more than merely getting the trolley off the main track.

In my view the reason why turning the trolley would be right in the loopback case is not because the one on the spur has no right comparable to the right of the fat man not to be shoved or toppled. There is a right not to be fatally interfered with that is violated by shoving or toppling the fat man, a right that would also be violated by turning the trolley in order to hit the body of the one on the spur, were it not for peculiar features of the loopback case.

To clarify the loopback, consider still another trolley case; let us call this the connecting spur case (Fig. 2).

In this case, one can let the trolley stay on the main track, killing five, or one can turn the trolley onto the spur in order to hit the body of the one, stopping the trolley so that the lives of the five will be spared. The trolley has to hit the one, otherwise it will go back on the main track and kill the five. One turns the trolley onto the spur in order to hit a body, in contrast to the Edward/Frank or bystander-at-a-switch cases where one turns the trolley simply to get it off the main track. Turning the trolley in this case would not be permitted in my view because the one on the spur

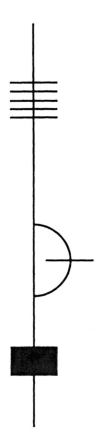

Fig. 2.

has a right not to be fatally used. The connecting spur case is morally parallel to the case of the one patient whose organs are used to save five others.

But in the loopback case, no matter what is done, someone's body (bodies) is (are) used as the means of saving others.[28] I would assume that this

28. Costa (1987, 462–63) also distinguishes these two sorts of cases in order to defend Thomson's original doctrine and relates (1986; 1987) Thomson's 1975 proposal to double effect along the same lines as I do here. Costa's account is close to mine but differs in some respects. First, I do not argue that the death itself of the one patient in the transplant case is a cause of the organs' being available (Costa 1986, 443). Costa himself also says that killing is not the means but "harm" to the person is; the means consist of "violating [the patient's] body and making use of his organs without his permission" (1986, 446); I would only add that the use is fatal. Second, to deal with the case of shields, I argue that it is causally necessary

is a case of a conflict of rights and that in such a case agents would agree to sacrifice as few rights as possible.[29] Thus, we can account for Thomson's conviction that the trolley should be turned in the loopback case without relinquishing her earlier view that individuals have a right not to have their bodies fatally used as the means of saving others. This case of a conflict of rights is the one that Tom Regan's "miniride" principle fits:

> Special considerations aside, when we must choose between overriding the rights of many who are innocent or the rights of few who are innocent, and when each affected individual will be harmed in a prima facie comparable way, then we ought to choose to override the rights of the few in preference to overriding the rights of many. (1983, 305)

Whereas in the connecting spur case, the right of the one would have been violated, in the loopback case of a conflict of rights, it seems appropriate to say that the right of one would be overridden.

Trolleys and Wars

So understood, Thomson's fatal-use doctrine can now be applied to the case of noncombatant deaths in a just war (cf. 1986, 106 n. 12). Taking action against military targets is like turning the trolley in the Edward, Frank, and bystander cases; in these cases the means save but also take innocent life. The threats are different, of course, for in the one there is a mechanical accident, in the other unjust aggression; moreover, when one turns the trolley (the threat), one turns it against the innocent, but when one attacks aggressors, it is ordinarily one's own defensive action that kills the innocent as a side effect, not a deflection of the aggressors' attack itself.

Does this difference show that the fatal-use doctrine is different and

---

for the bullets to pass through the shield in order to hit the assailant, but harm to the shield is not intended as a means (see the discussion on shields ahead). On the question whether a means would fail to satisfy double effect but still be justified, see Costa (1986, 446–48) and Chapter 5 on absolutism.

29. Because there is a metaprinciple that tells us what to do in the loopback case, the rights of the few are overridden, not violated; thus, the case is only one of a conflict, not a dilemma, where the latter involves not only incompatible, but also incommensurable, duties. See Santurri (1987) for this distinction, and Chapter 5 on absolutism. Cf. Kamm (1989, 230, 240–41, 256 n. 6) on the "prevented return" case. See also Kamm (1991a, 573–74).

indeed narrower than double effect? I argue, building on Thomson, but rejecting some criticisms of her earlier doctrine, that we are obligated to save five lives at the cost of one provided that we do not fatally use the one as the means; thus we are obligated to turn the trolley but prohibited from cutting up the patient.[30] Foot, Thomson, Michael J. Costa, and Eric Mack all insist, however, that we may only redirect an existing threat, not create a new one. Foot (1984, 179–80) argues that it would not be permissible to "run over" one individual trapped on a road in order to rescue five others; one may only "divert" the trolley, not start a "new . . . fatal sequence" (1984, 183). Thomson (1986) takes up another case of Foot's and makes a similar point: five patients could be saved by the manufacture of a gas, but this would release lethal fumes into the room of another patient who cannot be moved (1986, 107); for Thomson, in this "Hospital" case one would not be redirecting an existing threat but creating a new one.[31] Costa (1987, 464–65) takes up Thomson's point but sees it as an explanation of why the manufacture of the gas violates the provision of double effect that the act by means of which the good is produced not itself be an "evil"; for Costa (1987, 464), "one who brings some new threat or source of foreseeable harm into the world is engaged in an act that is itself a prima facie evil," for example, the manufacture of the gas. Mack (1988, 64ff.) argues that no one's right to life is violated when a deadly swarm of mosquitoes approaching New York is sprayed leaving a remnant of the mosquitoes which, having been deflected, will unfortunately destroy the smaller city of Worcester. But the right would be violated if you saved two patients in a hospital room by releasing a gas fatal to a third (who cannot be removed in time); for Mack, we do not have primary causal responsibility when there is an "antecedent peril" and we only intend to destroy it; in the hospital case, however, you are not "deflecting an already incoming gas. . . . [You] would be *introducing* the gas" (1988, 71).

In my view, however, the trolley and the hospital cases are morally similar. Foot says that in the hospital case you initiate the deadly process. But a deadly process was already present, the *illness* that threatened the five. To be sure, you do not literally redirect that illness when you manufacture

30. Thomson (1990, 177, 196–97) makes clear that she does not argue that one is "morally required" to turn the trolley, but only that it is "permissible" to do so. I do not think that making turning required is a remnant of utilitarianism; it is rather, in my view, a consequence of positing a general right to be saved and then deciding in what instances that right applies.

31. Thomson says that "the impermissibility of proceeding in Hospital seems to have a common source with the impermissibility of operating in Transplant, in which the surgeon would be [fatally] using the one" (1986, 107 n. 13). In regard to the gas case, I am assuming that there is no available way in which the various parties could be moved and that the agent has no special moral responsibilities to any of the parties. see Mack (1985, 22).

the gas, but you take a defensive action to keep the threat from the five, an action that is also fatal to the one. To neutralize a threat to some people you take an action that threatens another. Thus, even though manufacturing the gas and attacking the aggressor are literally not the same as turning a trolley (redirecting the antecedently existing harm), there seem to be no morally significant differences if the crucial considerations consist in one's duty to save and a Thomson-derived view of the prohibited means.[32] Neither the manufacture of the gas nor attacking the aggressor involves the prohibited fatal use of persons.

My quarrel with Mack's account (which in many ways overlaps with mine) is similar. He is willing to allow you to spray the mosquitoes, thereby deflecting some of them to Worcester, but he is not willing to allow the introduction of a gas to save two at the expense of a third; presumably he would not object if the gas merely deflected the *disease* onto the third roommate (see also Mack 1985). Mack himself notes (1988, 73 n. 11), however, that if he has to rule that the introduction of gas is impermissible in the hospital case, he cannot allow the indirect deaths of noncombatants in most wartime situations. Only a case of deflecting a missile back onto aggressors with some loss of innocent bystanders would be parallel, he says, to the Worcester case. But in "real world" cases do defenders, Mack asks, introduce a new peril, that is, their own "destructive efforts?" Says Mack: "If this is so, is such defensive action impermissible even when it is directed solely at aggressors and the defenders are not responsible for the location of the innocents?" (see Mack 1985). I hold to the view that the crucial issue is whether the innocents were fatally used; if not, then whether the deflected antecedent peril itself causes their deaths or whether our efforts (the spray, the gas, the defensive action) are causally responsible, is morally indifferent. Even if the spray killed the Worcesterians as opposed to the deflected mosquitoes killing them, one does not intend their deaths as the means to the greater good; nor does one use the Worcesterians in the sense one would (in another case of Mack's) if one dismembered them and used their bodies to make a medication in order to save the already infected New Yorkers. In both the mosquito and the hospital gas cases there is an antecedent peril and the deaths are unintended; the bystanders die as a consequence, not as a means, of what we do to deal proportionately with the threat.[33]

---

32. Nagel (1972) develops a distinction similar to Thomson's and applies it to war; I see Thomson's trolley argument as a way of clarifying and extending what Nagel suggests.

33. Mack argues that the principle of antecedent peril is a principle of "causal casuistry," which tells us when we are "primarily" or "robustly" responsible causally and hence morally. Thus, in the mosquito case "primary" causal and moral responsibility remains with the antecedent peril. See also Mack (1985). In my view, the agents in both the Worcester and the hospital cases causally contribute to the unintended results. The issue is whether there is moral blame. I agree with Mack that cases of the permissible deaths of innocents are not limited to

Thus, the trolley and war situations are morally similar in crucial respects: one turns the trolley away to save the five, but one is killed; one attacks the aggressors to save those they would have killed, but some innocents also die. One can imagine a case where the causal parallel is close: instead of attacking the aggressor's troops and also killing noncombatants, one deflects an enemy missile onto a smaller group of innocents in order to save lives.[34] One does not violate the rights of those killed, however, even if it is not the "antecedent peril" but one's own action that kills them. But just as it would be wrong to cut up a patient to save five lives, so it would also be unjust to kill noncombatants in order to weaken enemy morale and speed victory. It would be unjust to use noncombatant deaths even to save more innocent lives. Noncombatants, as the traditional doctrine of *jus in bello* teaches, have immunity from direct attack.[35]

The fatal-use doctrine, then, and its application to trolleys and wars, rests on assumptions about how we should deal with the distribution of

---

cases of defense against an aggressor; see Mack (1985, 13–17). On Mack, see Gruzalski (1988) and Levine (1988).

34. See Mack (1988, 73 n. 11). I heard this example first from Christopher Bache. Cf. an example of Audi's, which is parallel to the trolley (1978, 53); also Thomson (1986, 114). Cf. Costa's "missile I" (1987, 465) case where a missile is diverted from a metropolitan area to somewhere where it only takes twelve lives. Costa argues that neither double effect nor Thomson's redistribution principle would justify using an antiballistic missile ("II") to destroy an incoming warhead aimed at a metropolitan center, where the exhaust of the antiballistic missile would also kill a dozen, nor would either permit using a private plane (without permission of those inside) to collide with the incoming missile ("III"), thus also killing the occupants of the plane. If Thomson insisted on a literal act of diverting, then only case I would satisfy. However, my version of double effect would apparently apply to II and III; persons are not fatally used in either.

35. Walzer (1977) endorses noncombatant immunity (discrimination) but also wants to revise the traditional notion of proportion in the application of double effect to war. Instead of requiring only that the loss of noncombatant lives be outweighed by the value of the military objective, one must be prepared to accept grave risks for soldiers in order to lessen noncombatant casualties, so long as one does not risk the military venture or suffer losses such that one's actions (in the same general circumstances) could not be repeated. Thus, precision bombing in France was more costly to fliers than high altitude bombing but it saved French noncombatant lives; it did the job and raids could be repeated. Similarly a commando raid against a Norwegian heavy-water plant instead of an air attack was justified even though it took two tries. Thus "proportion" must do more than judge that the deaths of noncombatants are outweighed by military gains; one must weigh noncombatants' lives heavily and be prepared to lose more soldiers than strictly speaking is necessary. In reply, one could argue that one minimizes the risk to combatants because they could be used for other missions to shorten the war and save more combatant and noncombatant lives overall. See also Miller (1991, 164, 274 n. 65) who argues for a "thick" theory of intention, which would "include the duty to *reduce* the unintended but foreseen harms that accompany an act." My sense is that the criterion of proportionality not only demands that the good outweigh the bad, but that one seek the act with the best overall consequences. Cf. Brandt (1972) and Hare (1972).

evils. Even if circumstances are such that my body, my parts, my dismemberment, or my death itself could be used to save other lives, it would be unjust to kill me (unless I waive my right); but if circumstances are such that I will be killed when a threat is distributed so as to save more lives (or some other just distribution), my death is not unjust. I have, in other words, a right (at least prima facie, perhaps absolute) not to be fatally used, that is, not to have my body, bodily parts, dismemberment, or death itself used to save others, but I have no right not to be killed in other circumstances where a threat could be distributed.[36] That one would think it just in trolley-type circumstances to take a distributive action that would save some but not others would not necessarily commit one to saving the most lives (other valuational and distributive principles might be preferred) nor would it resolve the question—to be addressed in Chapter 5—whether the right not to be fatally used should ever be overridden. Donagan could still say it may not, and in this sense he could insist that one may not do evil that good may come. I have so far allowed only the "miniride" exception.

Problems of Application

The fatal-use motif, I argue, in effect furnishes the core of a doctrine of double effect. Where the tradition speaks of proportionate reason, Thomson speaks of distributing a good or evil; where the tradition speaks of direct and indirect, she speaks of doing something to persons in order to distribute something in contrast to distributing something and thereby also doing something to persons (1975, 215–16). Persons have a right not to be used fatally to further a distribution of good or evil. If we revise Donagan's theory of duty, one's duty to rational creatures would require one only to refrain from fatally attacking their persons in order to distribute goods or evils; it does not require us to refrain from killing in the course of distributing goods or evils. Donagan's prohibition, therefore, can be modified along the lines of Thomson's distinction. Thomson gives examples of the forbid-

---

36. If one did not want to argue in the cancerous uterus case that the woman's promise is conditional or that the burden exceeds the general duty to aid, could one use the doctrine of double effect for this case? One may attack the disease if saving the woman's life over the fetus's is proportionately justified? See Chapter 3 on Ramsey's reluctance to weigh lives in a case where the fetus would live if nothing is done.

den killing—the surgeon's use of a healthy patient's organs, shoving the fat man off the bridge. The difficulty lies in extracting what is common to these cases and deciding what counts as doing something to persons directly (fatal use) and what counts as indirect killing.

First, direct killing. Consider the case of craniotomy as a method of abortion. This has been interpreted in the Catholic tradition as an instance of direct killing. To save the woman's life, one has to disarm the fetus, neutralize its force, stop it from doing what it is doing to the woman. The only way one can do this is by destroying it. If killing is not the immediate means of saving the woman's life, it is the means to the means of stopping the unborn's threatening force. One has to intend the fetus's death to stop, narrow, or remove it, and that is never licit, since the fetus, it is assumed in the Catholic discussion, is not an unjust aggressor.

Other authors, however, argue that this traditional view of the craniotomy case is incorrect. Paul Ramsey as I interpret him (1971) argues that one incapacitates the fetus as the means; its death is an indirect consequence.[37] Susan Nicholson (1978) claims more broadly that in therapeutic abortions fetal death is not the means to the desired end (chap. 1, 47 n. 1; chap. 2). In a case of hypertension, the "removal" of the fetus is the means; in the craniotomy case, it is the "narrowing of the fetus's head" (1978, 25, 26–27, 37).[38] In the latter, Nicholson has in mind that forceps or other

37. Marquis argues that since "crushing a child's skull and killing a child *seem* to be the same action" (1991, 527), Boyle (1991a) is correct to define the intended means as a state of affairs, not an action: in the craniotomy the skull becoming smaller saves the woman's life, not death itself. (See also Boyle 1977b.) Thus, says Marquis, the means is defined solely in terms of "the actual *causal configuration* of what one does" (1991, 527). Marquis suggests, however, that Boyle's version of double effect would have to permit the use of the organs of one patient to save five, since the death of the one is not strictly intended (1991, 524). Marquis's point would be valid if the harm prohibited as a means were narrowly defined as death, but not if the prohibited means is defined more broadly as fatal use. The moral relevance of using in this sense depends on convictions about how threats should be distributed. See Marquis's (1991, 535ff.) discussion of Quinn's (1989b) Kantian rationale. See also Donagan (1991) on Boyle and Boyle's replies to critics (1991b). On Ramsey, see 102–3 n. 34.

38. Hoffman argues that one intends complex states of affairs that include effects one wants and effects one does not (1984, 390). Only if we identify intentions with motive would we say we do not intend to dull the knife when we carve a roast in order to have sliced meat (we do not want to dull the knife, we want sliced meat) (1984, 391). Thus, a craniotomy would cause both the death of a fetus and a lifesaving delivery (1984, 391–92); one prefers, and hence intends, that this state of affairs obtain. Traditional defenders of double effect, however, never deny that one *chooses* to bring about a state of affairs that has mixed results. The general issue between Hoffman and defenders of double effect would seem to be whether one intends both effects or chooses to bring them about as a complex state of affairs while intending only one.

instruments narrow the head, an action that also kills.[39] If Catholic thinkers
construe the forbidden direct killing as one where death itself is the means,
then, Nicholson argues, the prohibition does not cover the craniotomy
case.[40]

One can get a clearer sense of what Nicholson means by considering two
sorts of cases of self-defense. In some self-defense cases, death itself is
necessary to disarm. Suppose an attacker has a gun in each hand. You
could shoot one gun away, without injuring the attacker, but he or she

39. See also Geddes (1972, 94), Duff (1973, 17) and Bennett (1981, 106–7) who argue
that the death of the child is not the intended means in the craniotomy case. Cf. Anscombe
(1982, 22) and Norvin Richards (1984, 391–92). Kuhse (1987, 96ff.) also notes that one need
not intend death in the craniotomy and similar cases. Kuhse argues that death is not a "causally
prior means" either in the craniotomy case or in the case of the pregnant woman with a
"serious heart condition" who will die unless the fetus is "removed" (1987, 94, 102). Kamm
(1982, 105) distinguishes in regard to abortion 1) death as a consequence of loss of support,
e.g., dilation and curretage; 2) death in the process of removal, e.g., saline injection that causes
ejection; 3) fetus is attacked but death not intended, e.g., craniotomy; and 4) death intended
because necessary for removal. Cf. Boyle (1977b, 313). The idea that not death itself but only
removal is instrumental in the craniotomy appeared in early Roman Catholic debate (Connery
1977, 242).

40. McCormick (1989, 223–24) suggests that in one classic craniotomy case the "direct-
indirect" distinction of double effect is "redundant"; what really matters is what I call here
nothing is lost, namely, that if nothing is done both will die, but the life of one can be saved.
McCormick says this principle was at work in Grisez's revisionary thesis that the abortion is
"indirect" if "the very same act [abortion] is indivisible in its behavioral process [the saving
effect does not require a subsequent act]." Moreover, McCormick also suggests (1989, 224–
26) that for some the very distinction of direct/indirect may itself not be of moral significance.
He notes that certain moral theologians such as Scholz (1977) argue that some deaths, formerly
said to be indirect, were really directly willed, but with regret and for a "'proportionate
reason'." For example, in the case of an agent who escapes from an attack by riding down a
road occupied by crippled and blind individuals, thereby killing them, the deaths or injuries
are so significant, says Scholz, that they are an essential part of the means (McCormick 1989,
224–25; cf. Connery 1977, 126); in the case of an attacker who besieges a fortress with
explosives, thereby killing some noncombatants, the deaths are *conditio sine qua non* and
hence directly willed. I do not see, however, how the presence of the persons in the road is
part of the "essence or object" of the act. In the fortress case Scholz may be arguing that the
attacker must aim at an area containing both combatants and noncombatants, but as I argue
subsequently, the deaths of the noncombatants are still not intended as the means. Thus I
would argue that the deaths of innocents in both cases are indirect (discriminate); whether
proportionate, of course, is another question. On this point see Connery (1977, 197). Finnis
(1988, 178 n. 47) takes proportionality to mean morally proportionate, e.g., fair. I take it to
mean productive of good according to a standard, e.g., impartial maximization or some other
notion of justice. To fully specify the doctrine of proportionality, one needs to answer two
questions: which goods, such as lives or other values, and whose goods, that is, how the goods
are distributed (see McCormick 1989 on Schüller 1978). For some of McCormick's own
reflections, see (1989, 228ff.).

would get you with the other. You must therefore "shoot to kill." In this case, disarming the attacker is the means of saving your life, but the death of the attacker is the means of disarming. Nicholson herself identifies a case where death is the means: killing someone to prevent them from revealing information. Here it is the stopping of the person's talking, if you will, which is the immediate means, but death is the only way to accomplish that (1978, 25).[41]

There is a second sort of self-defense case, nonetheless, where the death of the attacker does seem to be an unintended result of the means. Imagine a case where you can shoot a gun away without injuring the attacker so long as the gun hand is away from the body. Unfortunately, the attacker moves the hand close to the body, so that when you shoot to knock the gun away, the bullet will also kill. You shoot to disarm, but given the position of the gun hand, death is the foreseen result. What Nicholson claims is that the craniotomy is closer to this case than the one above where one aims at death itself. You take an action to disarm the fetus (removal), an action that in the circumstances also kills (cf. Hart 1968, 122–23).

Now how would Thomson's doctrine bear on the dispute between the traditional view of craniotomy and the Ramsey-Nicholson critique? It seems to me that Thomson, were it not her view that in abortion cases it is justified to repel the fetus because the woman does not have a duty to aid the threatening fetus, would be committed to including the craniotomy in the class of forbidden killings. You must cut up or otherwise fatally attack the body of the fetus in order to narrow or remove it; you do something fatal to the fetus in order to distribute an evil (its threatening force). Death itself is not the means, but you have to attack its person fatally in order to dispel the evil. Thus, Thomson's prohibition is broader than the view that death in itself is the forbidden means. Attacks on bodily integrity, death resulting, are included, as well as cases where death in itself is the means.

One can see the point also by considering Thomson's example of the surgeon who needs organs and asking how Nicholson or Ramsey would construe it. It would seem that according to their critique the case is one of indirect killing, if death itself is the forbidden means, for it is not the healthy patient's death itself that is the indispensable means to saving others; the means consist of obtaining organs through surgery (see Marquis 1991, 524; and note 37, above). The only genuine instance of direct killing would be the case where you aim at the person's death itself as the means to your end. The example of Thomson's that comes closest to satisfying this criterion of the forbidden means is dismemberment. Slightly modify

41. Finnis, Boyle, and Grisez (1987, 310–18) argue that in using force against unjust attacks one does not "choose to kill a human being" (cf. 299 n. 1); the deaths are not intended and

this case so that it is not just the dismemberment but also the dying itself that sets off the lifesaving process (as in the terror bombing of noncombatants) and we have the sort of case in which death itself is the means.

It appears in any case that we have two notions of how to construe the direct/indirect distinction. One view (which Ramsey holds and Nicholson suggests Catholic thinkers may affirm) restricts "direct" killing to cases where you aim at death as a means because death itself is necessary in order to bring about the desired end. According to this view, in the actual circumstances in which craniotomy is called for, the death itself of the fetus is not necessary as a means although it is a necessary result in the circumstances. Similarly, Thomson's transplant case would count as indirect killing, for death itself is not necessary as a means. I would hold, in contrast, following Thomson, that a killing is direct if one has to attack fatally the bodily integrity of a person in order to ward off an evil. On this view, both the cutting up of the healthy patient and the craniotomy *ceteris paribus* would count as direct killing.

It seems, in sum, that if it is forbidden to intend death as a means to an end, then Ramsey and Nicholson are right: the death of the fetus is not the means in the craniotomy case. Insofar as the Roman Catholic tradition expresses the distinction between direct and indirect killing in this way, then the tradition is exposed to the Ramsey-Nicholson critique.[42] But in Thomson's doctrine the forbidden means is not characterized only as aiming at a person's death; the forbidden killing is defined in a broader way which would prohibit craniotomy, *ceteris paribus,* as well as cutting up the healthy patient.[43] Thus, it is crucial to note that double effect as it is often stated (the means must be morally good or indifferent, and so on) is only a formal statement of a moral view that limits the duty to aid, or more generally to promote the good, by one or more prima facie or absolute moral con-

---

hence not chosen. See also Finnis, Boyle, and Grisez (1987, chap. 4), and Finnis (1988, 148, 154, 178 nn. 46, 47, 48). In my view, one sometimes does intend death as a means in a just defensive action.

42. Uniacke (1984, 207–8) says that the question, "'Would the agent's end be thwarted if the death did not occur'" is not a "satisfactory criterion for determining intention." However, the case she offers does not prove the point. If a doctor gave an injection with the intention of killing the patient but instead the patient is mysteriously cured, the doctor would not try to kill the patient in some other way, for the circumstances have changed; the death of the patient was to be a means to ending suffering and it was assumed that death is necessary to that end. What the test question should reveal is whether the death *under the assumed circumstances* is a causal precondition of the intended end, or only a concomitant effect.

43. See Uniacke (1984, 204–11), on the ectopic pregnancy case. See also Kuhse (1987, 108–9) who maintains that removing the tube in an ectopic pregnancy is similar to removing the fetus in a heart condition case; in both cases, the fetus is the threat; the fetus and its means of survival have to be disconnected.

straints. Everything depends on what the constraint is: for example, death itself as the means, or, more broadly, fatal use (cf. Mack 1985, 20).

The first problem of application, then, has to do with how the forbidden means is understood. The doctrine of double effect, according to Ramsey and Nicholson, identifies the forbidden means as an action in which one aims at the death of innocents. This view leads these thinkers to a critique of what the tradition actually teaches on certain cases, for example, craniotomy. However, if the forbidden killing is understood along Thomson's lines, then aiming at death or dying as a means is only one way to violate the individual's right to life, one way to use fatally a person's body to distribute an evil.

A second problem of application has primarily to do with the other part of the doctrine: the distribution of an evil that results indirectly in the death of persons. Thomson's example is the trolley that one turns. I argue that taking action against combatants, where that action also kills noncombatants, is morally like turning the trolley onto the spur; one deflects the evil, but in such a way that one also kills the innocent. The question, however, is exactly what counts as taking action against military targets and killing noncombatants indirectly? What exactly is the permitted (or, as I argue, perhaps obligatory) action?

Advocates of the traditional doctrine of double effect have themselves debated the sorts of wartime cases to which it applies. For instance, in one sort of case one takes an action against a military target. In addition to the damage done to the target, the explosive force also kills noncombatants: an airstrike against a truck convoy also kills noncombatants in the nearby fields. These deaths in some cases are statistically foreseeable. What if, however, one needs to knock out a target located in a city (or village) where there are noncombatants, but either one does not know how to locate the combatants more precisely or the only weapon one has will obliterate the entire city? In the first case you aim at a combatant target, but the explosive force has a slightly wider range of dispersal that is lethal to those who happen to be in its range, for example, the noncombatants in the fields. But in the city/village case, one cannot be said to aim at the combatant target; one aims at an area containing the target and other things and people as well. Now the cases seem different and the apparent difference leads some interpreters of double effect, John C. Ford, for example, to say the doctrine is not applicable to the "obliteration" bombing of villages or cities (Ford 1970, 28–30).[44]

44. The issue, of course, is whether "obliteration" bombing in Ford's sense is justified in terms of double effect, not whether direct attacks on noncombatants can ever be legitimate. Ford argues that in effect obliteration or area bombing includes a direct attack on noncomba-

How different are the convoy case and obliteration bombing? As the dispersal area increases, the truck convoy case and the obliteration case seem less dissimilar. After all, in the convoy case one may be aiming at a combatant target but one's weapon hits a larger area. The convoy case is not like another sort of case where it seems that one could both aim at (discounting the possibility of error) and confine one's attack to the combatant target: one aims at a bridge and the troops on it, but the bridge fragments fall on refugees who happen to be passing underneath. Here the bridge fragments have the lethal force, not the explosive per se.

Ford's formulation of the doctrine of double effect, however, would seem to include the bridge and the convoy cases, but not obliteration bombing. In the convoy case the bullets used to shoot to kill or to disarm may also pass through or beyond soldiers or simply go astray, and thus cause death to noncombatants; the explosive force is wider than its object. In the bridge case, the explosive force per se does not kill the noncombatants but rather events set in motion by that force; one's force has effects beyond the target. In both the convoy and bridge cases, however, the circumstances permit one to define the means as the direction of force against a military target. The physical aiming one does is how one effectuates what one aims at as a means.

In the obliteration case, in contrast, one is not able to define the means in the traditional way. Either because one does not know where the enemy is, or even if one knows, because one's weapons cannot be directed at the enemy object, the means one is forced to use is the destruction of an area containing combatants and noncombatants; one has aimed destructive force at the area itself. By the nature of the circumstances, one has to define the means as the bringing of destructive force against an area that includes both combatants and noncombatants. To adopt this means is not the same as firing against a military target, even where one knows that the force will go through, extend beyond, go astray, or set up a chain of events harmful to noncombatants.[45] In the obliteration case, Ford claimed, circumstances

---

tants therein. See Palmer-Fernandez (1993, 59–60). Cf. Norvin Richards (1984, 395–96) who builds into the case the condition that there is an intention to kill noncombatants also.

45. As Nagel puts it, "If one makes no attempt to discriminate between guerrillas and civilians, as is impossible in an aerial attack on a small village, then one cannot regard as a mere side effect [of an attack on combatants] the deaths of those in the group that one would not have bothered to kill if more selective means had been available" (1972, 131). Nagel thinks, however, that there is a valid counterobjection to this argument. The means can be redescribed: the means is the obliteration of the area, the death of the noncombatants a side effect—one would have bombed the area even if the noncombatants had been absent. I argue ahead that this action does not constitute fatal use, but note the assumption that more selective means are not in fact available.

do not permit intending as a means something that is morally good or indifferent.[46]

Thus, insofar as the tradition requires that the intended means be defined only as the bringing of destructive force against a military objective, the doctrine cannot be applied to obliteration bombing. Ramsey, therefore, if he had stayed with the tradition as interpreted by Ford, would have had to retract his view that the destruction of villages in Vietnam was legitimate because the death of noncombatants therein was not intended as a means (1968, 428–40). The traditional view would not, according to Ford, permit one to adopt as a means an action that in the nature of the case cannot be understood as directed solely at a military target. For Ford, although it may have been no part of the plan to use the noncombatants' deaths as a means (the point Ramsey stresses), the nature of the circumstances is such that the deaths of the noncombatants are not a side effect of an attack on a military target but are part of a single act of obliteration.

I believe, however, that Ramsey is right that the noncombatants are not killed as a means, or more broadly, fatally used, in the obliteration case. (Ramsey also argues that some civilians are actually used as combatants, and that the enemy is responsible for placing military forces in noncombatant areas; see Lammers 1990, 69–70.) One can imagine the following version of the trolley case. Suppose that instead of turning the trolley (it now has no driver), you could stop it only by 1) dropping a bomb on the trolley, which destroys the trolley but whose range is broader and kills a bystander; 2) dropping a bomb on it which sets up a chain of events, such as knocking over a wall that kills a bystander; 3) dropping a bomb on an area that contains the trolley and also the bystander. Only in cases 1 and 2, according to Ford's view of the traditional doctrine, is your means the destruction of the evil force, for in case 3 you must intend to destroy a different object. On the fatal-use doctrine, however, it would seem that in neither case 1, 2, or 3 is the bystander being fatally used to save the others. The runaway trolley is an evil we have the capacity to distribute so as to save the most lives (or whatever distributive pattern we think just). In all three cases the step we take kills an innocent, but in no case does the fatal use itself of the innocent constitute the resource by which we save the others; the saving resource is the destruction of the trolley. Thus oblitera-

---

46. Thomson asks (1991, 293) whether, in debating the permissibility of bombing a place containing both military targets and noncombatants, one can decide by "looking inward" to determine one's intention. See Anscombe's (1982) criticism of the view that intention refers only to a mental condition, but see also Thomson's suggestion (1991, 295 n. 9) that Anscombe (1958) may have been concerned with "fault" rather than "permissibility."

tion bombing (in this sense) could be justified so long as the distributive criterion is satisfied.[47]

Objections

The consensus, therefore, needs a notion of double effect. I attempt to build on the fatal-use theme to provide such a notion. Two major sorts of

47. According to Kamm, one could not throw a grenade to stop a trolley if the shrapnel also kills a bystander Joe (1989, 229–31; see also 1991a, 573). Kamm's solution to this and other cases is the *"Principle of (Im)Permissible Harm,"* which turns on the following idea: "If an event is more intimately causally related to the harm than to the good, then we will perceive this as having achieved the good 'by' harming others"(1989, 232). The grenade has a "more intimate causal" relation to the death of the bystander (a "direct relation") than to the saving of the five since the grenade has to *turn* or *stop* the trolley and this is what does the saving (1989, 236–38) (an "indirect relation"). Thus Kamm's principle not only rules out taking the organs of one patient to save five or throwing someone off a bridge to stop the trolley (1989, 238–39), but also other cases where the "event" or what we do is "more intimately casually related" to the "lesser harm" than to the "greater good" (1989, 232). One could, however, use the grenade if its relation to *both* harm and good was indirect (1989, 236–37; 1992, 374), e.g., if the grenade that indirectly saves the five sets off a rockslide that kills the one. Her principle would not allow the use of a gas to save five if the gas "indirectly" saves (runs a machine that saves) but "directly" kills (is poisonous to the bystander) (1989, 237); but if the gas both directly saves and directly kills, it is permissible to use it because "its relation to greater good and lesser harm is causally equally intimate" (1989, 237; see also 1991a, 573). Kamm says "something that is an aspect of an event is more intimately connected to it than something that is a direct effect, and something that is a direct effect is more intimately connected to it than something that is an indirect effect" (1989, 242); in a Lazy Susan case, saving the five is an "aspect" of turning the Lazy Susan—the five are ipso facto moved to safety although one other is moved into an electric pole or simply crushed (see 1989, 234; 1992, 373–74).

Kamm's point (1989, 241, 244–45) seems to be that what is morally significant is not that the harm to the innocent causes the greater good and that we intend it as such, but that our degree of causal intimacy to the harm should not be greater than to the good. Kamm argues (1992, 380–81; see also 1989, 242–45, 258 n. 21) that double effect is neither sufficient nor necessary to explain why it is right to turn the trolley in the paradigm case: 1) Not sufficient, because it does not "explain why we may not also wiggle a bridge over the trolley when the vibrations thus created will stop the trolley from hitting five, if we foresee that the wiggling will also topple a bystander to his causally unnecessary death." For Kamm, the wiggling directly kills the bystander, but indirectly saves by stopping the trolley (1989, 230, 236), and this is impermissible in her view; it is not the introduction of a new threat (the wiggling) (1989, 229), but the degree of causal intimacy of our action to the greater and lesser harm that is morally significant. In my view, however, what is morally significant is whether the harm to the bystander is itself causally instrumental to our end. Hence I permit the wiggling. 2) Not necessary, because of the permissibility of intending harm to the one in the "Prevented Return" case. In the "Prevented Return" case (1989, 230), we turn the trolley toward the one (Joe) on the sidetrack "and we *require* that it actually grind itself into Joe because otherwise it would roll back and hit the five anyway." She believes this is justified because the trolley's

objections are commonly brought against double effect: problems about intention and morally normative criticisms.

First, objections about intention. It is claimed that the ordinary distinction between intended means or end and foreseen consequences is invalid; one intends all the foreseen consequences of what one does or refrains from doing, for example, the deaths of noncombatants. I do not argue directly against this objection as it is made, for example, by Kuhse (1987, 146ff.).[48] Following many writers, I assume a distinction between intended means or end and foreseen consequences.[49] However, even if I were forced to accept a "broad" concept of intention, which includes foreseen consequences in what is intended, the moral questions would still be open. Is it permissible to cause the deaths of noncombatants that occur in the course of an attack on a military target? Is it permissible to use the deaths of noncombatants as an instrument to weaken enemy morale and speed victory? The moral

---

hitting the one "maintains" the good of having the trolley turned away from the five; it is permissible to do so if what we do is "at least as intimately related to the greater good as to the lesser harm" (1989, 239–41). Kamm (1989, 256 n. 6) compares her prevented return to Thomson's loopback, but I think the cases are different. Thomson's loopback (1986, 101–2) seems to be a case where *either* the trolley hitting the five stops it from going around to kill the one, or where its hitting the one stops it from going around to kill the five. My intuition is that one may *not* turn the trolley in the prevented return, where unless the trolley hits the one it will roll back and kill the five, but where apparently it is not also the case that unless it hits the five it will come around and kill the one. In prevented return Joe is saved not by the injuries to the five but by allowing the trolley to roll back; but the five are saved by the trolley hitting Joe.

48. Kuhse (1987, 87) suggests that those who are against any intentional termination of innocent life by omission or commission, and yet want to allow some uses of lethal drugs and withdrawal of treatment, use the principle of double effect to show that such actions are not intended as end or means, and death results only as a side effect. Her strategy is to show that the conception of intention used in double effect is inadequate and thus she adopts the notion that an agent "intends all the foreseen consequences of her actions or omissions" (1987, 90). Kuhse (1987, 147, 153; cf. 149, 163), following Sidgwick, opts for a "broad" conception of intention. Kuhse notes that Anscombe rejects the notion of intention as an interior mental act we direct at will but says that Anscombe provides no substitute (Kuhse 1987, 159, 159 n. 146, 160–61; cf. 137 n. 103, 113 n. 62).

49. I do not argue here against Kuhse's view that one intends what one chooses (including all the foreseen or at least all the foreseen and seriously considered effects). But I would base my rejection of this view on a theory of intention such as that developed by Bratman (1987), who cogently deals with *"the problem of the package deal"* (if one considers and chooses A, knowing A will produce E, does not one intend E?) (1987, 143). Bratman distinguishes between our deliberation about and choice of a complex scenario that includes important effects, and our intentions (1987, 152–55). See Bratman (1987, 193 n. 24) on Sidgwick, whose view Kuhse accepts but Bratman rejects. Bratman (1987, 155ff.) also deals with the case where the "strategic" bomber does not intend deaths of children as a means, but learns that their deaths will also in fact weaken the enemy. Cf. Kamm (1989, 258 n. 15). For debate about the "belief-desire" view of intention, see Mele's (1988) criticisms of Audi (1973; 1986) and Audi's (1988) reply.

questions recur even if one favors a "broad" concept of intention. I feel justified, then, in continuing to employ the conventional distinction between intended means and end, and foreseen consequences.[50]

Another objection regarding intention holds that even if the conventional concept of intention is justified, the way it is put to work in double effect is morally vacuous, "limitlessly permissive," as Kuhse (1987, 147, 164) puts it; so long as death in itself is not aimed at as the means, the description of the means is in effect determined by the end: for example, in the craniotomy one *removes a threat* to the woman's life; death is described as a side effect. I admit and indeed use the distinction between intending death in itself and intending various other forms of fatal use, for it enables us to sharpen our concept of the forbidden means; as I argue, the forbidden means is broader than intending death in itself.[51] Although I agree then that death in itself need not be intended as end or means, for example, in the craniotomy case, the account of double effect I give does not endorse Kuhse's conclusion that "the [principle of double effect] will permit all those killings where the death in question is not intended as . . . ultimate end" (1987, 119ff.). The fatal-use view of the means is not determined by the description of the end but rather stands on its own as a conception of what is prohibited and what is not.[52]

50. See Macdonald (1984), who applies Kenny's (1966; 1975) framework to the case of the cancerous uterus; the removal of the uterus is the means; because the uterus is removed the woman lives and the fetus dies; these are "concomitant" effects (Macdonald 1984, 5). The death of the fetus is not intended if the removal is not for the reason that the fetus will die.

51. In my view, contrary to Kuhse, I believe one can independently distinguish what is done as a means, and thus it is at least *possible* to believe 1) that some actions (beyond intending death as a means) are prima facie wrong independent of their consequences, or 2) that some actions are absolutely wrong (see Kuhse 1987, 146 n. 122). Chandler (1990, 423–25) argues that moral beliefs determine whether one opts for a "wide" (utilitarian) or "narrow" (double effect) doctrine of intention. I assume here that there are independent reasons for approving the narrow view, but that does not determine the morally normative question.

52. Davis (1984b) raises a number of important points about double effect. 1) What does it mean to say that the death of the fetus is not required in the craniotomy? I would say that even in the actual circumstances the death itself is not causally necessary (see 1984b, 111–12). 2) In regard to her distinction between an "agent-interpretation" of double effect and an "event-interpretation," I use a notion of the intended means that incorporates both "event" or causal judgments, and elements of an agent's plan or purpose (see 1984b, 114). 3) Davis says the question of whether X would still "have a reason" to seek the death of Y if the desired end were secured without Y's death occurring is too broad; it tests whether the agent sought the death both as a means and a "supplementary end in itself" (1984b, 116–17). I agree that the formulation of the test question should make clear the assumption that the agent has no other end than saving life; the question then focuses on the means. 4) My account of the means agrees with points of Anscombe's that Davis (1984b, 118) notes, for instance, that intention is not merely an interior act of will. I disagree, however, with Anscombe's view that the death of the fetus is intended in the craniotomy. 5) In regard to the purported moral difference between giving a drug to ease the pain but also causing death, and giving a drug to cause death in order to ease the pain, Davis says the only difference in regard to the means

Yet even in cases where the intended means is commonly taken to be the harm of death itself, Jonathan Bennett (1981) suggests that one need not really intend death itself; thus in this additional sense, Bennett argues, the means-end distinction is morally vacuous: one never need intend death in itself.

What one intends, says Bennett, is determined by the beliefs that explain or give reasons for one's conduct (1981, 99–100). Thus, to identify intentions, we can ask how conduct would be different if beliefs were different (1981, 100). In the contrast between a tactical bomber who destroys a munitions factory, knowing that the raid will also kill civilians, and a terror bomber who kills civilians in order to demoralize the enemy, the difference in intention is brought out by asking this question: "If you had believed that there would be no civilian deaths, would you have been less likely to go through with the raid?" (1981, 100). The terror bomber presumably says yes and the tactical bomber no.

Bennett interprets the question to mean that in the counterfactual state no civilian deaths occur and whatever follows causally from that; that is, the question asks the terror bomber, would you have gone through with the raid if no civilians had died and morale would not have been lowered as a result (1981, 101)? The tactical bomber, however, is permitted to continue to assume that the factory is destroyed. Bennett has to interpret the question in this way because if the counterfactual state included what is causally "upstream" from the deaths (the destruction of the munitions factory) as well as "downstream" (the lowering of morale), then the question would not be answered differently by the two bombers. If the tactical bomber did not believe that the destruction of the factory would occur, then this bomber would answer *yes* as well. If both the destruction and the lowering of morale continue to be assumed, then both would answer *no*.

Tactical	*Terror*
1. deaths do not occur and factory is not destroyed	deaths do not occur and morale is not lowered

both answer yes (less likely to go through with raid)

---

is in the doctor's "occurrent intention or (actual) mental inventory" (1984b, 119). In my view, however, the difference is in part causal, for in the one death is not required to end pain, in the other it is necessary. Whether this has moral significance is the issue. Also see Davis (1984c) on problematic meanings of "using persons."

2. deaths do not occur and   deaths do not occur and
   factory is destroyed   morale is lowered

both answer no (not less likely to go through with raid)

Both sets of deaths are believed to be necessary in the circumstances, but Bennett's form of the question is designed to bring out whether the agent believes the deaths are a result or a precondition.[53] If both bombers believed that no civilian deaths would result from the raid, and the terror bomber believed that enemy morale could not be lowered without civilian deaths while the tactical bomber believed that the deaths of civilians were not causally necessary in order to destroy the target, then the terror bomber would call off the raid but the tactical bomber would not (1981, 101–2). Thus, on this test of what intentions are, Bennett accepts the thesis that the terror bomber intends the civilian deaths as a means while the tactical bomber does not (1981, 101).[54]

Bennett goes on, however, to question the supposition that the terror bomber intends civilian deaths while the tactical bomber does not. He first argues, as Ramsey and Nicholson do, that in the craniotomy case death is not intended as a means (1981, 106). According to the test question, says Bennett, "it is possible and even probable that the surgeon does not intend the child to die" (1981, 106). Thus, the craniotomy and the hysterectomy

---

53. Cf. Brock (1989, 349–51; 1993, 172ff.) on double effect. Note that although one would not continue to seek death if a supposedly lethal injection somehow relieved suffering (the end) in a nonlethal way, *in these circumstances* (it is believed) the injection must cause death in order to relieve suffering, whereas in the case of the drug that reduces pain but also causes an earlier death, death is not the instrument (1993, 173). The test question for determining what is intended as one's means must not ask what one would have *preferred* to do, or what one would rather have happen, for one could always say, for example, about the craniotomy that if one could have saved the woman's life without crushing the fetus's head, one would have (see Marquis 1991, 526). The test question—however stated—must reveal what the agent believes about the causal structure of the action he or she is prepared to take in the actual circumstances as the agent believes them to be. The normative question, then, is whether, in Brock's words, the "value judgments" that weigh the relief of suffering over causing death in both cases exhaust the morally relevant considerations, or whether it also matters morally how death occurs, as double effect claims. As I noted in Chapter 2, however, the issue where a single person is concerned is whether the patient yields the right not to be killed in either sort of case.

54. See Kuhse's (1987, 44ff., 53–54) critique of Bennett and her views (1987, 96, 102, 122, 129ff.) on the counterfactual test. She denies that there is a difference in intentions in a case where an iron lung is shut off and one in which a lethal injection is given (1987, 124–25, 129–31). She argues that both doctors intend the patient's death in the sense of doing what they on balance want, but neither would have the patient die if their objective could be achieved in some other way (1987, 134). See also Kuhse's (1987, 68) critique of Weinryb (1980).

(cancerous uterus) cases are symmetrical: "A prohibition of intention killing condemns both" or neither (1981, 107).[55]

Bennett then goes a step further. He presents a point he says has been implicit in his account. One cannot have beliefs about particular future events, for a "thought about a concrete particular must be an effect of that particular" (1981, 109). Furthermore, one can only intend what one can have beliefs about. Intentions are aimed at "kinds of events" rather than at "particular events" (1981, 110). By "particular" event, I think Bennett means actual event, as opposed to a concept or "kind" of event; he is not contrasting something general—for instance, the death of civilians—with something specific—the death of particular civilians. Thus, with this distinction in mind, Bennett then considers an example: a political leader takes action against a union, intending it to be inoperative, indeed dissolved, in December so that it cannot call a strike, but foresees that the dissolution will be permanent (1981, 110). Similarly the terror bomber did not intend the permanent dissolution (death) of the civilians, he only intended that "the people's bodies should be inoperative for long enough to cause a general belief that they were dead, this belief lasting long enough to speed the end of the war" (1981, 111). Because one cannot have beliefs and hence intentions about future particulars, the terror bomber could not intend the permanent dissolution, that is, the deaths of the civilians; the terror bomber can intend only a certain dissolution or "inoperativeness" that will cause the belief that they are dead, which will in turn weaken enemy morale (1981, 111). Even though the terror bomber knows that civilians will die, he does not intend their deaths (1981, 113).

Bennett has attempted, then, to show that even the terror bomber does not intend that the civilians actually die in the sense of permanent dissolution; indeed, the terror bomber *cannot* intend their deaths since their deaths would be concrete particulars; the terror bomber can intend only to "dismantle" or dissolve them (1981, 113). Yet surely the distinction in inten-

---

55. Even if one granted, says Bennett, that "if you do X by doing Y then your X-ing is identical with your Y-ing . . . , you can intend to do X without intending to do Y" (1981, 108–9; see also Boyle 1977b, 307ff.). Note also the important point made clear by Lichtenberg (1994, 351) following Bennett (1981): Neither the tactical nor terror bomber "regard civilian deaths as intrinsically desirable." However, Lichtenberg questions and ultimately denies the thesis that the fact that civilian deaths are a "temporally prior causal precondition," and hence the terror bomber can be said to use those deaths or those persons as a means, is morally significant (1994, 353). Where "probability and number of deaths is the same, the question whether you have intended or merely foreseen them is morally insignificant" (1991, 355–56). Lichtenberg (1994, 360ff.) notes, however, that other moral considerations may lead us to view double effect as a "useful rule of thumb" (1994, 355–56). See Lichtenberg also on Walzer and on the proportionality criterion (1994, 355, 361).

tions between tactical and terror bombing only requires what Bennett himself at one point seems to grant, namely, that the terror bomber intends to bring about "deaths of civilians or deaths of those civilians . . ." (1981, 110). Bennett must be supposing that if one intends "deaths of civilians or deaths of those civilians" as a kind of event, one is really intending merely dissolution, not permanent dissolution (death), which would be a "concrete particular." Yet why can one not intend a civilian death as a permanent dissolution, even if it is true that one does not intend it as an actual event but rather as a type of event? One intends that the bullet fly even if one cannot intend that flight (the actual flight) of the bullet (1981, 110). What one intends and what happens correspond even though the former is a kind of event, not a particular event.

Perhaps, however, Bennett's thesis could be restated: the *death* of a union or a person is simply the nonexistence of that entity; whether nonexistence is permanent is a further fact about a death. Thus, the union buster intends the death (kind of event) of the union and foresees that this dissolution or state of nonexistence will be permanent; the terror bomber intends deaths (kind of event), knowing that the dissolution of the properties on which personal identity rests is permanent. The terror bomber intends nonexistence but foresees permanent nonexistence. This revision, however, does not suffice, for the crucial difference between tactical bombing and terror bombing remains; only in the latter is death (even defined simply as nonexistence) necessary as a means. The terror bomber might believe in the resurrection of the dead, but he or she would nonetheless intend the nonexistence of civilians just as the political leader intends the dissolution of the union as the means of avoiding a strike. In both cases nonexistence is, in the circumstances, a necessary causal condition of achieving some state of affairs (for example, lowering morale or avoiding a strike) which is itself instrumental to the agent's goal (victory or maintaining production).[56]

56. Quinn (1989b) argues that neither Anscombe's test of whether something is intended as the means (to the question, Why this upshot, is the answer "to" do this or that, or "it can't be helped . . ."?), nor the view that "All aspects of an action or inaction that do not in the strictest sense contribute to an agent's goal will be trimmed away as unintentional" (1986b, 340), are satisfactory (the latter allows the terror bomber, following Bennett [1981], to say that the actual deaths of the noncombatants are not needed, only their seeming dead [Quinn 1989b, 337, 340–41; see his critique of Bennett 1989a, 295–96]). Quinn's suggested solution is that the terror bomber need not intend deaths but does intend "that they [the noncombatants] be violently impacted by the explosion of his bombs" (1989b, 342). Thus the terror bomber is a case "in which harm comes to some victims, at least in part, from the agent's deliberately involving them in something in order to further his purpose precisely by way of their being so involved" (1989b, 343). (Cf. Mack 1985, 5–6; Kamm 1992, 376, 379.) Over and above harming per se, Quinn says, the agent who harms as a means treats the victims "as if they were then and there *for* his purposes" (1989b, 348); they are "cast in some

I conclude, therefore, that the distinction between terror and tactical bombing does lie in whether death is intended as a means.[57] Whether the distinction has moral significance will depend on one's overall moral view.[58]

Second, then, the moral objection. The noncombatants will be dead: What moral difference does it make if their deaths are intended as a means

---

role that serves the agent's goal" (1989b, 349; on craniotomy, see 342–43). Thus, double effect "rests on the strong moral presumption that those who can be usefully involved in the promotion of a goal only at the cost of something protected by their independent moral rights . . . ought, prima facie, to serve the goal only voluntarily." The substantive assumption, in my account, is also that one has a right not to be fatally used without one's consent. Although I think the content of this assumption could be said to be Kantian because of the role of consent, I think the notion of such a right could be *justified* in other than Kantian ways; for instance, a neo-Aristotelian view that puts a high value on autonomy or self-determination and hence leaves it to the agent to decide when a standard harm or benefit is outweighed. For criticisms of Quinn's version of double effect, and in particular his Kantian justification, see Fischer, Ravizza, and Copp (1993).

57. See also Shun (1985) who argues that neither Nagel's (1980) nor Bennett's (1981) view of intending as a means is satisfactory. The test of intending as a means is not whether one aims at a certain state of affairs (in the sense of being willing to adjust one's action so as to produce it), or whether one would be less likely to act in the proposed way if the state of affairs (for example, civilian deaths) would not occur. The correct test is this: "Given that an agent does A [goes on a bombing raid] and believes that he will bring about S [killing civilians] by doing A, he intends to bring about S as a means if part of his motivation in doing A is dependent in the appropriate way on his belief that there are other things he can bring about [lowering enemy morale] by bringing about S" (Shun 1985, 221). Thus although Bennett acknowledges that intending as a means involves having certain beliefs, Bennett does not identify those beliefs correctly: "The test question Bennett uses to distinguish between the terror bomber and the tactical bomber shows that he thinks what matters is a dependence relation between the agent's motivation in doing A and his belief about *whether he can bring about S by doing A*. . . . My argument shows, however, that what matters is a dependence relation between the agent's motivation in doing A and his beliefs about *whether he can bring about certain other things by bringing about S*" (222 n. 8). My sense, however, is that Bennett wants to include the dependence relation Shun insists on in the notion of what is believed about the "causally downstream" effects. As Shun himself puts Bennett's view: "From the belief that there would be no civilian deaths, the terror bomber is supposed to have inferred in a causally downstream direction that there would also be no lowering of enemy morale" (217).

58. Bennett does not attribute moral significance to the putative difference in intentions. Even though the destruction of the factory is not brought about by the deaths of the civilians, the death of the civilians is brought about by the tactical bombing just as it is in the case of terror bombing (1981, 102); neither the terror nor the tactical bomber wishes the civilians to die (1981, 103); either situation could have been different—that is, the civilians near the factory could have been out of town or it could have been that it was not necessary to kill civilians to weaken enemy morale (1981, 103); nor does it matter that the tactical bomber will not try to kill you if you survive, for this bomber is willing to pursue a course that results in your death just as the terror bomber is (1981, 104); nor, Bennett suggests without developing the point, can it be said that the tactical bomber is not using people as means to his end (1981, 105); the distinction between intending as means and foreseeing should also not be confused with the distinction between doing and allowing to happen, even if the latter is

or not? This is the morally significant issue. The answer depends on one's web of belief; following the just-war tradition in general and the fatal-use idea in particular, I argue that my web of belief—and the consensus under development—requires a distinction between intentionally using the non-combatants fatally to further one's ends, and unintentionally causing their deaths; when they die as a side effect, one intentionally initiates the causal sequence that leads to their deaths and hence one "kills" them (see Chapter 1), but one does not intentionally use their bodies fatally. In particular, one does not intend their deaths as the means.

Thus, the framework of moral convictions renders the distinction among means, ends, and unintended consequences significant. The normative framework defines the "direct" and the "indirect" killing. The notion of intention provides only the tools with which the normative framework goes to work. The moral framework one endorses gives the doctrine of double effect content by identifying a particular species of impermissible actions. To reject double effect, then, the critic needs to argue for alternative moral convictions.

One way to defeat the concept of double effect that rests on a prohibition against intending a certain harm or set of harms is to show that the prohibition and the related concept of double effect cannot encompass the judgments its upholders want to make; thus, the prohibition or constraint is normatively inadequate. Shelly Kagan, for example, takes the case of a human shield to produce troubles for anyone who upholds a constraint against intending harm as a means:

> Suppose, for example, that the missile from my anti-tank gun must pass through the body of the shield in order to hit and destroy the tank. Unless I get at the tank itself I cannot stop it. Thus digging a path through the body of the shield is a necessary *means* to accomplishing the end of stopping the tank. But having a missile go through a body is obviously a harm; therefore when I shoot at the shield in order to hit the tank, I am intending harm to the shield as a means. (1989, 139)

---

of moral significance (1981, 105). Having surveyed these considerations, Bennett concludes that the distinction between intending as a means and foreseeing has no moral significance. Bennett does not consider, however, except in his brief dismissal of the notion of using as a means, any substantive moral views that would attach significance to how deaths occur, even when "degrees of good and bad" in regard to consequences and "probabilities" are the same (1981, 98).

Kagan himself suggests a modification of the constraint. There is another case:

> Consider this gruesome variation on our tank example: Suppose I have no gun powerful enough to destroy the tank, but by shooting and killing the shield I can spatter the blood over the tank's window—blinding [the driver], and allowing me to escape. Were it not for the shield conveniently located on the tank, I would be *unable* to escape. (1989, 140)

We can now, says Kagan, distinguish two sorts of means:

> In the original case, the harm to the shield is a means to an end which I would have been able to achieve even were it not for the existence/state of the shield. All along I was capable of stopping the tank with my gun; now the shield blocks the tank—but harming the shield only puts me back where I would have been otherwise. The shield's presence—and eventual harm—doesn't make me any better off than I would have been without the shield altogether. It is different for the second case, where the presence—and eventual harm—of the shield itself *benefits* me. It makes me better off than I would have been without the shield altogether. Without the shield I would have been incapable of stopping the tank; harming the shield puts me ahead of where I would have been otherwise. Let us say, for cases of this second kind, that harm is a *strong* means to the desired end; in contrast, for cases of the first sort, the harm is merely a *weak* means to the end. (1989, 140–41)

However, says Kagan, even if one holds that only a strong means is forbidden, this standard for the forbidden means would allow harms the upholders of the constraint do not want to permit:

> The modified constraint itself may have implications which are unacceptable. . . . Restricted to cases of intending harm as a strong means, the constraint may excuse too much. For example, imagine that the only way to avoid the tank racing toward me is to push an innocent bystander over the cliff—enabling me to stand in safety where the bystander is currently standing. . . . It seems plausible to think that the constraint against intending harm should rule out such a reaction. Yet on the account I have suggested, pushing the bystander apparently is merely a weak means to my end, for I am

no better off for the bystander's presence: were he not there, I could simply move to the safe spot. Thus it seems that the modified constraint excuses too much . . . (1989, 143).

Now how should I respond to Kagan's objections? First, I do not think our accounts differ substantially in regard to the concept of intention or means.[59] I have assumed the rough intuitive view that X is a means (intended as a means) if and only if X is a causally necessary precondition that one purposively brings about in order to accomplish one's end. Similarly, Kagan says:

A vehicle to some end functions as a means to that end if and only if the fact that the event is a vehicle is the agent's *reason* for countenancing it. (1989, 130)

Thus, he renders the constraint against intending harm as follows:

The constraint forbids countenancing harm where the agent's reason for doing so is that the harm is an end or a *vehicle* to some end. (1989, 128 n. 2)

Second, my account agrees with Kagan that the upholder of the constraint will make use of the idea that what Kagan calls a strong means involves in some sense "using" a person:

Perhaps an advocate of this account might argue as follows: "Each agent has, or is able to acquire, certain abilities; he is capable of accomplishing certain goals, avoiding certain harms, and so on. Now in some cases—cases where harm is merely a *weak* means— some other individual has (unfortunately) become so situated that he will be harmed by the exercise of the agent's capabilities. In effect, however, the agent only accomplishes what he is already able to do: the harm to the other bestows no real benefit; it only frees the agent from the paralysis imposed by the presence of the other. In contrast,

---

59. See Kagan (1989) on what he regards as an alternative justification for the purported moral distinction between intending and foreseeing harm, namely, the view that one should not aim at evil or what is bad; we should not turn our minds to evil (1989, 131–32). I agree with Kagan that "it does not follow from the essence of *evil* that it is fundamentally incorrect to aim at" (1989, 168); it could be necessary, as in Kagan's example, to use pain itself as part of the cure of a disease, in which case the pain would not be a "side effect" but an "essential means" (1989, 168).

when harm is a *strong* means, the agent literally gains at the other's expense. His capabilities are *increased;* he is able to take what he could not otherwise take—by virtue of the loss inflicted upon the other. So it is only in cases where harm is a strong means that the other person is actually being used, only in such cases that the agent is genuinely profiting from the misfortune of another. Therefore the constraint against intending harm should be restricted to cases of intending harm as a strong means." (1989, 142–43)

Third, however, my view diverges from Kagan's in the representation of the original shield case. Kagan says, we remember:

> Digging a path through the body of the shield is a necessary *means* to accomplishing the end of stopping the tank. But having a missile go through a body is obviously a harm; therefore when I shoot at the shield in order to hit the tank, I am intending harm to the shield as a means. (1989, 139)

The question here seems to be whether we must describe digging harmfully, indeed fatally, through the shield as the intended means. On Kagan's view, since the missile must go through the shield to hit the tank, the harmful digging is the intended means because it is a "vehicle" and the agent's "reason for countenancing it": "I shoot at the shield in order to hit the tank."

The contrary view, which I adopt here, is stated as follows by Warren Quinn:

> Another problematic kind of case involves innocent hostages or other persons who physically get in the way of our otherwise legitimate targets or projects. Does our shooting through or running over them involve a direct intention to affect them? I think not. It is to our purpose, in the kind of case I am imagining, that a bullet or car move through a certain space, but it is not to our purpose that it in fact move through or over someone occupying that space. The victims in such cases are of no use to us and do not constitute empirical obstacles (since they will not deflect the missile or vehicle in question). If we act despite their presence, we act exactly as we would if they were not there. If, on the other hand, we needed to aim at someone in order to hit a target, that person would clearly figure as an intentional object. (1989b, 345; cf. 341–44)

I do not "shoot at the shield *in order to* hit the tank" (my italics), I shoot at the tank, foreseeing that my missile will in fact pass through and harm the shield on its way to the tank.[60] The harm of digging through is temporally before the good effect but not causally instrumental in the requisite sense (see Boyle 1977b; and note 11, above). It is true that it must be possible for the missile to dig through the shield; the shield must not be able to obstruct the missile. But the digging through does not itself make any positive contribution to the flight of the missile. For the harm, or fatal use as I put it, to be the intended means, it must play a positive role in the execution of our purpose. As Quinn said, the shield must not be an obstacle—the missile must pass through—but this fact does not constitute the positive instrumentality we ascribe to a means: "we act exactly as we would if they were not there."

Suppose Kagan were right, however: since the fatal digging through is a causal precondition of the missile speeding on to the tank, and it is accepted by the agent for that very reason, then let us suppose that as a matter of the theory of action we must describe it as the intended means. I would then be forced to accept Kagan's distinction between weak and strong means. I would have to amend my notion of fatal use, as Kagan expects the defender of the constraint against harming to do, so that it signifies only a strong and not a weak means. I would now say that what double effect forbids is fatal use in the strong means sense.

Fourth, would I then be left with the difficulty Kagan finds with the "strong means," namely, that it excuses too much? Kagan says that "pushing the bystander apparently is merely a weak means to my end, for I am no better off for the bystander's presence: were he not there I could simply move to the safe spot" (1989, 143). Thus, presumably, if only a "strong means" is forbidden, it is not prohibited to push the bystander aside.

My first response is that the means here does seem to lie in a fatal attack on a person, although it is not a person's presence but rather their absence that is necessary. Although death in itself is not intended, I fatally attack the person in order to accomplish my end. In the circumstances, getting the person off the space involves their dying. In Kagan's own words, one agent "gains at the other's expense . . . by virtue of the loss inflicted on the other" (1989, 142–43).[61]

60. In Regan's innocent shield case (1983, 291–92) a terrorist with a tank is killing hostages but has strapped another hostage to the tank. In this case, if nothing is done the hostages will apparently die but the one on the tank will live. Regan suggests only that blowing up the tank will kill the hostage, not that one has to shoot through the hostage to blow up the tank. Cf. Nicholson (1978) and Reynolds (1985) on the cases where one has to go through the fetus to operate on the diseased organ of the woman.

61. Cf. Brown's (1987) use of the "at the expense of others" theme in his application of oppression as "just cause" for violent revolution. Cf. also Boorse and Sorenson (1988) on the

Thus, the prohibited means is not limited to cases where the presence of the one injured confers the benefit. I must amend Kagan's "strong means" so that it includes not only the sort of case where the shield's presence (and subsequent harm) confers a benefit, but also cases where the absence of the innocent serves the same purpose; a fatal injury serves my purpose in either case. Thus, the view I take here would not *ceteris paribus* legitimate killing in shield cases where one would have to inflict a fatal injury first on the shield *in order to* clear a field of fire to get at the threatening force (the tank, a person with a gun) (cf. Ramsey 1973). In this sort of shield case, one does not merely shoot through the shield, one has to remove the shield, procure the shield's *absence,* through a fatal injury.[62]

Second, however, even if one had to accept Kagan's view that pushing the bystander off the safe spot is not a "strong means" (since one does not benefit by the bystander's presence), another feature of the case may explain why we oppose throwing the bystander off. In Kagan's case it is apparently only a case of saving *my* life at the bystander's expense. In Kagan's description of the shield cases, proportionality seems to be satisfied since one is defending not only oneself but one's "family." However, in the innocent bystander case, Kagan's description seems to suggest that one would be saving only oneself. Even if it were permitted, as Thomson argues, for the trolley to be diverted in order to save five at the expense of one, it would not be right to divert the trolley in order to save only oneself (assuming, of course, no other relevant moral claims). Thus, even if pushing off the bystander met the criterion of "discrimination"—it was not in itself an

---

ducking/sacrificing distinction (in the former, one escapes harm, allowing it to fall on another; in the latter, one uses the other as a shield). See their comments on the case where one has to shove someone fatally in order to escape (1988, 130).

62. Thus, if the fatal injury inflicted on the fetus in order to remove it in the case of the misplaced appendix or the aneurysm were parallel to Kagan's bystander, then in none of these cases is killing permissible. According to Ramsey (1973), in these cases one must first take an action to remove the fetus, and then take a separate medical action to deal with the condition of the woman—in contrast to the craniotomy, where one action removes and saves. In these cases one would be doing a fatal injury in order to clear a space, as it were, to save another. See also Connery's (1977, 242; also 177, 269) discussion of de Lugo on the child used as a shield by an unjust aggressor: it is one thing to kill the child as a side effect of an act of defense, another to kill the child first "in order to get him out of the way, and then kill the assailant. . . . The person assailed would intend the death of the innocent person as a means to his defense, and hence he would be intending it directly. It would be a separate act, and he would be defending himself in another act aimed at the assailant." Note, however, that Ramsey's (1973) defense of abortion in both the craniotomy and the appendix/aneurysm case (in the former sort of case, a single act presumably removes and saves, whereas in the latter two acts are required) depends apparently on the fact that if nothing is done both would die (nothing is lost). The difference, therefore, in sorts of actions does not seem morally relevant to him in the context of these cases. (See notes 10, 11, and 12, above; Grisez 1970b, 341.)

instance of the prohibited means—it does not satisfy the criterion of proportionality, provided we not, as Ramsey, and apparently Thomson, insist, weigh the lives of two individuals.

At Least a Prima Facie Right

In summary, I try, then, to show that Donagan's critique of double effect should be formulated as a moral critique, not as a critique of a traditional assumption about action. The difficulty with Donagan's normative position, however, is that it does not allow for the indirect deaths of noncombatants. I attempt, therefore, to modify the fatal-use doctrine as a version of double effect. Donagan's prohibition would limit severely what we can do to repel unjust attacks; the fatal-use doctrine of what we owe others would provide a normative basis for a distinction between direct and indirect noncombatant deaths. Finally, I try to show how this revised doctrine of double effect can be applied to difficult cases. In regard to the forbidden killing, I argue that the prohibition is broader than cases where one intends death as a means (*ceteris paribus,* craniotomy would be forbidden); in regard to what counts as indirect and hence permitted, I note that traditional defenders of double effect such as Ford do not allow "obliteration" bombing, but I argue that my way of drawing the distinction would permit it. Of course, even if my version of double effect can be sustained and used to distinguish indirect from direct deaths of noncombatants, the question remains, as Anscombe (1970) and others ask, whether it is ever permitted or obligatory to override the prohibition: for example, Is it ever right to attack noncombatants directly to further the aims of a just war? I allow so far only for the "miniride" exception; the question whether there are other instances in which the prohibition can morally be set aside is still before us. I will attempt to deal with this in Chapter 5.

5

Absolutism

What Is Absolutism?

I have argued that against the aggressor it is licit to intend fatal use, even death itself as a means. I agree with Paul Ramsey and others that death itself is not the means in the craniotomy, but I count action against the fetus in the craniotomy as direct because it inflicts fatal injury as a means; only if the fetus is an aggressor in a relevant moral sense is craniotomy justified.

Repelling the aggressor in an unjust war and repelling a runaway trolley, even if the innocent die as a side effect, are justified so long as the means are permissible and the cost is proportionate. In war, provided my means are permissible and the cost is proportionate, I can both defend myself and fulfill my duty to defend others (this duty could be interpreted as part of a general duty to aid, and as a special commitment to a political community). Similarly, if I were one of the five on the track in the path of the onrushing trolley, I also could and should turn the trolley, provided that it is the turning that saves and not fatal use, and that the loss is proportionate.

In contrast, it is at least prima facie wrong to fatally use noncombatants, either through "terror bombing," where one intends their deaths or through any other form of fatal use. And it would be equally wrong to save five from the trolley by the fatal use of one, except in the "miniride" case, where I can either save five by the fatal use of one or one by the fatal use of five.

In this chapter I argue that except for the miniride and one other case— a Nazi-like threat—the right against fatal use should be absolute. But what does this mean? By absolutism I do not mean, of course, that the killing of the "innocent" is never justified. This sense of absolutism would preclude that individuals could be killed when they are nonvoluntary or involuntary pursuers, when they yield their right, when nothing is lost, and when their deaths would be indirect. Against the background of a distinction between "killing" and "letting die," I have tried to specify the meaning of the rights in question by distinguishing those instances of killing or letting die that are morally forbidden from those that are not.[1]

My method, then, is to qualify the meaning of the rights, practicing a combination of what Judith Thomson calls factual and moral specification (1976; cf. Feinberg 1980b, 225ff.). I do not deny that in some circumstances where rights are involved we may find it more convenient to speak of a "prima facie" right that can be "overridden."[2] The right is said to be "actual," or decisive, unless it is overridden by a "more stringent" right. In Chapter 4 I identify a sort of case (the loopback) where one would, in Thomson's words, distribute a threat by doing something (fatal) to a person, no matter what one did; this seems to me to be one case where we justifiably *override* the right not to be killed (the miniride principle).

Furthermore, there may also be, as Feinberg suggests, cases where a right (not merely prima facie but actual) is justifiably "infringed," in Thomson's

1. Note that my absolutism is different from the view of those who draw the line at intending death as means or end. Cf. Fried (1978, 27–28, 32ff., 40–42), who argues that one does not violate the agent's categorical or absolute right not to be harmed unless one intends death as end or means. Nor do I insist that the broader fatal-use constraint has no exceptions. Cf. my approach to Nielsen (1973; 1990) who insists that on the basis of what is good for the greatest number (his qualified utilitarianism) and facts relevant to certain situations, exceptions could be made to the rule against "deliberately" harming or killing the innocent. He holds open the possibility of exceptions even in cases where he now would hold the line— for example, the judicial punishment of the innocent—and he could hold the line where he now allows exceptions; empirical beliefs may change. Cf. Evans (1968) and Outka (1968).
2. Feinberg (1980b, 226) cites Frankena (1955); see also Childress on war (1982a).

vocabulary; in these cases we feel moral regret and owe compensation. Feinberg (1980b, 230) gives this case:[3]

> You are on a back-packing trip in the high mountain country when an unanticipated blizzard strikes the area with such ferocity that your life is imperiled. Fortunately, you stumble onto an unoccupied cabin, locked and boarded up for the winter, clearly somebody else's private property. You smash in a window, enter, and huddle in a corner for three days until the storm abates. During this period you help yourself to your unknown benefactor's food supply and burn his wooden furniture in the fireplace to keep warm.

As Feinberg and Thomson use this example, it is not a case where aid might be owed. What is taken and used, for example, furniture, is seen as beyond what one owes or ought to give as a Minimal Samaritan. The case is an emergency where property rights are justifiably infringed and later the expended resources must be made up in kind or through compensation.

My sense, however, is that an infringed actual right is really another class of overridden rights, for it is hard to see how the right is *actual* (in the sense of decisive) if it can be justifiably set aside; perhaps it would be simpler to say that on some occasions when rights are overridden, or even when they are not, because of how the rights are specified, we owe compensation, as Thomson (1976) and Feinberg (1980b) argue is the case when we kill an innocent hostage in the course of repelling an aggression.

My thesis, in any case, is that once properly understood, the right not to be killed and the right to be saved do not fall into the class of rights that can be overridden or justifiably infringed except in the miniride case and one other possible instance—a Nazi-like threat—considered in this chapter. I endorse absolutism, then, in the sense that once the meaning of the rights is suitably qualified, and the two legitimate overrides identified, no further qualifications or overrides are allowed; the rights are closed, in other words, to further future "exceptions."

---

3. Thomson refers (1980, 15 n. 3) to a similar example of her own; see her 1976, 10–11; and 1986, 105–6, 112. Cf. Foot (1983a, 384, 393–94) on the notion that sometimes an obligation can stand even if it cannot morally be discharged. Thomson (1990, chap. 3; 1993a, 160) argues that where one may infringe a claim, one ought *ceteris paribus* to try to "obtain a release," and if that is not possible, "compensate." On Thomson's advocacy of infringement rather than override (where apparently the right overridden leaves no "traces"), see Davis (1988, 808–9, 815). Davis questions (1988, 817–18) whether one can redress or compensate the innocent person (in contrast to their heirs) justifiably killed in cases such as the trolley. Thus, she suggests, while infringement "may work well enough for property rights, it seems to have problems accommodating rights to life" (818).

Note, however, that this is a *revisable* absolutism. No further future exceptions are expected so far as one *now* sees. One endorses this system and its constraints. But moral beliefs are revisable, and other adjustments could be needed to cover other cases. (I will need in any case to extend my account to suicide and capital punishment, for example.) Thus I aim for closure in one sense, but not another: I aim for closure now, for a view that determines what the "evil" is that we may not do even that good may come. But I do not claim that my view seeks closure in the sense of unrevisability.

Supreme Emergency

Should the traditional prohibition against direct attacks on noncombatants be absolute?[4] Should only combatants surrender their immunity from attack? Or are there reasons why the protection should be violated or overridden? Michael Walzer holds that the prohibition should be disregarded in a "supreme emergency." A supreme emergency consists in a situation where a Nazi-like threat hangs over all humankind or even over only one political community, and direct attacks on noncombatants, for example, terror bombing, are a last resort against the threat. In the actual case:

> Nazism was an ultimate threat to everything decent in our lives, an ideology and a practice of domination so murderous, so degrading even to those who might survive, that the consequences of its final victory were literally beyond calculation . . . evil objectified in the world . . . a threat to human values so radical that its imminence would surely constitute a supreme emergency. (Walzer 1977, 253)

But even if the Nazi threat had been directed at Britain alone, it would have been reason enough to put aside the prohibition:

> Can a supreme emergency be constituted by a particular threat—by a threat of enslavement or extermination directed against a single nation? Can soldiers or statesmen override the rights of innocent

4. For the sake of simplicity, I discuss attacks on noncombatants as killings, although one could imagine a letting-die case as well. For example, a group of noncombatants is about to be massacred by their own soldiers; should one fail to save them in order that their deaths induce terror in the population at large and shorten the war?

people for the sake of their own political community? I am inclined to answer this question affirmatively, though not without hesitation and worry. (1977, 254)

Walzer argues, then, that the enslavement or extermination of the members of a political community constitutes the supreme emergency and justifies attacking noncombatants.[5] It is not required that our action also save the most lives, because large nations would then have an advantage:[6]

Perhaps it is only a matter of arithmetic: individuals cannot kill other individuals to save themselves, but to save a nation we can violate the rights of a determinate but smaller number of people. But then large nations and small ones would have different entitlements in such cases, and I doubt very much that that is true. We might better say that it is possible to live in a world where individuals are sometimes murdered, but a world where entire peoples are enslaved or massacred is literally unbearable. For the survival and freedom of political communities—whose members share a way of life, developed by their ancestors, to be passed on to their children— are the highest values of international society. (1977, 254)

Walzer seems to mean that if the maximization of life were also a criterion of a supreme emergency, if we can save a nation "only" if we also save the most lives, then since larger nations have a better chance of meeting the criterion there would be an asymmetry between the entitlements of large and small nations; the larger nation could save itself because more lives overall would be saved than lost, but the small nation could not meet a threat of extermination or enslavement if more lives overall would be lost. Maximization alone, he says, does not override noncombatant immunity,

5. In this chapter I am dealing with instances in which the same right (the right not to be killed) or perhaps a right with an equivalent moral status (the right not to be enslaved) are putatively in conflict. A rights theory must also deal with the conflicts of other rights, for example, the right not to be killed with the right not to be harmed in some lesser way. Gewirth uses his basic moral principle to order rights in conflict; since the "Principle of Generic Consistency" protects and promotes the "necessary conditions of action . . . that right takes precedence which is more necessary for action" (1982, 219–20).

6. Walzer (1977, 262) argues that if one were calculating utilities, other things besides lives would count. On Walzer see Childress (1982a, 84ff.). See Lammers (1983, 99–100, 109) on Walzer's theme that the Nazis were a threat to Western values and the danger of introducing supreme emergency as a social practice. See also Finnis, Boyle, and Grisez (1987, 181–89) on arguments by Mavrodes (1975) and O'Brien (1981) against the absoluteness of noncombatant immunity.

nor even maximization along with a threat to the community. The latter alone justifies us in overriding the prohibition.

Walzer seems to be saying then that a threat of the massacre or enslavement of a political community is both a necessary and a sufficient reason to disregard noncombatant immunity. He would allow a very small nation to inflict direct noncombatant casualties in excess of the number saved. But for Walzer large as well as small nations must wait until their very existence is at stake.[7] If it were not that the massacre (or enslavement) of an entire nation were at stake, the mere fact that more lives (or liberties) could be saved by attacking noncombatants would not justify doing so; and if the nation really is at stake, saving more lives is not required. Walzer argues, in effect, that in one sort of case proportion is alone sufficient; here proportion overrides noncombatant immunity. But this judgment of proportion identifies the maintenance of political communities as the highest value, not mere maximization of life or liberty. When proportion in this sense is satisfied, on this interpretation of Walzer, then noncombatant immunity can be set aside. It is crucial to note as well that it is not mere defeat—a threat to political sovereignty or territorial integrity—that justifies direct attacks on noncombatants; the nation must be threatened with massacre or enslavement, conditions that destroy its ability to continue as a political community. Short of massacre or enslavement, I believe Walzer assumes, the community can survive even if conquered and its fundamental institutions suppressed; massacre and enslavement, however, can end its very existence.

When noncombatant immunity is set aside, however, wrong is done; Walzer seems to argue that one violates, not merely overrides, the rights of noncombatants. Walzer seems to hold that although a threat to a political community somehow justifies disregarding or setting aside the prohibition, the political leader nonetheless violates rights. The leader has two obligations, saving the community and respecting noncombatant immunity, and to fulfill one duty is to fail to fulfill the other; Walzer sometimes speaks of an override but seems to mean violation, for the two duties are not merely conflicting, but incommensurable; there is no metaprinciple to decide which overrides the other:

> What are we to say about those military commanders (or political leaders) who override the rules of war and kill innocent people in a

---

7. Note, for example, that Walzer's supreme emergency would not necessarily justify terrorism. Terrorists would have to believe not only that an "oppressor" had unjustly appropriated their homeland (violated their "territorial integrity and political sovereignty") but that their exile or defeat will lead either to extermination or enslavement; moreover, they would have to argue that terror attacks are the only way (last resort) to redress the situation.

"supreme emergency"? Surely we want to be led at such a time by men and women ready to do what has to be done—what is necessary for it is only here that necessity, in its true sense, comes into the theory of war. On the other hand, we cannot ignore or forget what it is they do. The deliberate killing of the innocent is murder. Sometimes, in conditions of extremity (which I have tried to define and delimit), commanders must commit murder or they must order others to commit it. And then they are murderers, though in a good cause. In domestic society, and particularly in the context of revolutionary politics, we say of such people that they have dirty hands. I have argued elsewhere that men and women with dirty hands, though it may be the case that they had acted well and done what their office required, must nonetheless bear a burden of responsibility and guilt. They have killed unjustly, let us say, for the sake of justice itself, but justice itself requires that unjust killing be condemned. (1977, 323)

Were there no guilt involved, the decisions [political leaders] make would be less agonizing than they are. And they can only prove their honor by accepting responsibility for those decisions and by living out the agony. A moral theory that made their life easier, or that concealed their dilemma from the rest of us, might achieve greater coherence, but it would miss or it would repress the reality of war. (1977, 326)

Objections

The first objection to Walzer's doctrine to raise is this: If the rights of political entities are derived from the rights of individuals, as Walzer at times seems to say they are, then why should a threat to political community override noncombatant immunity?[8] For Walzer all noncombatants (yours and your enemy's) have the same moral status. One cannot attack some

---

8. One might also ask whether massacre and enslavement are necessary to destroy a political community or way of life. Would not forced deportation and resettlement over a period of time not only violate political sovereignty and territorial integrity but also erode the community's sense of itself, its very identity? If so, then would aggression of a lesser magnitude than massacre or enslavement constitute a supreme emergency? Cf. Palmer-Fernandez (1993, 57–58, and passim) on Walzer's view of supreme emergency and the tension between individual rights and communal survival.

enemy noncombatants simply to save a much greater number of your own people from massacre or enslavement. Then why should the line be crossed if suddenly it is not merely a great number of your own people in danger but the massacre or enslavement of the community itself?

One might reply that the rights of individuals to life and liberty are not safe unless states (the "union of people and government" [1985, 220]) are permitted to protect their own communities. Even had Britain been the only object of Nazi aggression, attacks on German noncombatants would have been justified; for not only was Britain's political community at stake, but because of a kind of domino danger, other communities and hence other clusters of the rights of individuals would have been threatened—if not by Hitler, then by some other tyrant in time to come; if political communities can be ravaged, then adherence to nonaggression in the international community is weakened. This reply, however, depends on an empirical judgment of awesome generality; it could have been that Hitler only wanted Britain, and other tyrants would not have been encouraged. Moreover, the reply would seem to commit Walzer to a justification in terms of the numbers of rights protected; one would be justified in disregarding noncombatant immunity in order to preserve the rights of many in the long run. But Walzer seems to have rejected the appeal to "greater numbers" as a sufficient or even as a necessary condition for violating noncombatant immunity. If a numbers condition is not sufficient or necessary in the particular case, then why should it apply when extended by way of a domino clause to other future cases? Walzer indeed, as I have suggested, seems to rest his doctrine of supreme emergency on another basis, namely, the overriding value of political community. This could be taken to mean that the value of community in a transindividual sense is overriding, or that there is another sort of individual right, the right to form political associations, which overrides rights to life or liberty (Doppelt 1980).[9]

Whether one finds convincing Walzer's thesis about the supremacy of political community, I believe he also introduces another independent sense of supreme emergency: an immediate threat to any observance of basic rights. He suggests:

---

9. See Luban's critical discussion of Walzer's view of the moral standing of states (1985a) and Walzer's (1985) reply to Luban and other critics (Beitz 1979; Doppelt 1978; Wasserstrom 1978). Beitz (1980), Doppelt (1980), and Luban (1985b) reply to Walzer's reply (1985). Doppelt (1980, 398) argues that Walzer shifts from the argument that the rights of states rest on rights to life and liberty (Walzer 1977) to the argument (Walzer 1985) that the rights of states (governed nations or political communities) rest on the rights of people to work out their form of "'historic community'" and political association. Cf. Holmes (1989,169ff.).

Nazism was an ultimate threat to everything decent in our lives, an ideology and a practice of domination so murderous, so degrading even to those who might survive, that the consequences of its final victory were literally beyond calculation, immeasurably awful. We see it—and I don't use the phrase lightly—as evil objectified in the world. (1977, 253)

James Turner Johnson in fact interprets Walzer to argue that we can override the immunity of noncombatants "in order to protect the very values that ultimately guarantee the safety of such persons" (1981, 26, 223). On this view, supreme emergency connotes not a danger to a particular political community, but a threat of such magnitude that the very observance anywhere for the foreseeable future (the thousand year Reich) of basic rights to life and liberty would be eradicated (see also Childress 1978a).

The claim is not, I suppose, that respect for rights would never again arise, but in contrast to the claim that large numbers of innocents in many communities would have their rights violated, the theory now is that the entire practice of respect for rights would be, at least for the time being, everywhere threatened. This construction of supreme emergency, however, may suffer from the defects of the domino appeal: there is a daunting empirical claim, and ultimately the argument seems to appeal to numbers; violate some rights now to preserve rights for others. I am inclined to think, however, that it is not an appeal of the sort that antimaximizers traditionally fear: the practice of doing injustice in order to prevent greater injustice has seemed to many people to erode the basic commitment to rights. But presumably under a Nazi-like threat one attempts to preserve not merely more rights, but rights themselves. I am inclined, then, given the rarity of these circumstances, to endorse the notion that a Nazi-like threat is a justifiable override, a supreme emergency.[10]

10. See Kamm (1989, 227ff.) where she argues that one should not violate a right to life even to minimize violations of that right. Kamm (1989, 252ff.) argues against a "utilitarianism of rights"; if one can minimize "violation of a right by transgression of that very right," by so doing one "essentially eliminates that right from the system." If we endorse the killing we change our moral system, and our conception of ourselves that we believe "represents the truth" (254–55). See also Kamm (1992, 389) on the distinction between violating the right not to be harmed in order to maximize utility (save more lives) in contrast to violating the right to prevent a greater number of comparable rights violations; Kamm argues that if there is a constraint against harm based on "personal inviolability of a certain sort" then "it would be simply self-contradictory for it to be morally permissible to minimize violations of the constraint itself for the sake of showing concern for it" (1992, 384). My view is that we should not violate rights in order to minimize rights violations. The state of affairs or system we want to preserve is one in which agents do not violate certain rights even if by doing so they would prevent others from violating more of these rights. But we should be prepared, so I argue, should the system *as a whole* be at stake, to do what we would not otherwise view

A second objection has to do with Walzer's insistence that the political leader who attacks noncombatants violates their rights and hence has "dirty hands." If noncombatant immunity is justifiably put aside for moral reasons, however, then it is hard to see why the leader has dirty hands (see Walzer, 1973). Walzer seems at times to assume that there is some specific moral judgment in this situation that warrants the choice of which duty to fulfill. If the choice is morally warranted, then the judgment should be presented as an override. The rights of noncombatants have been overridden, not violated; the priority of one duty over another in the situation is morally authorized. The duties in the case are conflicting but not incommensurable. One can have moral regret and even acknowledge a duty of reparation, but one need not feel that what one did was morally wrong (see Santurri 1987).

The notion of a justified override would thus preserve the sense in which the rights of the innocent were intact. Their rights were justifiably overridden, in which case regret and perhaps reparations are required.[11] Once a judgment is made to override, we would henceforth assume a principle about when this could take place, that is, in situations of supreme emergency. Unless the right is held to be open to further overrides then it is absolute in the sense that it is never to be set aside in any circumstances other than those provided for in the principle.

Walzer insists, however, that people who disregard noncombatant immunity are guilty; they have apparently violated, not overridden, the rights of innocents. He could have argued that political leaders should sometimes put a nonmoral reason, such as national self-interest, above moral considerations. However, he wants to hold on to the thesis that the leaders have a moral obligation to protect their communities in times of supreme emergency; they act for a moral reason. It would seem natural, then, for him to adopt the view he attributes to Thomas Nagel (1972) that the moral life can present us with two incompatible duties for which no ordering principle exists (Walzer 1977, 325–26). Walzer nevertheless does not seem to want to take that course:

> I have tried to avoid the stark indeterminacy of that description [Nagel's] by suggesting that political leaders can hardly help but choose the utilitarian side of the argument. (1977, 326)

---

as justified. In other words, I am suggesting that the Nazi-like threat version of supreme emergency is not equivalent to a utilitarianism of rights.

11. Gewirth (1982, 219), using terminology he says he borrows from Thomson (1976), distinguishes between violating a right (an unjustifiable infringement) and overriding it (a justifiable infringement); a right is absolute when it cannot be justifiably overridden.

He seems to suggest that there is an underlying principle that justifies the political decision and hence provides coherence to the moral life. If political leaders can "hardly help" but preserve their political communities (their decision is "utilitarian" in this way, not in the maximizing sense), however, then it would seem that they justifiably override, and not violate, the rights of noncombatants.

Walzer's doctrine of supreme emergency seems to rest, then, on the supremacy of the right to political community; but he also seems to offer a different view: the Nazi-like threat to the very practice of rights. Moreover, if the setting aside of immunity were morally justified, then we do not have a moral dilemma in the sense of incompatible and unrankable directives, but rather an authorized override. The question of the adequacy of the justification aside, we would be dealing with a morally justified override or infringement, not a violation.

Nothing Is Lost and Proleptic Agreement

Suppose, however, that we rejected either the political community or Nazi-like threat views of supreme emergency. Are there any other conditions under which noncombatant immunity could be set aside? Are there wartime situations in which nothing is lost would apply, for example, and hence the right not to be killed would be suspended?

There is a case we can imagine that would parallel, *mutatis mutandis,* the cave where the head of the one stuck in the entrance is facing inside, or the raft where all will die unless the load is lightened. Suppose a village has military targets and we propose a conventional attack; we believe, however, that virtually *all* of the noncombatants in the village will be killed indirectly; nonetheless the attack satisfies not only the discrimination but also the proportionality criteria of double effect. We also believe, however, that a terror attack on some of the noncombatants in the village would undermine the resistance of the combatants, saving the other noncombatants. Thus, we reason that since all or most of the noncombatants would die indirectly if we were forced to mount a conventional attack, there is no unfairness done, as Brody would put it, to the few we directly kill. Doubts aside about the empirical effectiveness of a terror attack, or whether we have no other alternative if we are to save any of the noncombatants, the case seems to parallel in morally relevant ways the nothing-is-lost cases. In this wartime situation, then, noncombatant immunity is suspended. (Cf. Kamm 1989, 248ff.; 1991a, 583.)

The nothing-is-lost suspension of the right not to be killed seems more difficult to apply, however, to a broader range of cases. Let us suppose that a massive number of noncombatant casualties in a country were to be expected from a conventional invasion (they would die indirectly as a result of ordinary military operations). Suppose also that a terror attack on a smaller number would undermine combatant resistance and save noncombatant lives. Would we be justified in setting aside noncombatant immunity in this case as well?

The difficulty here is that, as the case is described, the smaller number who would die as a result of terror bombing, or some of them at least, may not be identical with the ones who would die indirectly in the invasion. We can imagine two scenarios: 1) the two groups do not overlap at all; the suitable targets for terror bombing are physically removed from the noncombatants who would be killed in the invasion, and none of those killed in terror bombing would have died anyway; 2) the two populations overlap, but not completely; some at least of the ones killed in terror bombing would not have died anyway in the invasion. In either case, the situation apparently would not permit us to apply the nothing-is-lost rationale. Not all would die anyway.

We could, however, perhaps argue that a proleptic agreement is assumed. Would we be justified in assuming that the noncombatants in the country in question explicitly or tacitly agree that should the situation arise a smaller rather than a larger number should die? We would, in effect, be assimilating the wartime case to the cave where the head of the one stuck is facing out. The noncombatants like the potholers are said to have agreed proleptically to yield their rights should the situation arise in which the direct killing of a few is necessary to save the lives of many. We would assume that the attackers are cognizant of the agreement and that, although they are not part of the agreement, in contrast to the potholers in the cave who carry out the deed, they are also justified in doing the killing.

My sense is that it is reasonable to assume a proleptic agreement in a body of noncombatants who are at risk even as indirect casualties. The noncombatants of a particular country share presumably a common culture as well as common dangers. Given these commonalities, it is plausible to suppose that they could be envisaged to reason, as Donagan's potholers do, that it is in their individual interest so far as the preservation of their lives is concerned, assuming certain probabilities, to agree that a few should be sacrificed if necessary for the many. If we assume an additional independent interest in the preservation of as large a part of the community as possible, the argument for a proleptic agreement is even stronger.

Let me now deal with several possible difficulties in this attempt to construe instances in which noncombatant immunity can be set aside as cases of nothing is lost or proleptic agreement.

First, would the moral judgment be different if the initial threat to noncombatants did not come from outside attacks but from their own government or military? Suppose the noncombatants were already being terrorized by their own rulers and then the question of terror as a tactic arises for revolutionaries. My sense is that our application of nothing is lost or proleptic agreement would not turn on how the initial threat to the noncombatants arises. It would nevertheless be difficult to hold the empirical assumption that terror attacks on the part of revolutionaries would somehow galvanize the population to resist the government when the terror attacks of their own government had not cowed them into submission.

Second, a number of ancillary conditions would have to be satisfied if we are to apply the notions of nothing is lost or proleptic agreement. I have already mentioned the problem of the empirical effectiveness of terror bombing: as many writers note, terror bombing (or terrorism more generally) may in many instances actually strengthen, rather than weaken, enemy resistance. Last resort is also difficult to satisfy: As Walzer notes (1977), in the case of the use of the atomic bomb in the attacks on Hiroshima and Nagasaki it is widely held that not all alternatives for negotiation or demonstration had been exhausted. In addition, as Walzer observes about the Japanese case, the predictions about the casualties that would be sustained may well depend on one's war objectives, in this case unconditional surrender; if that objective is unjustified, then one cannot assume that the choice lies between extensive casualties in a land invasion necessary to achieve unconditional surrender and a lesser number of casualties achieved through terror bombing. Walzer also notes that the allies had already begun terror bombing with conventional weapons, a policy that figured in the calculation of potential noncombatant casualties (1977, 266–67). Finally, there is the issue of other consequences, along with the number of lives, which might have to be factored into the judgment of proportion. For example, in the Japanese case the introduction of nuclear weapons as a type of weapon has seemed to many to outweigh the noncombatant lives saved.

Third, we have to ask about the scope of cases to which the nothing-is-lost or proleptic agreement cases apply. So far, I limited the calculation to enemy noncombatants. Now let us imagine the case as follows: suppose that in the course of our conventional attack a certain number of noncombatants of the enemy would die. Suppose also that if we kill the same number directly through terror bombing we can save many more of our own noncombatants who are now exposed to death as indirect casualties as a result of conventional enemy attacks. (I bracket here the issue of whether reprisals would be justified as a response to the enemy's terror bombing of our noncombatants.) The first thing to note about this case is that the enemy noncombatants who would die indirectly are not necessarily the same as those we would kill in a terror attack. We do not know so far, as the case is stated, whether the ones subject to terror would have died anyway in a conventional attack, or whether they would have survived. If, however, somehow the individuals who would die in any case indirectly are those whom we would terror bomb, then, I would assume, there would be no objection to terror; the nothing-is-lost justification would take into account both enemy and friendly noncombatants.

But what of the case where the enemy noncombatants who would have to be killed by terror are not the same as those who would die in a conventional attack? Would it fall under proleptic agreement? Would it be reasonable to suppose that a proleptic agreement to yield exists among the entire class of noncombatants, ours and theirs? My sense is that it would not be reasonable to suppose such an agreement. It may be reasonable to suppose that a body of noncombatants in a particular political community who share a common identity, parallel to a particular group of potholers, could be supposed to have an agreement (probably implicit) that a lesser rather than a greater number should be killed; but there seems no reason to suppose that a similar agreement would exist between politically disparate groups of noncombatants.

Fourth, would we be justified in counting combatant casualties saved? The allies may have been principally concerned about the loss of allied combatant lives if a land invasion of Japan was necessary; presumably they also factored in Japanese noncombatants and combatants. It seems to me that combatants could and should be counted in a strict nothing-is-lost case. If a nothing-is-lost situation obtained such that a certain group of noncombatants would die in any case, then that group could be directly attacked to save a greater number of combatants, either enemy, friendly, or both, considered alone or in conjunction with noncombatants saved. This would seem to be required by proportion if, again, the crucial condition that the particular individuals would die anyway is satisfied. If this did not obtain, then we would be thrown into the other sort of situation where only a proleptic agreement will do.

Can we envisage a proleptic agreement to yield on the part of noncombatants should the direct deaths of some be necessary to save a larger number of *their own* combatants? Could the war itself be envisaged as a common risky endeavor on which all are embarked and hence they agree to yield their rights if necessary? For example, could we assume a proleptic agreement among compatriots (noncombatant and combatant) that as few as possible should die? Could we assume that Japanese noncombatants would have agreed to yield their rights, should the circumstances arise, so that as few as possible of their compatriots (including combatants) should die? Perhaps we could transfer the notion of a proleptic agreement to yield to an entire national community, if we have sufficient historical knowledge of that community's culture. However, it hardly seems likely that noncombatants in one political entity could be envisaged to have a proleptic agreement with the attacking combatants of the *other*. The notion of a proleptic agreement, it again seems plausible to suppose, would have to be limited to political communities.

I argue, then, subject to the fulfillment of certain standard conditions, that nothing is lost or yielding through proleptic agreement may apply in some war cases. Among enemy noncombatants, either some particular ones would die anyway, or a proleptic yielding can be assumed. Nothing is lost judgments would seem, moreover, to encompass both enemy and friendly noncombatants as a class, but a proleptic agreement between noncombatants of warring countries seems farfetched. Nothing is lost would also seem to allow, and even require, counting combatants saved. We could perhaps even envisage a proleptic agreement among noncombatants and combatants of one country, but again the idea of an agreement across national lines seems unlikely. Nothing is lost, then, rests on whether unfairness is done to those subject to the terror, on whether they would die anyway; if this condition is satisfied, then only proportion remains (on the assumption that the duty to save applies across borders). Proleptic agreement, though, rests on the contingencies of historical alliance and communal identity.

The Intervening Action

Finally, my development of the supreme emergency, nothing is lost, and proleptic agreement motifs can be usefully contrasted with the principle of the intervening action as stated by Alan Gewirth. Gewirth uses a hypothetical terrorist example to show that the right to life is absolute; unless someone ("Abrams") tortures an innocent person to death, terrorists will drop a nuclear bomb on a city. For Gewirth the innocent's right is absolute (1982b, 225, 232–33). But what of those who are killed?

> It may be argued that the morally correct description of the alternative confronting Abrams is not simply that it is one of not violating

or violating an innocent person's right to life, but rather not violating one innocent person's right to life and thereby violating the right to life of thousands of other innocent persons through being partly responsible for their deaths, or violating one innocent person's right to life and thereby protecting or fulfilling the right to life of thousands of other innocent persons. (Gewirth 1982b, 226)

Gewirth has to show that Abrams is not violating the rights of the people in the city because the terrorists—and not he—are morally responsible for their deaths (227–28). His answer is the principle of the intervening action (on the part of the terrorists):

> The required supplement is provided by the principle of the intervening action. According to this principle, when there is a causal connection between some person A's performing some action (or inaction) X and some other person C's incurring a certain harm Z, A's moral responsibility for Z is removed if, between X and Z, there intervenes some other action Y of some person B who knows the relevant circumstances of his action and who intends to produce Z or who produces Z through recklessness. The reason for this removal is that B's intervening action Y is the more direct or proximate cause of Z and, unlike A's action (or inaction), Y is the sufficient condition of Z as it actually occurs. (1982b, 229)

The terrorists who drop the bomb after Abrams refuses to torture are the intervening agents, and they, not Abrams, are responsible.

First, I do not think that B's intervening action Y (the terrorists' dropping the bomb) is in fact a sufficient causal condition in the circumstances. Following Green (see Chapter 1), I would say that A's refraining is also a necessary causal condition in the circumstances of the terrorist case. The moral question still remains, however: Is A blameworthy for refraining?

Second, even if we grant that the intervening action was the sufficient cause, the one who fails to torture could still be held morally blameless for a different reason. The individual is relieved of responsibility not because of the intervening action, but because one has no duty to save the city at the cost of violating the innocent's right.[12] The agent is not morally respon-

---

12. Gewirth says that the choice to preserve absolutism is premised on a high degree of certainty that the terrorists will keep their word, that is, they will bomb if Abrams does not torture and not bomb if he does. If Abrams is not so certain, then he could take a risk and try other steps to stop the terrorists (1982b, 231–32). On probability and responsibility for consequences dependent on the choice of others, see Lichtenberg (1994, 357–81) and her comments (1994, 357, 367 n. 18) on Holmes (1989, 193–211).

sible, for one may not "do evil that good may come" (cf. Gewirth 1982b, 230).[13] If we do not terror bomb the few (where nothing is lost or proleptic agreement do not obtain) in order to save the many, we are not responsible (in the sense of blameworthy) for their deaths, not because there is some other intervening action, but because we are only responsible for saving by morally permissible means.

Third, if the innocent person would die anyway in the nuclear explosion, or if we could assume a proleptic agreement, then the torture is perhaps justified (cf. Gewirth 1982b, 231). One would have to believe, however, that the method of the innocent's death—by torture—does not change the moral situation; perhaps one would assume that the death the victim would suffer if nothing is done—death in a nuclear explosion—is equally horrible.

Fiat Justitia, Ruat Caelum

I suggest then that only two overrides are acceptable: the miniride and the Nazi-like threat. If nothing is lost or proleptic agreement were applicable to the war cases, these "exceptions" are already provided for within the meaning of the right not to be killed; when these circumstances obtain, the right is suspended or waived. Once the right is defined in these ways, and the two legitimate overrides identified, then noncombatant immunity must be observed; in this sense, it is now absolute. We would have to be prepared to lose our lives and to allow the lives of many to be lost rather than to violate the rights of even a lesser number; in this sense we would be prepared to let the heavens fall rather than not preserve justice. We would stand in the long tradition of those who have said it is better to suffer, and to allow others to suffer, than to commit injustice (see Kenny 1966). If the situation is not one where nothing is lost, and there is no proleptic agreement, and where the overrides do not occur, then we cannot save ourselves or others by directly attacking noncombatants. Individuals who refuse to

13. Gewirth argues that double effect does not explain why Abrams is not responsible for the deaths of the innocents. I agree, for the victim's right itself is decisive and not the fact that Abrams does not intend the deaths of those he fails to save (1982b, 228). Gewirth also argues that the distinction between killing and letting die does not explain why Abrams is not responsible; according to Gewirth, the right to life also includes a duty to save up to comparable cost, and thus Abrams would be responsible "to this extent" (1982b, 228–29). Gewirth could still say that the negative duty in the right to life outweighs the positive responsibility therein, but he is drawn to the principle of the intervening action as a solution. Gewirth also argues that "respect for persons" is too vague to settle the question.

engage in terror bombing are expressing the view, which they believe the people they fail to save should share, that it is better for some to suffer injustice rather than for others to commit it. The refusing agents commit themselves to a view that would require they not be saved were the roles reversed.

Thus, absolutism ranks duty over temporal good. If there is no hope for an afterlife where wrongs are righted, then the loss is permanent. For believers whose view of rights is based on God's dominion, or even for other adherents of rights who encompass morality within a theism that provides for the transcendent destiny of the individual, only temporal good is lost precisely because the heavens will not fall.[14] But without such a "sacred canopy," the refusal to sacrifice some innocents even to save a greater number must rest on the inherent appeal of respect for rights.[15] The agent in the end may value over all else the way of life in which absolutism is a part.[16]

---

14. Finnis, Boyle, and Grisez (1987, 380–82) argue that although humans are not allowed to "bring about the greater good and permit the lesser evil" when this would require the choice as means of the destruction of an intrinsic basic good, such as life, God will nonetheless bring good from evil and thereby secure the greater good in the long run. Cf. Stout (1991, 233–34) on Ramsey and the theological assurance that the heavens at least will not fall, although absolutism could mean earthly disaster. See Gustafson (1981) for a criticism of the anthropocentrism of this sort of theological assumption.

15. Cf. Donagan (1977, 206–7) on *Fiat justitia, ruat caelum,* and Gewirth on the "minimal conditions of a worthwhile life" (1982b, 225, 225–26 n. 7); he refers to Donagan (1977, 156–57, 183). See Murphy's argument (1973, 547–48, 550) on the right to noninterference as absolute, and Baier (1985) on "secular faith." For opposing views, see Kuhse who argues that absolutism makes no sense outside of a theological framework (1987, 15) and Paul W. Taylor (1986, 243) who also argues that no moral rights are absolute. See also Santurri 1987.

16. Even if the ultimate basis of this absolutism were stated in utilitarian form—it is for the greatest good of the greatest number that the right to life be absolute—the judgment is not necessarily that such absolutism maximizes life or other goods; the appeal could be to the intrinsic good of this pattern of life itself. See Introduction, note 3. See also Kamm (1992, 388–89) who says that "if we conceive of deontological constraints as expressions of the status of each person and this status of inviolability is itself a good, then to some extent we narrow the distinction between consequentialism and deontology." Note I do not discuss here whether the good or value at stake in absolutism rests principally in the putative victim's inviolability or in what violating rights, even to preserve them in other cases, does to the violating agents. See Kamm's (1993, 94–96) criticism of Sen (1982) from the perspective of her "rights-based deontology." On these issues I am indebted to discussions with Gene Outka. See also Nagel (1986) and Finnis (1991). On the search for an ordering principle, in contrast to the view that the moral life presents us with intractable conflict, see Cahill (1988) on Gustafson (1988).

Conclusion

A Modest Consensus

I have tried to systematize and modify some of the views of Donagan, Foot, Ramsey, Thomson, and other writers; I express the resultant view as two basic rights, and present them, once properly qualified—and with the "miniride" and Nazi exceptions—as absolute. Perhaps rights could be dispensed with under utopian conditions. My own inclination is to think that the discourse of rights could be left behind if humans were different (see Reeder 1992). But even if superceded, I would argue that there are values expressed in these common convictions about rights that we are not likely to jettison: we would still insist on the respect for the freedom and well-being of individuals that rights promote.

We have found in any case an overlap of convictions about killing and saving. My argument has been that the overlap rests fundamentally on a common commitment to the maintenance of the good of life for all. However, this commitment does not translate into a straightforward utilitarian calculus (save the most lives). Rather the commitment to equality is qualified—its meaning specified—by the view that the lottery of events should

How killing or letting die or saving arrangates w/ Outka's Agape.

Conclusion   173

be left standing in those cases where, to change it, one or more persons would have to be fatally used to save a greater number of others. When life is threatened by events in the natural order or by unjust human causes, you may not *take* my life directly in order to save others; nor am I required to *give* it; but I, or others, am required to help at some cost. There is a commitment to equality, but it is limited by a resolve to allow the lottery of events to stand rather than purchase the survival of many at the expense of using even a smaller number of others (see Brock 1981; cf. Alexander 1976). Whether in the circumstances my life would be taken or given, our judgment is that your life need not be maintained against threats through the fatal use of mine. The equal consideration of the interests of all, then, is here construed as a commitment to do what is possible to secure lives against threats, but to rule out fatal use whether that use would come about through an act of direct taking or a required act of giving. Thus, while a greater number of lives might be saved, one life (or more) would have to be used to save others; one life would have been "subordinated" to others. The lottery of events is therefore not to be changed so as to maximize the number of lives saved; rather we are to uphold lives short of other people taking our lives, or our giving our own, even to save many.

There is thus an "asymmetry" between the cost we have to suffer rather than kill, in contrast to the cost we have to suffer to help (Morillo 1977, 35): I should be prepared to die rather than kill you to save myself (to get your only kidney), but I do not have to die in order to save you (give you my only kidney). But these costs are only asymmetrical from the point of view of one agent's responsibilities; the moral judgments regarding not killing and saving are the opposite sides of the same coin: I cannot *take* your life (to save mine or others) and you do not have to *give* it.[1]

This sense of a commitment to the equality of lives, then, is expressed in the right not to be killed and the right to lifesaving aid. I can, however,

---

1. I think this underlying symmetry also provides part of an answer to Kagan's difficulty (1989). See Kagan's (1991a) "précis," the comments of various critics (Kamm 1991b; Brock 1991; Slote 1991), and Kagan's reply (1991b). Kagan argue to allow to die because of the cost to the giver, there is a not to suffer the same loss, unless there is a "logically disti (1991a, 899). My response here, roughly, is that there is su distinct, for it rests on a conviction that underlies both c to aid; we have no duty to give our life and hence no on or others. There is another question, though: Am I perm you in order to save my life? If the starving need a loaf then *ceteris paribus* the poor have a right to appropriat It seems to me that a failure to save, as well as an act (deadly force. See Lichtenberg (1982).

yield either my right not to be killed or my right to lifesaving aid; the common ground also includes the value of the agent's self-determination. Thus, the twin expressions of commitment to the equality of lives are expressed as the *right* not to be killed and the *right* to lifesaving aid.[2] Moreover, in nothing-is-lost situations my rights will be suspended. Furthermore, if you voluntarily try to secure your advantage (even your life) at the expense of mine, I am permitted to resist you and others are obligated to assist me. If you become a nonvoluntary or involuntary pursuer, I have no obligation to assist you (to let you live) by sacrificing myself. Finally, if to protect myself and others from a threat to life I must deflect that threat, and either the deflected threat itself or the action I take to deflect it causes a smaller number to die, I am obligated to act. The common commitment rules out the fatal use of others, but not their deaths as an unintended result of lifesaving action.[3]

These, then, are the elements of the consensus I have tried to uncover and develop. Yet the traditions diverge at critical points; although they all ground rights not to kill and to be saved—rights (or their close relatives) that constitute a core of moral agreement—their differing moral descriptions and justifications come into play in regard to some of the hardest cases.[4]

The common commitment is itself threatened, moreover, from two major

2. Quinn's normative criterion is stronger than mine: A person's body or person "is, morally speaking, his only if his say over what may be done to it (and thereby to him) can override the greater needs of others" (1989a, 308–9; see also 1989b). On my view, consent or yielding is not required if one owes it to someone to suffer some injury (depending on where the standard of aid is set) on their behalf. I agree, however, with the direction of Quinn's thought where he focuses on one's title or "say" over one's body and life. My sense is that both negative and positive rights are ways in which 1) we guard or secure goods for persons and 2) we allow persons some measure of decision-making control for cases in which a standard good (for example, medical treatment or a form of aid) may under the circumstances be an evil (we allow the individual to make the judgment when competent). I explain the precedence of the negative right as part of a view about how misfortune is to be distributed: if I need a kidney, you are the only person around, and you have one, I may not kill you by *taking* your only kidney; nor am I obligated to *give* my only kidney to you; nor would the moral situation be changed if there were two of you in need and I had two kidneys (two lives to be saved at the cost of one). We intervene in the lottery of misfortune in order to secure the lives of all, short of sacrificing one life (by taking or giving).

3. The shape of the moral consensus I try to develop here also extends to how these sorts of situations are related: roughly, if agents yield rights, or if nothing is lost, then the use of ̶e categories of pursuer or double effect is otiose (even if these categories obtain); but where ̶er yielding nor nothing is lost apply, then only if the conditions of pursuit or double ̶e satisfied is it licit to kill (or let die).

̶debates about justification, see, e.g., Boyle (1991a; 1991b), Chandler (1990), Foot ̶is (1991), and Quinn (1989a; 1989b).

directions. On the one hand, some versions of nontheological Enlightenment traditions uphold a strong barrier to taking life, even to save many others, but advocate a very weak injunction to help, such as Thomson's Minimal Samaritanism. Not only was its cost to be minimal, but it was not clear, we remember, whether Minimal Samaritanism was even a requirement or whether it signified merely optional kindness. The consensus requires at least that saving be a requirement. On the other hand, some of the theological traditions uphold a duty to sacrifice one's goods, even one's life, in order to save others from a similar loss. Thus, even though there would still be a strong commitment against taking life, these two camps would respectively pull away from the consensus either by weakening the demand to assist or by strengthening it beyond even the up-to-comparable-cost standard.

Here, again, I believe we are pushed back to a foundational level of argument. To the nontheological argument for nonrequired Minimal Samaritanism, one would need to present nontheological reasons for holding that aid is required. I believe that the view that proposes a duty not to kill *and* a duty to save does not rest necessarily on theological grounds—equal value or status before God—and hence it can survive translation to a nontheological "narrative." To the theologian who holds to self-sacrifice in regard to the good of temporal existence, other theologians would have to present reasons to move the advocate of self-sacrifice back to the norm of temporal equality. The theological advocate of earthly self-sacrifice, we should remember, holds to the norm of ultimate equality in any case. Equality of well-being will be secured in the eschaton; earthly self-sacrifice is part of the role penultimately assigned to the believer in some versions of the drama whereby all are brought ultimately to eschatological fulfillment. Thus, the theological quarrel is about how to construe earthly duty.

Even if the consensus is maintained against these threats, there is still the question of the standard of aid. I have indicated I would argue for a strong standard of aid (up to comparable cost) but not self-sacrifice. There is, of course, much more to be said. My suspicion is that some people would endorse up to comparable cost where property is concerned (even capitalists can endorse the notion that all should have necessities before anyone has luxuries), but they would balk at the idea that one should, as a matter of general duty, incur serious physical injury even to save life. I leave this question open as an issue that divides those who otherwise agree. Life should be preserved, but the lottery of events need not be disturbed in cases where to save many the lives of fewer would have to be directly taken or given; this much is agreed. How far we should go to save life, however, varies between the standards of up to comparable cost and Minimal Samaritanism.

My sense is that we should not despair at these differences between traditions. The agreements are deep and important; on reflection, many of us have convictions about taking and saving lives that seem to have a definite shape that specifies the limited class of circumstances in which killing is justified in order to save. We have a basis for public policy, and even where there is disagreement there is common ground. Thus, there is connection even where there is difference; we should lose sight of neither.[5]

---

5. I should end as I began with an acknowledgment that I have made only a "selective retrieval" from a vast literature. I have deliberately saved some authors and works for the task of trying to justify (in secular or in theological terms) the pattern of convictions outlined here. My list is not limited to these, but I have in mind in particular: Jean Bethke Elshtain, Stuart Hampshire, Gilbert C. Meilaender, J. Giles Milhaven, and Edward C. Vacek.

Appendix

Moral Status

Who has the right not to be killed? The right to be saved? Which beings, in other words, are included in the scope of these rights? I concentrate here on issues about the "first of life." Although some individuals no longer have even the potential to have those capacities that constitute personhood and personal identity, the unborn and newborn have the potential that will, in the normal course of development, mature into the actual capacities in question.[1] Our society is divided, roughly speaking, between those who think that potentiality at the first of life is sufficient for moral status and those who insist on actuality. I agree with Beverly Wildung Harrison (1983) that the issue of the status of the unborn has often masked male attempts to control female sexuality, but as Harrison herself notes, the question still has to be asked. One can also agree that women should have the legal right to make the moral decision one way or the other, as Harrison argues, but still acknowledge that the issues involved concern everyone.

I want to examine three versions of the argument that full status in the moral community of rights depends on having certain actual capacities; all three purport to show in particular that entities who do not have certain actual capacities cannot have the right to life. (Arguments such as these are usually framed in regard to the right not to be killed, but I believe that they could be taken to show that if there were a right to lifesaving help, *actual* capacities would also be necessary for having that right.) The arguments are said to rest on assumptions about the nature and function of rights; these assumptions are thus said to be "self-evident," or "logical," or "conceptual." The aim of some of these arguments is to identify a necessary condition for having a right to life; in this sense "moral status" simply means being capable of having the right ascribed. The aim of other argu-

---

1. See Brock (1989, 145–47; 1993) on the definition of death, which today is generally taken to require the cessation of all brain activity.

ments is to suggest that having certain actual capacities is both necessary and sufficient for having the right to life.[2]

The Argument from Self-Evidence

In discussions of abortion, the term *person* often is used in very different senses. First, the term is used simply to signify something human, a member of the species homo sapiens. Second, it is also used in a moral sense to signify someone with duties or rights. Third, it has two important metaphysical meanings: personhood in general (being a sort of thing that has certain attributes), and personal identity (being a particular person).[3] Mary Anne Warren asserts that whatever is a metaphysical person "is the sort of entity to which it is proper to ascribe moral rights" (1984, 102); "it is or should be self-evident that the moral community consists only of people," that is, persons in a metaphysical sense (1984, 110–11, 112–13). Warren also argues that what a person is in the general metaphysical sense will probably be "obvious," at least to those who share "our conceptual scheme" (1984, 112). Thus, since a person has some of a set of certain actual capacities—for example, self-consciousness or rationality—and since

2. See Feinberg (1980a, 191). Instead of speaking of necessary and sufficient conditions for having the right, one could distinguish two sorts of conditions: enabling conditions and ascribing conditions; each of these could be further broken down into necessary and sufficient components. See White (1984, 75ff.) who discusses the question of whether there are characteristics "necessary or sufficient for the possible possession of a right." See also Buchanan (1984, 77) who distinguishes the questions: "(a) can we coherently ascribe rights to beings who lack moral agency; and (b) are we morally justified in ascribing rights to beings who lack moral agency?" Santurri (1992) addresses the question of moral standing in the second sense, that is, to whom do we ascribe equal worth in the moral community. He criticizes, for example, Engelhardt's (1986) thesis that status in this sense rests on one's ability to participate in the process of moral deliberation and judgment, arguing in effect that we are justified, in Buchanan's terminology, in ascribing full status to beings who lack moral agency, that is, a certain set of cognitive capacities necessary for moral deliberation.

3. See Green and Wikler (1980). Cf. Lomasky (1984, 162ff.) on these sorts of definitions of person. I agree with Brock and Buchanan (1989, 161) who argue that the metaphysical (personal identity) and moral senses of a person cannot be "neatly distinguished." Our metaphysical and moral assumptions are closely related in our webs of belief, indeed our operative concepts often include both; we may be motivated by moral concerns, and we may even be prepared to let moral considerations shape a metaphysical view (1989, 174). However, it seems to me these insights do not collapse the distinctions between 1) personhood and moral agency (the capabilities of interacting persons), 2) personal identity (one's history, one's sense of an ongoing self), and 3) a "moral person" in the sense of someone who has a particular set of duties or rights. Cf. Macklin (1984).

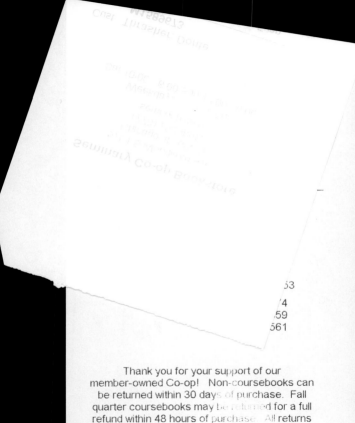

it is self-evident that only metaphysical persons have rights, she reasons that a fetus is a human being that is not yet a person, and thus it "cannot coherently be said to have full moral rights" (1984, 113).[4] (I use the term *fetus* to signify various stages of the unborn.) I interpret Warren, then, to say that being an actual metaphysical person is both necessary and sufficient for being a full member of the community of rights and having the right to life.

This way of proceeding, however, masks the moral character of judgments about the status of the unborn or newborn. There is an assumption that all entities that are metaphysical persons have the right to life; on the basis of this assumption, then, apparently only a *metaphysical* question remains: What is a person? Understandably the hope is that the abortion debate can be settled on metaphysical grounds. If you could show metaphysically that entities that have certain potential capacities are or aren't persons, then you would show that such entities have or don't have the right to life.

The difficulty is that the metaphysical question does not seem to have an obvious answer; furthermore, it is not self-evident that the metaphysical class of persons is coextensive with the class of entities that have the right to life. One can see this by contrasting two metaphysical views of persons and then asking a moral question. On one metaphysical view, "a person is a thing which is such that it is physically possible (it is not contrary to the laws of nature) that there is a time at which that thing consciously thinks" (Chisholm 1977, 181); on this view, as I construe it here, one is a person when one has the potential or the actual capacity for conscious thought. On another view, apparently Warren's, the metaphysical intuition is that one should not think of there being persons until certain capacities, or some of them at least, are actual; the entity does not exist until its characteristic properties actually exist (Engelhardt 1974; 1983).

These, then, are two metaphysical views. We may ask the one who says that persons are those in whom certain properties—the capacity to think, for instance—are either potential or actual whether all persons should have the right to life or only those whose capacities are actual. We may also ask the one who argues that persons are those in whom certain properties are actual whether potential persons should have the same rights persons do. If the one who includes those with potential capacities in the metaphysical class of persons also grants them the right to life, then this is a moral

---

4. Warren (1977, 276) accepts the view that a "viable sexually mixed pair of gametes" is a potential person; cf. Hare (1975, 212). Warren nonetheless does not accept Hare's argument that not only abortion but also contraception is prima facie wrong.

judgment; if the one with this metaphysical view wants to limit the right to life to those persons whose capacities are actual, then this also is a moral judgment. If the one who limits metaphysical persons to those whose capacities are actualized wants to limit the right to life to them, this is a moral judgment; if the one who holds the actualist metaphysic wants to extend the right to life to potential persons, this also is a moral judgment.

Thus, if one argues that only persons in some metaphysical sense have the right to life, then one is really saying that only certain sorts of beings should have the right to life. In the guise of correlating a metaphysical class with a right, one is really making a moral judgment to the effect that certain entities with certain characteristics should have the right. The burden of making this moral judgment cannot be evaded by assuming that one simply must correlate the metaphysical class of persons with the class of those who have full moral rights, and then trying to solve the moral status question by appeal to metaphysical considerations. The moral correlation is not "self-evident" as Warren assumes.

Thus, assuming that persons and the right to life are coextensive and then proceeding to make a metaphysical determination conceals a moral argument to the effect that certain beings with certain characteristics should have the right to life. Why this is the case is the issue, that is, why actual or potential capacities of some sort should ground the right to life. In sum, one cannot say that the unborn or newborn should not have the right to life because they are not metaphysical persons unless one makes clear what the moral significance of metaphysical personhood is, and to do that is to explain the *moral significance* of certain actual or potential properties.[5]

The "'Logical Point'"

Joel Feinberg does not assume it is self-evident that whatever satisfies the criteria (characteristics C) of "commonsense" personhood should have the right to life, for he asks:

> What is the relation, if any, between having C, and being a person in the normative (moral) sense, that is, a being who possesses, among other things, a right to life? (Feinberg 1980a, 190; cf. 191; see also 1986; and Feinberg and Levenbook 1993)

5. See Ronald M. Green (1974) on going "straight" to the moral question and for the view that rights can be conferred; see the response by Childress (1974).

He asks, in other words, what the relation is between what I have called metaphysical personhood and moral status, being a person in a moral sense. He argues there is a logical objection to both the "strict potentiality criterion," the view that those and only those who either actually or potentially possess C have the right to life (1980a, 193), and the "modified or gradualist potentiality criterion," the view that potential possession of C confers stronger claims the closer to actual possession the entity comes (1980a, 194, 196). Feinberg argues that "the merely potential possession of any set of qualifications for a moral status does not logically insure actual possession of that status" (1980a, 193); only actual qualification confers actual rights (1980a, 194, 196, 201). Thus he insists on the "actual possession criterion." He is maintaining that being an actual person (characteristics C) is both necessary and sufficient for having the right to life.[6]

But Feinberg seems to beg the question in the very way the "'logical point'" is phrased. Of course one must *have* whatever qualifications are necessary or sufficient; in this sense the qualifications must be actual. The issue, however, is whether potential or actual capacities constitute the qualifications. The phrase, the "merely potential possession of any set of qualifications for a moral status," seems to assume that the qualifications consist in actual capacities. If the qualifications are in fact actual capacities, then potential possession of those capacities would not suffice. But the question is whether the qualifications must be actual capacities or whether merely potential ones will do.

Conceptual Conditions for the Right to Life

Michael Tooley argues that an entity cannot have a right to life unless it is capable of having an interest in its own continued existence. This is a conceptual requirement, he says, not a "substantive moral theory" (1983, 96). The sorts of beings who can have rights are the sorts of beings who can have interests (1984, 123). There are, moreover, connections between particular interests and rights; entities cannot have particular rights unless they are capable of having the interests that are furthered by having such rights (1984, 125). The right to life, furthermore, should signify not merely the continued existence of a biological organism, but also the continued

6. Feezell (1987) notes a tension between Feinberg's earlier view that rights can be predicated of unborn children because of their future interests and the "'logical point'" (1987, 45–56). See Feinberg (1976).

existence of a subject of experiences and other mental states, for, if the Pope could be reprogrammed as Bertrand Russell, "someone" would have been destroyed; thus, the "'right to life' refers to the right of a subject of experiences and other mental states to continue to exist" (1984, 125). The right to life, then, is not just the right of a metaphysical person in Warren's sense to continue to exist, but the right to continue to exist as a particular person. Thus, to have a right to life one must be capable of having an interest in continued existence as a particular subject or person.[7]

Tooley tries to show, moreover, that an entity is not capable of having an interest in its continued existence unless it possesses at some time the concept of a continuing self. If entities such as the unborn and newborn were to have the right to life, they must have an interest in their continued existence, so the question is "what must be the case if the continued existence of something is to be in its interest" (1984, 125, 127). Tooley's answer is that such entities must have at some time the concept of a continuing self, which, Tooley assumes on empirical grounds, the unborn and newborn do not.[8]

How does Tooley argue that for the continued existence of something to be in its interest it must have at some time the concept of a continuing self (1984, 128–30)? First, he argues that nothing could be in an entity's interest unless it has some desires (1984, 129):

> A subject of interests, in the relevant sense of "interest," must necessarily be a subject of conscious states, including experiences and desires. (1984, 128)

> To be a subject of rights one needs to be capable of having interests in the sense that involves the capacity for having desires. (1983, 117; see also 112, 118–19)

7. Tooley's definition of a right (1983, 115–16) combines elements of a "respected choice" and a "beneficiary" theory of rights (cf. Lyons 1979, 8–9).

8. Petchesky (1984, 342–44) argues that the right to life belongs to those who have self-consciousness, but she emphasizes that self-consciousness develops in relation to others; Tooley would have no reason to disagree. Bassen (1982) argues versus Tooley's 1973b essay that a newborn is "victimizable," that is, it "is a being (prospective) harm to which by itself gives reason to prevent an action" (316ff.). I think Tooley (1983; 1984) could agree with this, provided that the individual who will have the later desires can be shown to be the same individual who does not have the present desire to live or the capacity to have such a desire. Bassen also argues that the embryo is not yet victimizable (1984, 326); against the view that future potential victimizability confers present victimizability (1984, 328–29ff.), he argues that our intuitions require a present "sake" before future prospects are relevant (1984, 332–33); only an "agent" or a "subject" can be a victim (1984, 334).

Thus, to have an interest one must at least be capable of having some desires. It would "generally be sufficient" for having an interest in continued existence if an individual actually desired or was capable of desiring its own continued existence (1984, 129). However,

> it also seems clear that an individual's continued existence can be in its own interest even when such a desire [the desire for continued existence] is not present. What is needed, apparently, is that the continued existence of the individual will make possible the satisfaction of some desires existing at other times. But not just any desires existing at other times will do. . . . It is crucial that they belong to one and the same subject of consciousness. (1984, 129; cf. 123–24)

The entity that does not desire or is not yet capable of desiring to continue to exist could have an interest in its continued existence if we could say that the entity in question is over time the same subject of consciousness. But to say this, Tooley argues, one needs to be able to attribute the concept of a continuing self to the entity. One needs it because one cannot connect stages in the life of an individual without memory or other psychological links. To have such links the entity has to be capable of connecting itself to former stages (1984, 129). This requires that the entity was at least a conscious subject of experiences and desires in a former state, and that it thinks (or has the capability to think) of itself as itself, that is, it has or is capable of having the concept of a continuing self and thinking of itself as such. Thus, for continued existence to be in the interest of an entity it must have or be capable of having the concept of a continuing self in order to attribute "desires existing at different times . . . to a single, continuing subject of consciousness" (1984, 129). (One must be careful to distinguish potential capability from actual capability; Tooley is requiring the actual capability to have the concept of a continuing self, not the potential capability that the unborn or newborn has. I also generally speak in what follows of an actual capability simply as a capability.)

One can say, then, that continued existence is in an entity's interest even if it were not capable of desiring it, provided one has an individual who developed from that entity and now thinks or is capable of thinking of itself as a continuous self and remembering or having other links to earlier stages. Of Mary, to use Tooley's example, who remembers the experiences of the newborn baby she was, one can say that it was in Mary's interest as a baby not to have been destroyed; of the baby itself, one could not, until it develops the capacity to have a concept of a continuing self (1984, 130–31). The individual who develops from this entity and who has the concept of a continuing self can say retrospectively that it was in his or her interest not to have been destroyed because this individual can identify itself with that former stage.[9]

In sum, a conceptual requirement of a right is that one have an interest in what one has a right to. To have a right to life one needs an interest in continued existence as a particular person; to have an interest in continued existence one would need either the capability of desiring it or it must be the case that continued existence would make possible the satisfaction of desires at some other time of the same subject of consciousness; but an entity must have a concept of a continuing self in order to be the same subject of consciousness; thus, only the individual who actually develops and has (or has the capability to have) the concept of a continuing self can look back and say it was in its interest not to have been destroyed. On its own, the newborn baby (or stages of the unborn) could have a right not to be tortured, for it, like a kitten, is capable of having the relevant desire and, hence, interest. But since it cannot have an interest in continued existence as a particular subject, it cannot have a right to life.

Here is schematic way of putting Tooley's argument:

1. To have a right an entity must be capable of having some interest furthered by that right.
2. The right to life is the right of a "subject of experiences and other mental states to continue to exist."
3. To have a right to life it must be in the interest of an entity to continue to exist as a subject of experiences.
4. To have any interests, an entity must be a subject of conscious states, including experiences and desires.
5. To have an interest in continuing to exist, an entity must not only have some desires, but a) desire or be capable of desiring its continuing existence; or b) the continued existence of the entity must make possible the satisfaction of desires existing at other times of the same individual.
6. A necessary condition of being the same individual is to remember oneself as a continuing self.
7. To remember oneself as a continuing self one must possess or be capable of possessing the concept of a continuing self.
8. Thus for continued existence to make possible the satisfaction of the

9. Santurri (1992) asks whether Tooley (1983, 110–11, 118–21) is consistent in saying that an infant has an interest in not being castrated and a woman an interest in not being socialized so as to desire only to be a helpmate, but the unborn or newborn does not have an interest in continued existence. Cf. Trammel (1976) and Pahel (1987).

desires of the same individual for an entity that does not have the capability to desire to continue to exist, and thus for continued existence to be in that entity's interest, the entity must conceive or have the capability of conceiving of itself as a continuing self.

9. The unborn and the newborn do not conceive or have the capability of conceiving of themselves as continuing selves (subjects of experiences), and hence it cannot be said that they have an interest in continued existence.

10. Since an interest in continued existence is a necessary condition of the right to life, the unborn and newborn cannot have the right to life.

There are a series of objections to Tooley's view. First, he argues that only beings who can have interests can have rights and only those beings that are "subjects of consciousness and desires" can have interests. Tooley grants that once an entity has consciousness, an interest in continued existence could be based not on a present desire or capability to desire continued existence, but rather on the possible satisfaction of future desires. In other words, to have any interests at all, one must have reached the stage of having conscious desires; once there, one can have an interest in something one does not yet desire or have the capability to desire. But if this is so, why can't interest be attributed to beings before they are capable of having *any* consciousness or desires? Tooley insists on the second of two senses of "can have interests": 1) only those beings can have interests who are capable or can be capable of having consciousness and desires; 2) only those beings can have interests who are capable of having consciousness and desires. Sense 1 is the thesis that to have an interest one must be the sort of being that at some time can be capable of having consciousness and desires, as opposed to speaking of an interest whenever something merely has "needs, a good, and a capacity to be benefitted or harmed," for example, a tree (Sumner 1984, 78).[10] Sense 2 stipulates that the capability must

10. Sumner says that "if morality has to do with the promotion and protection of interests or welfare, morality can only concern itself with beings who are conscious or sentient" (1984, 79; cf. 83). However, even if we agree with Sumner to link "interest" or "welfare" to the psychological state of sentient beings, we need not agree that morality or, more narrowly, rights have only to do with those in whom the capacity for sentience is actual. It is not clear, moreover, why sentience for Sumner is a criterion of moral standing defined as the right to life, as opposed merely to a right not to suffer (1981, 83–84; cf. Tooley 1983, 100, on the right of kittens not to suffer pain). Cf. Feinberg's analysis of an interest, upon which Tooley builds (Feinberg 1974; Tooley 1983, 96–97; Tooley 1984, 124–25). I argue here, in effect, that one need not have the actual capability to "take" an interest in order to "have" an interest. For this distinction, see Lomasky (1987, chap. 7, p. 163).

be actual. One can agree with Tooley that it is a "conceptual requirement," in the sense that our concept of rights expresses our beliefs about rights, that only beings for whom it is possible to have consciousness and desires at some time can have rights, without agreeing that only beings actually capable of these states can have rights. I assume there would be no need for rights if there were no beings capable at some time of having desires.

Second, even if we bracket momentarily Tooley's basic condition for what it means to be capable of having an interest, he also argues that an entity must be the same subject of consciousness if it is to have an interest in and hence a right to continued existence even when it has not yet come to desire or be capable of desiring to continue. Tooley claims that to remember myself as the same individual is a necessary ("crucial") condition of personal identity, and that to remember, one must possess or be capable of possessing the concept of a continuing self. Yet why should we assume that memory and self-consciousness are conditions of personal identity? Perhaps they are sufficient but not necessary? Perhaps other criteria of personal identity would allow us to predicate identity of the conscious, but not self-conscious, entity and the self-conscious subject of experiences it could become.

Furthermore, even if one were to assume Tooley's metaphysic of personal identity, the moral question is still open: Should we attribute the right to continued existence only to entities who meet the criteria of personal identity or should we extend it to those who would satisfy the criteria later given certain assumptions about their development? Not only are Tooley's criteria debatable, but also the argument would not establish what it sets out to prove: we could extend the right to continued existence to beings with the potential to become individuals with particular personal identities (on Tooley's criteria) even if we could not attribute personal identity to them in early stages of their development. All we would need is some way of relating the potential person to the person it would later become; we would not be claiming *personal* identity (the same subject of consciousness), but we would use some other fact, such as genotype, to identify the stages. If we can relate the unborn or the newborn to the particular person it will later become, then we could say that continued existence is in its interest.

Thus, why must the right to life be defined as the right of a particular subject or person to continue to exist? Why not the right of an entity that will under certain conditions become a particular subject? I see nothing in the concept of a right that prevents us saying an infant has a right to inherit property, for example, although the infant does not have the actual capacity to desire property and does not meet Tooley's criteria of personal identity since it is not capable of conceiving of itself as a continuing subject; such a right can be protected and exercised by proxies.[11] Why should the right to life be different? Thus, Tooley's appeal to personal identity would not establish his case; despite his effort to use a metaphysical argument he would have to fall back simply on a moral conviction that the right to life should be limited to actualized individuals.[12]

Tooley himself offers an explicitly normative critique of the moral relevance of fetal potentiality. He first attempts, as we have seen, to refute the thesis that the right to life is the right either of a potential or actual individual by an analysis of the concept of a right and hence of interests and personal identity. He also wants to refute the claim that the "destruction of potential persons is, in general, prima facie seriously wrong." This claim, he says, is entailed by the right-to-life thesis above. However, because Tooley believes that some moral theories do not employ the concept of rights, the claim that the destruction of potential subjects is intrinsically *wrong* has to be countered on its own ground (1984, 127).[13]

11. Cf. Petchesky (1984, 345) and Carrier (1975, 396–97). See Melden (1977, 147–49, 152–53) on the rights of infants. See also Macklin (1984), Nelson (1985), and Taylor (1986).

12. Marquis's "future-like-ours" argument seems open to a Tooley-like objection: on a plausible account of what such a future is, it will be that of a "subject of experiences and other mental states." The question, then, for Tooley is whether the fetus can be identified as the same subject as the entity that would experience the future state. Marquis first denies, however, that the notion of a "future-like-ours" even has to imply a "future as a person"; it might only signify a future of "enjoyments" (1994, 355–56). Moreover, even if he were to concede that the future in question is that of a person, he also argues, as I do here, that it is not necessary to identify the fetus as already a *personal* subject (having personal identity); one need merely assert that the fetus can be identified as a "human being" that is deprived of its future if it is killed (1994, 357). In my view, Marquis and Tooley can be interpreted as offering two opposing *normative* arguments: for Marquis, deprivation of a future like ours is *sufficient* for the prima facie wrongness of killing; Tooley, as I argue here, can be revised to make a normative argument to the effect that the wrongness of killing rests on the loss of the future of a person *to* a person, rather than a metaphysical argument about why the fetus is not the same "subject" as the entity it would become. These normative accounts ultimately require, it seems to me, some justification of why one property or set of properties underlies the wrongness of killing (cf. McInerney 1994; Paske 1994).

13. In 1983 Tooley first says that because not all moral theories endorse rights and rights are generally less well understood than other moral concepts, he proposes to determine the descriptive content of the concept "person" by establishing "what relatively enduring non-potential properties make it intrinsically wrong to destroy something, and do so independent of its intrinsic value" (1983, 95; cf. 51–52, 57–58). However, he also says that because "most people" believe the reason such destruction is intrinsically wrong is that entities with certain properties have a *right* not to be destroyed, the best way to proceed is to discuss the notion of a right and, in particular, the right not to be destroyed (1983, 95–96). Section 5.2 (1983) contains the discussion of rights and employs the thesis that the unification of desires in a single subject requires the concept of a continuing self; this thesis is defended in 5.3 (1983, 120–23; cf. 1984, 128–29). Chapter 6 (1983) takes up the claim that "the destruction of potential persons is intrinsically wrong"; Tooley's counterarguments were not included by the editor in the 1984 essay (1984, 132 n. 15).

Tooley develops this characterization of a potential person (persons being those with nonpotential properties such that it is intrinsically wrong to destroy them):[14]

> X is a *potential person* if and only if X has all, or almost all, of the properties of a positive sort that together would be causally sufficient to bring it about that X gives rise to a person, and there are no factors within X that would block the process in question. (1983, 168)

The "conservative" moral claim Tooley focuses on, then, is this: "the destruction of potential persons is intrinsically wrong, and seriously so" (1983, 173).

Tooley's first major argument is that the conservative's position requires acceptance of the "Unrestricted Potentiality Principle," and this "has consequences which are clearly unacceptable." The claim the conservative accepts is the "restricted" one that it is intrinsically wrong to destroy a biologically unified potential person (1983, 178). Tooley's contention is that if this principle is acceptable, then so is the unrestricted principle:

> The destruction of a potential person is intrinsically wrong, and seriously so, where X is a potential person if and only if X is an entity, or system of entities, that has all, or almost all, of the properties of a positive sort that together would be causally sufficient to bring it about that X gives rise to a person, and where there are no factors present within X that would block the causal process in question. (1983, 179)

Thus, in this form the principle applies to "nonbiological" entities and to "systems of entities that are causally interrelated in the appropriate way"

---

14. X is a *latent* person if something could block the process; X has an *active* potentiality if no outside factors are necessary; a merely *possible* person is one who would have existed if certain actions were or were not performed (Tooley 1983, 167–68). Note that Tooley's general proposal for the use of "person" is to specify the concept as descriptive on the one hand, but to determine its content by moral considerations on the other. The question is whether certain properties that in their actualized form ground the assertion of the intrinsic wrongness of destruction—and hence determine the descriptive content of "person"—also ground such a claim when merely potential. On the potentiality argument, see Kluge (1975), Brody (1975), and J. C. Fletcher (1979).

(1983, 179).[15] The reason one must accept the unrestricted principle is that the grounds of the intrinsic wrongness of destruction rest in the destruction of a certain potentiality in itself, not in how that potentiality is embodied (1983, 179). Electronic or mechanical potential persons are possible, and it is "logically possible for a person's body to be a whole that is unified causally, rather than spatially, and for its parts to be of different general types" (1983, 182).

Thus, if the unrestricted potentiality principle is true, it would be intrinsically wrong to disrupt a mechanical system programmed to bring together a human ovum and sperm cell (1983, 182). Very few people, says Tooley, would accept this view; nor would they accept the view that it is wrong to interfere with a "system" of a "woman together with a collection of spermatozoa" (1983, 183).[16] (Such a system is not an "active" potentiality as the mechanical system is, for it does not possess within itself all the necessary causal factors. But neither is a zygote on its own an active potentiality.) Thus, the unrestricted principle would make contraception as well as abortion intrinsically wrong. Those unwilling to accept the unrestricted principle because of its moral consequences must also reject the restricted principle as well, for the latter is merely a "version" of the former (1983, 178, 183).

In addition to this argument from the unrestricted potentiality principle, Tooley's other major objection to the intrinsic wrongness of the destruction of potential persons rests on this idea:

> Let C be any type of causal process where there is some type of occurrence, E, such that processes of type C would possess no intrinsic moral significance were it not for the fact that they result in occurrences of type E. (1983, 186)

15. Langerak argued that spermatozoa and ovum are only possible persons because it is not the case that "in the normal course of its development" a particular sperm or egg will become a person (1973, 415). In a revised essay, however, Tooley argued that ovum and spermatozoa together constitute a biological system of causally interrelated objects that possess the relevant potentiality (Tooley 1973b, 82 n. 28; Tooley mentioned the "generalized" potentiality principle elsewhere [1973a, 431] but did not apply it against Langerak). One is not dealing with a "collection of objects" that have certain possibilities: "The objects must already be interrelated in such a way that in the absence of external interference the laws governing their future interaction and development will bring it about that the system will develop the property in question" (1973b, 82). Tooley maintains this idea of spermatozoa and ovum as a system in 1983.

16. The woman-spermatozoa example of an almost active potentiality is discussed as a separate argument, but I treat it as part of the argument from the unacceptable consequences of the unrestricted potentiality principle.

If this is the case, then the "moral symmetry principle" (MSP) follows: intervening in C so as to prevent E is "intrinsically wrong to precisely the same degree" as not starting C when it was in one's power to do so (1983, 186). The MSP asserts that "being a case of killing, and being a case of failing to save, are equally weighty wrong-making characteristics" (1983, 187); they are equal with respect to the "degree of moral wrongness" (1983, 189); it is equally wrong (or right) *ceteris paribus* not to start up a causal process in a person's body necessary for life as it is to disrupt (interfere with) such a process (1983, 186–87). The common conviction that killing is more serious can be accounted for as a consequence of the fact that, generally speaking, acts of killing and failing to save tend to differ in other respects (1983, 187–88).

Tooley now uses the MSP and his kitten example to show that if intervening with a process that produces persons is intrinsically wrong, it is intrinsically wrong to the same degree not to start the process, that is, if abortion is wrong, contraception is equally so (1983, 191ff.). Tooley asks us to imagine that there is a chemical that would make kittens into potential persons. He then argues that the MSP "entails" that the actions of not injecting a kitten with a chemical that would make it a potential person is of equal moral weight (no more seriously wrong *or* right) with the action of neutralizing one that has been injected. If it is no more wrong to kill a neutralized kitten than a noninjected one, then it is no more wrong to neutralize and kill than to refrain from injecting and then to kill (neither kitten has the potentiality to become a person). Then, on the further assumption that it is no more wrong just to kill the injected kitten than to neutralize it and then to kill it, we have the following result: "it is prima facie no more wrong to kill a kitten that has been injected with the special chemical, but that has not yet developed into a person, than intentionally to refrain from injecting the special chemical into another kitten and then to kill it" (1983, 192). If we grant that there are no morally relevant differences between a potential cat-person and a human organism that is a potential person, then, Tooley concludes,

> the destruction of a human organism that is a potential person, but not a person, is prima facie no more seriously wrong than intentionally refraining from fertilizing a human egg cell, and destroying it instead. (1983, 193)

Because many people, including conservatives who oppose abortion, do not think "intentionally refraining from procreation" is wrong, then "neither is the destruction of potential persons" (1983, 193).[17] Conservatives who do not think it wrong to refrain from procreation must revise their view on abortion.

Tooley has advanced, then, two major arguments against the thesis that it is wrong to interrupt or destroy potential persons. Both of his arguments have the following form: Since potentiality resides in systems as well as entities, then if abortion is wrong (right) so is contraception; but this is clearly morally unacceptable. Since not starting and stopping in themselves are morally equivalent (the moral symmetry principle), contraception is wrong (right) if abortion is; but it is not wrong to refrain from procreation (193–94 and chap. 7). I now present objections to both arguments and consider some of Tooley's responses to similar criticisms.[18]

The key to Tooley's claim that if one accepts the restricted potentiality principle one must accept the unrestricted is that it is morally irrelevant whether a potential person is unified "spatially" or "causally," or whether it is biological in whole or in part. Thus, if it is wrong to destroy a biologically unified potential person, it is wrong to destroy a system of entities that has the relevant potentiality. The unrestricted principle applies to entities or systems of entities that have all or almost all of the properties causally sufficient to produce a person. Thus, the system of "a woman together with a collection of spermatozoa that could be used to bring about fertilization" qualifies; like a zygote within a woman such a system possesses "almost all" of the requisite causal properties; both require "external assistance" and any difference is only one of degree (1983, 183). Tooley then apparently has shown that the use of spermicide or other forms of contraception is wrong if abortion is.

The issue is whether Tooley is right to consider sperm and ovum as a system that possesses the relevant potentiality. Is the potentiality that re-

17. Tooley also deals with the "moral comparability" principle that leads to the conclusion "there is some number n such that intentionally refraining from bringing into existence n persons is in itself at least as seriously wrong as destroying a potential person" (1983, 195).

18. Pahel (1987) has made the same or similar points against Tooley. Following the structure of Tooley's own argument, he focuses first on the theory about rights and then, as I do, on the third and fifth of Tooley's subarguments on the intrinsic wrongness of destroying potential persons. I especially agree that Tooley's position must be evaluated as a substantial moral view, not one "entailed by our ordinary concept of a right or the right to continued existence" (1987, 96). We differ in some points of detail as regards the interpretation and criticism of Tooley, however. In regard to the restricted and unrestricted potentiality principles, Pahel focuses as I do on the difference between possible and potential persons, but on the moral symmetry principle his argument is different; in regard to step 2 of Tooley's argument, he wants to insist that there could be a morally relevant difference between neutralizing an injected kitten and neutralizing a human fetus (1987, 103); my argument focuses rather on the difference between neutralizing and not starting.

sides in the system really the *same* as that which resides in the organism? I believe we can identify a sense in which the potentiality of a fertilized egg (and further states) distinguishes it from spermatozoa and ovum considered as a causally interrelated system of objects (see Langerak 1973). The fertilized egg, due to its genetic makeup, has the potentiality to become a particular individual. Tooley himself construes the right to life not as the right to exist as *some* personal subject but the right to exist as a *particular* subject. Now it seems justified to assume that the potential to become a particular person rests in part at least on having a particular genetic identity. In addition, it seems justified to assume that genetic identity comes into existence first with the fertilized egg. It is not necessary to claim that genetic identity means a strictly unchanged genetic structure, since, as Engelhardt (1974, 326) puts it, "one undergoes mutations in a number of one's cells." Moreover, genetic identity still seems to be a necessary condition for personal identity even if a fertilized egg splits into two individuals (see the last section of this appendix on Ramsey). The argument merely asserts that in the fertilized egg one has the genetic package that along with other causal factors has the "almost active" potentiality for developing into a particular individual.

Thus, the fertilized egg has the requisite genetic identity but the concatenation of spermatozoa and ovum does not. Hence, in virtue of this identity, the fertilized egg has a different potentiality than the potentiality possessed by a system of objects.[19] My conclusion is that neither the disruption of a system programmed to bring sperm and ovum together, nor the destruction of either alone, constitutes the destruction of the relevant potentiality, the potentiality to become a particular individual. Thus, I accept Tooley's point that a system of causally interrelated entities could hypothetically be a potential person (1983, 182) if it possessed genetic identity or some analogue; but I argue that the "system" of sperm and egg does not possess the relevant factor of genetic identity. Given that genetic identity is a necessary condition of personal identity (at least for humans), this system itself is not a potential person.[20]

19. Feinberg (1980a, 194) apparently accepts this point: "The defender of the potentiality criterion will reply that it is only at the moment of conception that any being comes into existence with exactly the same chromosomal makeup as the human being that will later emerge from the womb, and it is *that* chromosomal combination that forms the potential person, not anything that exists before it comes together." Cf. Lomasky (1984, 165) on the conceptus as genetic individual.

20. Note that my argument does not assert that only biologically unified entities can be potential persons; my claim is that only with a certain genetic makeup, or whatever the functional equivalent would be for electronic or mechanical persons, does one have a potential person (cf. Tooley 1983, 197–98, on Devine 1978, 7ff., 75); neither biological form nor spatiotemporal unity are necessary. See also Feezell (1987, 44–45), who speaks of an identifiable potentiality that will develop into a person; and Marquis (1989, 201–2), who defends his argument that abortion is prima facie wrong (because it deprives fetuses of a valuable

My objection to Tooley's use of the moral symmetry principle is similar to a point made by Lawrence Davis, whom Tooley tries to refute (1983, 198ff.). Davis argues that since the MSP states (in Tooley's pre–1983 formulation) that only the result has intrinsic moral significance, it begs the question to apply the principle to the abortion case; if only the *result* were at stake, then the only relevant factor would be whether a *person* is produced; but in fact the issue at stake is whether it matters morally that the process is not started or disrupted (Tooley 1983, 199). Tooley says, however, that his 1983 statement of the MSP does not claim that only the result has intrinsic moral significance but that if the process C were not causally related to outcome E, "such *processes* would have no intrinsic moral significance" (1983, 199; italics mine).

The difficulty with Tooley's response is that it is not clear what he could mean by saying that the processes would have no intrinsic significance were it not for the outcome. If the process gets its significance only from the outcome, then its significance is derived and *not* intrinsic. Thus, it is natural to think that despite its new wording Tooley's MSP is really consequentialist, and thus that by applying it to the potential cat-person and by extension to human potential persons he has begged the question.

Suppose, however, that Tooley were successful in putting his principle in a way that is compatible with a nonconsequentialist ethic. This is evidently his contention:

> The moral symmetry principle is perfectly consistent with the claim that the rightness or wrongness of action cannot be reduced to the goodness or badness of resulting states of affairs. The moral symmetry principle says only that if causing something to happen is intrinsically wrong, so is allowing it to happen, and to the same degree. (1983, 212)

Even if there are wrong-making characteristics other than consequences, the characteristics of not starting and interfering are not among them.

I argue in Chapter 1 that the general moral significance that attaches to the distinction between killing and letting die (in the broad sense) is a function of the normative framework that distinguishes between the duty not to kill and the duty to save, and gives priority in a case of conflict to the former. But someone can still agree with Tooley that the narrower distinction between "causing" and "allowing" is not significant in itself, but only because of other factors. Thus, someone who believes that there is a morally significant distinction between not starting a potential person

---

future like ours) from the objection that if abortion is wrong, so is contraception; his thesis is that "there is no nonarbitrarily identifiable subject of the loss in the case of contraception."

(allowing it not to exist) and stopping one does not have to hold that general moral significance attaches somehow to the not-starting/stopping distinction itself. Whoever holds that contraception is not wrong, but abortion is, only has to hold that there are morally significant reasons for the distinction in this case.

Tooley's MSP, however, seems to deny categorically that there could be moral *reasons* for holding that it is wrong to destroy but acceptable not to start potential persons. The critic might grant that in regard to other sorts of cases no moral significance attaches to whether one fails to start or interrupts.[21] But the critic would insist that it begs the moral question, against those whose views of their responsibilities in regard to potential persons do attribute asymmetrical significance to not starting and stopping, simply to assume that the MSP applies to this case. That Tooley assumes the MSP applies in this case is clear in step 2 of the kitten argument (1983, 191) where he says that the MSP "entails" that not injecting a kitten with the special chemical is no more seriously wrong (or right) than neutralizing one that has been injected.[22] The MSP entails this conclusion, however, only if one makes the moral judgment that the principle applies in this case; the individual who is against abortion but permits contraception would presumably think it is wrong to *neutralize* the potential cat-person, while it is permitted not to inject in the first place. Tooley claims that if abortion is wrong, so to the same degree is refraining from conception, and if contraception is right, so is abortion. If the MSP applied to the kitten case his conclusion would follow, but those who hold different moral views contest precisely its applicability here.

The Historical Context

I argue, then, that Warren, Feinberg, and Tooley in the end rely on substantive moral beliefs to link the possession of actual capacities to the right to life. It makes historical sense, furthermore, that these thinkers would argue that the right to life rests on actual capabilities. Many versions of the natural rights tradition suggest that agents have rights "in virtue of" actual capacities, for example, to suffer or to choose. The capacities in themselves,

---

21. Tooley deals with those who attack the MSP itself in contrast to its applicability (1983, 198, 205ff.). In fact, he does not think it is a question of applicability at all, for the principle is "extremely general" (1983, 202).

22. Cf. Langerak (1973). Bassen (1982, 331) makes essentially this same argument against Tooley.

linked, for example, with values, prudential rationality, and consistency, are supposed to justify the ascription of rights (see Gewirth 1978). If one accepts such a theory of the justification of rights, then only entities with certain actual capacities can have rights. On my view, the "actual possession criterion" requires such a theory.

Some proponents of an "in virtue of actual capacities" theory of rights have nonetheless attempted to show that one can have weaker rights as one develops the capacities in question and thus entities that are only potential moral persons—that is, potential possessors of full moral status—can have some rights. Norman Gillespie, for example, argues that if rights are based on properties that admit of degrees of development, then the strength of these rights will vary with the stages of development (1977, 238–39). Thus, if abortion cases are seen as a conflict of rights, the woman's right to life would be stronger than the fetus's (1977, 241–42). Gillespie's thesis is based on Gewirth's "Principle of Proportionality" (Gewirth 1978, 141ff.; see also 374 n. 1). By arguing that those who are not actual agents can nonetheless have "generic rights in proportion to . . . degree of attainment of agency," or "preparatory rights," Gewirth gives the fetus "such a right to well-being as is required for developing its potentialities for growth towards purpose fulfillment" (1978, 141–42). However, if there is a conflict of rights, then the woman's rights to freedom and well-being are stronger (1978, 141–43). Where the woman would suffer even a "sizeable loss," the fetus's rights are overridden regardless of its stage of development (1978, 143). The difficulty with Gillespie's and Gewirth's argument is that if it were indeed true that only actual capabilities justify rights, then as Feinberg would argue it is hard to see how the potential or partial possession of these properties could do so; one either has the actual properties, and hence the rights, or one does not.

There are other alternatives to the "in virtue of actual capacities" theory. If one held an actual convention or contractarian theory of rights, for example, rights would be construed as bargains struck by self-interested agents. (For an actual convention theory of morality, see Harman 1977.)[23] These agents could take an interest, however, not only in their own well-being and liberty but in that of their offspring not yet capable of entering into conventions.[24] Thus, their agreements could include rights for the un-

23. Lomasky (1984, 170ff.) argues that it is not being a person—i.e., an entity with higher cognitive capacities—that matters but the modes of "identification" and social relationships into which the entity is immersed after birth. See also Harrison (1983, 224, 228–29) for the view that moral status depends on the establishment of social bonds.

24. Ronald M. Green (1983, 159ff.) argues that a judgment to ascribe moral personhood is not made because of qualities an entity possesses or does not possess, but is a decision based on our interests, including our liberty of action, to protect and assist such a being. Judgments about metaphysical personhood or personal identity are part of the nexus of beliefs

born or newborn; the actual agents would have struck a bargain *between* themselves, but *for the sake of* those who do not yet have the actual capacity to strike bargains.[25] The actual convention theory would therefore justify the moral and legal rights of those for which others—parents or courts— act as proxies. On this view, right-holders would not have to be persons or even have sentient capabilities. Such a theory, moreover, could also explain the modern evolution and growth of "natural" or "human" rights; current social friction about abortion could be explained not only as a disagreement between those who hold certain theological views and those who do not, but also as part of the same process of social adjustment and bargaining since the Enlightenment whereby rights have been established and to whom they apply delineated.[26] The current debate would be settled when a consensus is reached on when and how offspring should be protected.

Still another way of understanding "human" or "natural" rights and their ascription is to see them as instruments that loving or caring persons adopt in their relations. Harrison argues:

> A "pro-life" movement that invites us to "respect" fetal rights from conception or genetic implantation onward actually undermines us by tempting us to imagine that personal rights inhere in natural processes, apart from any genuine covenant of caring, including the human resolve to create viable conditions of life for all who are born among us. Human rights are qualities that ought to inhere in our social relations. (1983, 224)

Harrison also claims—parallel to the extension of rights by actual agents in the contractarian tradition—that loving agents can extend rights to those who are not full participants in the moral community.

The issue, then, is why any one point in the development of the unborn or newborn is chosen for such an extension. Harrison (1983, 216–18; cf.

---

we employ, however; Green notes that part of the moral judgment rests on the "nature of the entity" (1983, 161). Cf. Green's (1974) notion of the rights that agents who have "basic" rights "confer" on nonmoral or nonrational beings.

25. Lomasky (1987) attempts to supply a theory of the foundations of rights; he argues not for a standard contractarian basis but for an evolution of arrangements accepted by partly self-interested and partly altruistic beings. See esp. chap. 4; for a summary statement, see page 154. Note that a contractarian mode of justification would not necessarily aim to protect those incapable of making bargains in order to increase the virtue or happiness of those who bargain; the contractors can aim at the well-being of the nonbargainers for their own sake. See Santurri (1992) on "rationalist" reasons for protecting those without full moral status.

26. See Lomasky (1987) on the notion of an evolution of rights through a process of reciprocal agreements.

207) argues that a necessary condition for the ascription of moral status is that the unborn have the sort of "functional biological complexity commensurate with the degree of functionality required for discrete biological existence." Viability, therefore, is the earliest "plausible" point at which this sort of complexity is said to be present in brain and lung functioning (1983, 216–17). Harrison herself seems, moreover, to favor birth as the "critical developmental mark" (1983, 217–18; cf. 220). The question, though, is why a certain degree of functioning is required before rights can be ascribed.[27] Even if one admits that birth makes "identification" easier, as Loren Lomasky (1984) also argues, it still seems that social relations ("bonding") can be established with an early fetus. The unborn can be identified, loved, and, in my view, granted rights at any stage. Lomasky tries to prevent his own "piggyback" argument, which extends the rights of adult project pursuers to infants (we confer rights on prospective project pursuers), from being extended to the unborn by claiming that until birth we do not have sufficient knowledge to identify the individual (1987, chaps. 7, 8). As I note, however, we have enough biological information to relate the unborn to the infant and the particular person it would normally become.

God's Dominion

Whatever the outcome of these debates, their basic parameters are not theological. In an early essay on abortion, Paul Ramsey (1971) argues (as I interpret him) that genetic identity is a sufficient criterion for the existence of a particular person.[28] At conception one has the "essential constitutive features of a human individual" (1971, 7):

> The human individual comes into existence first as a minute informational speck. . . . (1971, 4)[29]

27. For Harrison the neonate is not yet a moral person, for personhood requires reflection and intention (1983, 220–21), but the neonate has "joined our society" in the sense that it has been ascribed rights. Harrison suggests that rights are ascribed in a "covenant of caring" (1983, 224). It is "morally wise," moreover, to extend respect, indeed the right to life, to late stages of the fetus (1983, 224–25), but abortions can still be justified for the sake of the woman's well-being (229).

28. Cf. Ramsey's later views on abortion (1973; 1978, Part One). On the themes of stewardship and dominion in his thought, see also Ramsey (1978, 146–48). See Meilaender (1991) on Ramsey's covenantal ethic.

29. Ramsey adds a footnote on identical twins who he says have the same genotype but each is "a unique, unrepeatable human person" (1971, 5 n. 1). This admission seems to suggest that genotype is not a sufficient criterion.

Ramsey notes, however, that this metaphysical claim does not entail a moral conclusion:

> One can, of course, allow this and still refuse to affirm that the embryo is as yet in any sense the bearer of human rights. (1971, 10)[30]

Moreover, he argues that from a theological point of view the metaphysical debate was not relevant:

> Having begun with all these distinctions and theories about when germinating life becomes human, it is now necessary for me to say that from an authentic religious point of view none of them matters very much. . . . Strictly speaking, it is far more crucial for contemporary thought than it is for any religious viewpoint to say when there is on the scene enough of the actuality of a man who is coming to be for there to be any sacredness in or any rights attached to his life. This is the case because in modern world views the sanctity of life can rest only on something inherent in man. It is, therefore, important to determine when proleptically he already essentially is all else that he will ever become in the course of a long life. Respect for life in the first of it, if this has any sacredness, must be an overflow backward from or in anticipation of something—some capability or power—that comes later to be a man's inherent possession. . . . One grasps the religious outlook upon the sanctity of human life only if he sees that this life is asserted to be *surrounded* by sanctity that need not be in a man; that the most dignity a man ever possesses is a dignity that is alien to him. . . . It becomes *relatively* unimportant to say exactly when among the products of human generation we are dealing with an organism that is human and when we are dealing with organic life that is not yet human (despite all the theological

30. Contrary to Petchesky's interpretation, Ramsey does not conflate biological genotype and personhood in a moral sense (Petchesky 1984, 335; cf. 338). He does seem to say that genotype is a sufficient condition of personal identity in the metaphysical sense. Donceel (1984, 18) would apparently dispute Ramsey's (1971) claim that genetics endorses the view that metaphysical personhood, indeed personal identity, begins at conception; for Donceel, the presence of the genetic code of an individual does not constitute an actual person; the human person is only "virtual," not actual, at conception; the soul as the "form" of the body develops over time (1984, 16). Donceel (1984), like Feinberg or Warren, believes one is a metaphysical person (and hence a moral person with a right to life) only when there is a certain *actual* state of affairs. But unlike Feinberg or Warren, he argues the metaphysical thesis that this state occurs sometime during fetal development when the body is actual (physiological structure is complete and only growth remains) and the "soul" is "infused."

speculations upon this question). A man's dignity is an overflow from God's dealing with him, and not primarily an anticipation of anything he will ever be by himself alone. (1971, 11).

On this view, life is a gift, a loan, or a trust from God with conditions attached; the right to life is not something an individual possesses in virtue either of potential or actual capabilities or any human agreement. God has sovereignty or dominion over life; to acknowledge an interhuman right to life or to respect life is to acknowledge God's right over life (Ramsey 1971, 12–16). Furthermore, one knows somehow at what stage God wills that *homo sapiens* "organic" life has full moral status. In this essay of Ramsey's, for example, one learns from revelation—that is, what is communicated through scripture—that full status begins at conception (1971, 12–13).[31] Ramsey's point is not that God reveals a metaphysical truth about when personhood or personal identity begins but that God reveals when human creatures are to be regarded as moral persons, that is, individuals with the right to life.[32]

The Judaic tradition, based also on a complex view of revelation (the written and the oral law revealed at Sinai), locates full moral status only after the head or greater part of the fetus emerges at birth (Feldman 1974, 225ff.).[33] Nonetheless, the tradition protects fetal life on the grounds of its

---

31. See Harrison's (1983, 69–70) critique of Ramsey's exegesis. See also Feinberg and Levenbook's objections (1993) to the homo sapiens criterion for moral status. Feinberg and Levenbook argue that such a criterion (even if adopted by God) would exclude aliens who have the "common sense" or descriptive characteristics of personhood, and include humans who have irretrievably lost any capacity to have them. Ramsey could perhaps have revised his view and said: God loves and gives full moral status (a more specific love than for the whole creation) not only to homo sapiens but to all creatures with the potential capacities to have a relation to God. It would be religiously indifferent to Ramsey whether these potential capacities did or did not make an entity a metaphysical person, but Ramsey's new criterion would be close to the strict potentiality criterion: all those with either potential or actual capacities to be persons have full moral status. At this juncture, Ramsey would have to defeat the "'logical point'" (see my arguments in the text). Would Ramsey be open to the objection that it is now something inherent in the creature that justifies moral status? No, Ramsey would say, for neither being homo sapiens, nor having certain potential capacities in themselves, directly grounds moral status; it is God's act of creating and loving such creatures, giving them the gift of life and entrusting them with responsibilities toward one another.

32. In some instances the religious traditions suggest that God communicates a metaphysical truth about metaphysical personhood or personal identity either through revelation or reason; on the basis of that knowledge, and assuming like Warren that whatever has metaphysical personhood or personal identity has full-blown moral status, one then draws moral conclusions. See Donceel (1984).

33. According to Feldman, talmudic traditions assume that the fetus is not a *nefesh adam*, a "human person" (1974, 254f.). After the head or the greater part emerges, "we do not set aside one life for another" (1974, 275 n. 45). Apparently other laws, such as laws of mourning, do not categorize the newborn as a *bar kayyama* (a viable, living thing) until thirty days after

source and value.[34] Despite the disagreement between the view Ramsey enunciates in the essay quoted and segments of Judaic tradition, there is a common assumption that God is Lord of life; the disagreement is about when the Lord of life grants full moral status. There is thus a disagreement about the content of revelation. Some contemporary Roman Catholics side with Ramsey on when full status begins, but they would appeal to "reason" as the source of their knowledge.[35] However, to appeal to reason as opposed to revelation as the source of this knowledge is not necessarily to change the structure of the argument: the right to life derives not from inherent human capacities but is based rather on God's right over human creatures.

Tooley might argue that insofar as the religious traditions want to speak of a right to life, such an idea must pass the same test as any right; that is, if to have a right to life an entity must have an interest in continued existence and that requires the capacity to have a concept of a continuing self, then this requirement would also apply to a right derived from God's dominion.[36] Tooley might also argue that even if one does not accept his notion of personal identity, which requires the actual capacity for self-consciousness, one will have to admit that the right to life can be ascribed only to individuals with personal identity, whatever that consists in.

But Ramsey could reply that in order to ascribe the right to life it is not necessary to ascribe personal identity (on whatever criterion). God makes

---

birth unless it is certain that the pregnancy had run a full nine months (1974, 254). Rosner says that although one has a *nefesh* at birth, it does not have full legal rights; if one kills the newborn one is not liable for the death penalty until it is clearly viable (1978, 261). See also Bleich (1960).

34. See Feldman (1974, chaps. 14 and 15) on various views in the tradition about reasons for abortion, such as a threat to the life of the woman. Note that once full status is assumed, the life of the woman is not a sufficient reason, unless, as one ruling adds, both will die (Feldman 1974, 283–84; cf. Brody 1975, 18, 151 n. 14). See Chapter 2 on nothing is lost.

35. See Cahill who identifies rights based on inherent human capacities with the natural law tradition in contrast to the idea that rights are established in virtue of a relation to God (1980, 279ff.). The view I identify as theological here sees the right to life as derivative from God's dominion, but this is known by natural reason according to some theologians, and in that sense it is part of the natural law tradition as well. Cf. 294–95 where Cahill also mentions God's dominion. Cahill puts rights within a neo-Aristotelian theory of the good; assuming a duty (based on God's claim) to seek the good, rights are claims to the necessary conditions of doing so (1980, 283–86). See Jerald H. Richards who argues versus Donagan that an adequate justification for respect for rational creatures requires a theological argument (1980, 321–22ff.).

36. Tooley (1973b, 81 n. 27) suggests that some might claim that God's right, as opposed to the fetus's right, is violated when the fetus is killed. But if the theologian sees the interhuman right as derivative from God's right—an ascribed right, if you will, such as a donor bestows on a beneficiary—then it is still not the sort of right that is based solely on the agent's inherent capabilities or interests.

known through revelation or reason that homo sapiens organic life is to be given full moral status (a right to life) at a certain point; this ascription does not rest on the ascription of personal identity in the full metaphysical sense. God's right over life is exercised in such a way that God gives full protection to entities that on Tooley's view of personal identity are only potential particular individuals since they do not yet fully satisfy the criteria of identity. Even if the unborn did satisfy some other set of criteria of personal identity, this ascription would not be necessary in order for God to assign the right to life. As I argue, it is morally possible to ascribe a right to continued existence even to entities that do not actually possess the features of personal identity.

Of course, even God—and humans following divine instructions—have to be able to *relate* the entities to the persons they will later become, but it is not necessary to relate them as individuals with personal identity. Ramsey later (1973) makes clear that he thinks that genotype is not metaphysically sufficient (because of the possibility of twinning at segmentation—already noted in 1971—or of two fertilized eggs becoming one individual). He stresses instead the identification of a time when "it is *settled* whether there will be one or two or more distinct human individuals," and adds the requirement of "morphological humanity and major, functioning organ systems." Here Ramsey seems to propose metaphysical status, not as the *grounds* of respect for life, but as the means of identifying the entities that should be respected. However, as I have argued, Ramsey's theological view requires only some way of identifying the entity in question even if the entity does not satisfy criteria of personal identity. Some point of individuation, if not identity, would be required.

Thus, there appears to be little common ground between Tooley's view and theological views of the right to life such as Ramsey's. Moreover, if my criticisms are correct, arguments such as Warren's, Feinberg's, or Tooley's cannot successfully settle the question of which entities can have the right to life. These authors must produce a full theory of rights and their justification in order to insist on "actual possession." The issue regarding necessary or sufficient conditions for having a right to life must be faced in terms of our moral beliefs about rights; there is no shortcut through morally neutral "conceptual" or "logical" requirements.[37]

37. Theories that justify rights in terms of actual capacities ("in virtue of" justifications) have been subject to severe criticisms by neo-Aristotelians and others. See Schwartz (1979) and MacIntyre (1984) on Gewirth. See McCloskey (1975) on Locke and Aquinas and the difference between a theistic account and an account based on inherent human capacities. (Using the latter, McCloskey wants to include a right to be saved in the right to life.) Cf. Feinberg and Levenbook (1993), who argue that the state should not legally endorse a view that gives potential persons moral status because such a view is contrary to "common sense" and rests on theological premises (228; also Feinberg 1986, 291). My broader point is that a view such as Feinberg and Levenbook's requires substantive premises that are at home in

However, the consensus on the right not to be killed and the right to be saved is not entirely exploded by disagreements about moral status. The theologian who sees full moral status as a matter of divine gift would still presumably need to have some notion of the sorts of beings to whom God grants this status. A theologian could hold, for example, that God grants moral status to beings that at some time *can* have consciousness and desires, or even self-consciousness and the capacity to relate (in some minimal sense at least) to others. While this theologian would hold that it is ultimately God's loving act that grants moral status—we do not possess status in virtue of our capacities alone, potential or actual—nonetheless the theologian could grant that having certain capacities at least potentially is a necessary condition:[38] Without these capacities, the argument would go, God's loving purpose cannot be fulfilled. Thus although this theologian and the "in virtue of inherent capacities" theorist may ultimately appeal to different grounds, and although the "in virtue of" theorist may insist on actual possession, there could be agreement on certain necessary conditions that all beings with full rights must possess; the theologian might agree, therefore, with the "in virtue of" theorist that anencephalic infants cannot have full moral status. Thus even in a setting of profound moral disagreement about abortion and infanticide, there could be agreement about some cases.[39]

"systems" of belief, just as the theological argument is. This seems to me to make the problem of a moral consensus on abortion in a pluralistic setting much more difficult.

38. See Santurri (1992), who adroitly contrasts a "humanist" and a "rationalist" criterion of moral standing (in the sense of characteristics sufficient for having equal worth, that is, having the same moral protections as anyone else); the former requires only that one be born of human parents, the latter that one have some set of capabilities.

39. Harrison (1983) insists on the right to "bodily integrity, or the power of self-direction as an embodied human being" (197; cf. 198–99); this self-control is an essential part of human well-being (199). Harrison also has another independent argument, I believe (in addition to supporting utilitarian considerations): women must have the right to moral choice because without it they are not accorded equal status as moral agents (195). Women are denied "full standing as moral persons" when they do not have "the authority to make fundamental moral choices over [their own lives]" (228). Because women do the childbearing (and still most of the childrearing), they should have the right to make the moral decision. Harrison is arguing, therefore, not only for a right to decide what happens in and to your body, for a zone of self-determination protected from interference from others; she is also postulating a right to make *moral* decisions concerning the use of reproductive capacities. Note how the two rights differ: the right to bodily integrity gives the woman discretionary control over the use of her body; as Thomson would say, one has a right to decide what happens in and to one's body. The right to make a moral decision would be a broader right that presumably would allow for the moral point of view embodied in the notion of a right to bodily integrity, *or* for a moral point of view that either did not acknowledge this right or severely limited it by duties to the fetus. This broader right rests on the argument that since the woman *bears*, the woman should make the moral decision about the rights and wrongs of abortion. In a matter that affects

---

women so fundamentally, Harrison argues, to deny them the sole right to decide is to deny their moral competence (cf. 114ff. and chaps. 1–2). There should therefore be no law that limits women's moral freedom in this respect. I think this is a powerful argument, but see Brody (1975, chap. 3) for the objection that we limit moral freedom when we believe basic rights of others are at stake. Brody also examines other sorts of arguments for legal freedom. Compare also Dworkin (1993) who argues that the basic issue in the abortion dispute is the clash of views on the value or sanctity of life, rather than the right to life; and since such sanctity is a form of religious belief, no one interpretation should be legislated. I cannot pursue these issues here but one wonders 1) whether values and rights are so distinct, and 2) even if the dispute is between religiously based interpretations of intrinsic value, why these should not be expressed in our views of public policy. On Dworkin, see Tribe (1993). For another treatment that gives values primacy, see Steffen (1994).

Bibliography

Adler, Rachel
    1978   "The Jew Who Wasn't There: Halacha and the Jewish Woman." In *Contemporary Jewish Ethics,* edited by Menachem Marc Kellner, 348–54. New York: Sanhedrin Press.

Aiken, William
    1977   "The Right to Be Saved from Starvation." In *World Hunger and Moral Obligation,* edited by William Aiken and Hugh LaFollette, 85–102. Englewood Cliffs, N.J.: Prentice-Hall.

Alexander, Lawrence A.
    1976   "Self-Defense and the Killing of Noncombatants: A Reply to Fullinwider." *Philosophy and Public Affairs* 5(4): 408–15.
    1993   "Self-Defense, Justification, and Excuse." *Philosophy and Public Affairs* 22(3): 53–66.

Allen, Joseph L.
    1979   "Paul Ramsey and His Respondents Since *The Patient as Person.*" *Religious Studies Review* 5(2): 89–95.

Anscombe, G.E.M.
    1958   "Modern Moral Philosophy." *Philosophy: The Journal of the Royal Institute of Philosophy* 33(124): 1–19.
    1966   "A Note on Mr. Bennett." *Analysis* 26(2): 208.
    1970   "War and Murder." In *War and Morality,* edited by Richard A. Wasserstrom, 42–53. Belmont, Calif.: Wadsworth.
    1982   "Medalist's Address: Action, Intention and 'Double Effect.'" *American Catholic Philosophical Association Proceedings* 5(54): 12–25.

Arthur, John
    1977   "Rights and the Duty to Bring Aid." In *World Hunger and Moral Obligation,* edited by William Aiken and Hugh LaFollette, 37–48. Englewood Cliffs, N.J.: Prentice-Hall.

Audi, Robert
    1973   "Intending." *Journal of Philosophy* 70(13): 387–403.
    1978   "The Moral Rights of the Terminally Ill." In *Contemporary Issues in Biomedical Ethics,* edited by John W. Davis, Barry Hoffmaster, and Sarah Shorten, 43–62. Clifton, N.J.: Humana Press.

1986   "Intending, Intentional Action, and Desire." In *The Ways of Desire,* edited by J. Marks, 17–38. Chicago: Precedent.
1988   "Deliberate Intentions and Willingness to Act: A Reply to Professor Mele." *Philosophia* 18(2 and 3): 243–45.

Baier, Annette
1985   "Secular Faith." In *Postures of the Mind: Essays on Mind and Morals,* 292–308. Minneapolis: University of Minnesota Press.

Bassen, Paul
1982   "Present Sakes and Future Prospects: The Status of Early Abortion." *Philosophy and Public Affairs* 11(4): 322–26.

Beauchamp, Tom L., and James F. Childress
1983   *Principles of Biomedical Ethics.* 2d ed. New York: Oxford University Press. 3d edition, 1989. 4th edition, 1994.

Beitz, Charles R.
1979   "Bounded Morality: Justice and the State in World Politics." *International Organization* 33(3): 405–24.
1980   "Nonintervention and Communal Integrity." *Philosophy and Public Affairs* 9(4): 385–91.

Belliotti, Raymond A.
1978   "Negative Duties, Positive Duties, and Rights." *Southern Journal of Philosophy* 16(1): 581–88.

Bennett, Jonathan
1971   "Whatever the Consequences." In *Moral Problems: A Collection of Philosophical Essays,* edited by James Rachels, 43–66. New York: Harper & Row.
1981   "Morality and Consequences." In *The Tanner Lectures on Human Values,* edited by S. M. McMurrin, vol. 2, 45–116. Salt Lake City: University of Utah Press.
1983   "Positive and Negative Relevance." *American Philosophical Quarterly* 20(2): 185–94.
1994   "Negation and Abstention: Two Theories of Allowing." In *Killing and Letting Die,* 2d ed., edited by Bonnie Steinbock and Alasdair Norcross, 230–56. New York: Fordham University Press.

Bleich, David
1960   "Abortion in Halakhic Literature." *Tradition* 10: 72–120.
1976   "Karen Ann Quinlan: A Torah Perspective." *Jewish Life* 1(3): 13–20.

Blumenfeld, Jean Beer
1981   "Causing Harm and Bringing Aid." *American Philosophical Quarterly* 18(4): 323–29.

Boorse, Christopher, and Roy A. Sorensen
1988   "Ducking Harm." *Journal of Philosophy* 85(3): 115–34.

Boyle, Joseph M., Jr.
1977a   "On Killing and Letting Die." *New Scholasticism* 51(4): 433–52.

1977b "Double-effect and a Certain Type of Embryotomy." *Irish Theological Quarterly* 44: 303–18.
1980   "Towards Understanding the Principle of Double Effect." *Ethics* 90(4): 527–38.
1984   "The Principle of Double Effect: Good Actions Entangled in Evil." In *Moral Theology Today,* edited by D. McCarthy, 243–60. St. Louis: Pope John XXIII Center.
1991a "Who Is Entitled to Double Effect?" *Journal of Medicine and Philosophy* 16(5): 475–93.
1991b "Further Thoughts on Double Effect: Some Preliminary Responses." *Journal of Medicine and Philosophy* 16(5): 565–69.

Brandt, R. B.
1972   "Utilitarianism and the Rules of War." *Philosophy and Public Affairs* 1(2): 145–61.

Bratman, Michael E.
1987   *Intention, Plans, and Practical Reason.* Cambridge: Harvard University Press.

Brock, Dan W.
1979   "Moral Rights and Permissible Killing." In *Ethical Issues Relating to Life and Death,* edited by John Ladd, 94–117. New York: Oxford University Press.
1981   "Moral Prohibitions and Consent." In *Action and Responsibility,* edited by Michael Brodie and Miles Brand. Bowling Green Series in Applied Philosophy. Bowling Green, Ohio: Bowling Green State University.
1985   "Taking Human Life." *Ethics* 95(4): 851–65.
1986   "Foregoing Life-Sustaining Food and Water: Is It Killing?" In *By No Extraordinary Means: The Choice to Forego Food and Water,* edited by J. Lynn, 117–31. Bloomington: Indiana University Press.
1989   "Death and Dying." In *Medical Ethics,* edited by R. Veatch, 329–56. Philadelphia: Jones and Bartlett.
1991   "Defending Moral Options." *Philosophy and Phenomenological Research* 51(4): 909–13.
1992   "Voluntary Active Euthanasia." *Hastings Center Report* 22(2): 10–22.
1993   *Life and Death: Philosophical Essays in Biomedical Ethics.* Cambridge: Cambridge University Press.

Brock, Dan W., and Allen E. Buchanan
1989   *Deciding for Others: The Ethics of Surrogate Decisionmaking.* New York: Cambridge University Press.

Brody, Baruch A.
1972   "Thompson on Abortion." *Philosophy and Public Affairs* 1(3): 335–40.
1973   "Abortion and the Sanctity of Life." In *The Problem of Abortion,* edited by Joel Feinberg, 104–20. Belmont, Calif.: Wadsworth.
1975   *Abortion and the Sanctity of Life: A Philosophical View.* Cambridge: MIT Press.

1978   "The Problem of Exceptions in Medical Ethics." In *Doing Evil to Achieve Good,* edited by Richard A. McCormick and Paul Ramsey, 54–68. Chicago: Loyola University Press.

1988   *Life and Death Decision Making.* New York: Oxford University Press.

Brown, Robert McAfee
1987   *Religion and Violence.* 2d ed. Philadelphia: Westminster Press.

Buchanan, Allen E.
1984   "What's So Special About Rights?" *Social Philosophy and Policy* 2(1): 61–83.

Cahill, Lisa Sowle
1977   "A 'Natural Law' Reconsideration of Euthanasia." *Linacre Quarterly* 44(1): 47–63.

1980   "Towards a Christian Theory of Human Rights." *Journal of Religious Ethics* 8(2): 277–301.

1981   "Teleology, Utilitarianism, and Christian Ethics." *Theological Studies* 42(4): 601–29.

1984   "Abortion, Autonomy, and Community." In *Abortion: Understanding Differences,* edited by Sydney and Daniel Callahan, 261–76. New York: Plenum Press.

1988   "Response to James Gustafson, 'The Consistent Life Ethic: A Protestant Response.'" In *Consistent Ethic of Life,* edited by Thomas G. Feuchtmann, 210–17. Kansas City, Mo.: Sheed and Ward.

1994   *Love Your Enemies: Discipleship, Pacifism, and Just War Theory.* Minneapolis: Fortress Press.

Camenish, Paul F.
1976   "Abortion, Analogies, and the Emergence of Value." *Journal of Religious Ethics* 4(1): 131–58.

Carney, Frederick
1978   "On McCormick and Teleological Morality." *Journal of Religious Ethics* 6(1): 81–107.

Carrier, L. S.
1975   "Abortion and the Right to Life." *Social Theory and Practice* 3(4): 381–401.

Casey, John
1971   "Actions and Consequences." In *Morality and Moral Reasoning,* edited by John Casey, 155–205. London: Methuen.

Chandler, John
1990   "Killing and Letting Die—Putting the Debate in Context." *Australasian Journal of Philosophy* 68(4): 420–31.

Childress, James F.
1974   "A Response to Conferred Rights and the Fetus." *Journal of Religious Ethics* 2(1): 77–83.

208   BIBLIOGRAPHY

1978a   Review of Michael Walzer, *Just and Unjust Wars*. *Bulletin of the Atomic Scientists* 34(8): 44–48.
1978b   "Who Shall Live When Not All Can Live?" In *Contemporary Issues in Bioethics*, edited by Tom L. Beauchamp and LeRoy Walters, 389–98. Encino, Calif.: Dickenson.
1982a   *Moral Responsibility in Conflicts: Essays On Nonviolence, War, and Conscience*. Baton Rouge: Louisiana State University Press.
1982b   *Who Should Decide? Paternalism in Health Care*. New York: Oxford University Press.
1986   "The Meaning of the Right to Life." In *Natural Rights and Natural Law: The Legacy of George Mason*, edited by Robert P. Davidow, 123–72. Fairfax, Va.: George Mason University Press.

Chisholm, Roderick M.
1977   "Coming into Being and Passing Away: Can the Metaphysician Help?" In *Philosophical Medical Ethics: Its Nature and Significance*, edited by S. F. Spicker and H. T. Engelhardt, 169–82. Dordecht: D. Reidel.

Churchill, Larry R., and José Jorge Simán
1982   "Abortion and the Rhetoric of Individual Rights." *Hastings Center Report* 12(1): 9–12.

Connery, John
1977   *Abortion: The Development of the Roman Catholic Perspective*. Chicago: Loyola University Press.

Costa, Michael J.
1986   "The Trolley Problem Revisited." *Southern Journal of Philosophy* 24(4): 437–49.
1987   "Another Trip on the Trolley." *Southern Journal of Philosophy* 25(4): 461–66.
1974   "Paul Ramsey and Traditional Roman Catholic Natural Law Theory." In *Love and Society: Essays in the Ethics of Paul Ramsey*, edited by James T. Johnson and David H. Smith, 47–65. Missoula: Scholars Press.

Curran, Charles
1974   "Paul Ramsey and Traditional Roman Catholic Natural Law Theory." In *Love and Society: Essays in the Ethics of Paul Ramsey*, edited by James T. Johnson and David H. Smith, 47–65. Missoula: Scholars Press.

Daube, David
1965   *Collaboration with Tyranny in Rabbinic Law*. London: Oxford University Press.
1987   "Appeasing or Resisting the Oppressor." In *Appeasement or Resistance and Other Essays on New Testament Judaism*, 75–119. Berkeley and Los Angeles: University of California Press.

Davis, Grady Scott
1992   *Warcraft and the Fragility of Virtue: An Essay in Aristotelian Ethics*. Moscow: University of Idaho Press.

Davis, Nancy (Ann)
1980   "The Priority of Avoiding Harm." In *Killing and Letting Die*, edited by Bonnie Steinbock, 172–214. Englewood Cliffs, N.J.: Prentice-Hall.

1984a "Abortion and Self-Defense." *Philosophy and Public Affairs* 13(3): 175–207.
1984b "The Doctrine of Double Effect: Some Problems of Interpretation." *Pacific Philosophical Quarterly* 65(2): 107–23.
1984c "Using Persons and Common Sense." *Ethics* 94(3): 387–406.
1988 "Rights and Moral Theory: A Critical Review of Judith Thomson's *Rights, Restitution, and Risk.*" *Ethics* 98(4): 806–26.
1993 "The Abortion Debate: The Search for Common Ground, Part 2." *Ethics* 103(4): 731–78.

Devine, Philip E.
1978 *The Ethics of Homicide.* Ithaca: Cornell University Press.

DiIanni, Albert
1977 "The Direct/Indirect Distinction in Morals." *Thomist* 61(3): 350–80.

Dinello, Daniel
1971 "On Killing and Letting Die." *Analysis* 31(3): 83–86.

Donagan, Alan
1977 *The Theory of Morality.* Chicago: University of Chicago Press.
1985 "Comments on Dan Brock and Terrence Reynolds." *Ethics* 95(4): 874–86.
1991 "Moral Absolutism and the Double-Effect Exception: Reflections on Joseph Boyle's 'Who Is Entitled to Double Effect?'" *Journal of Medicine and Philosophy* 16(5): 495–509.

Donceel, Joseph F.
1984 "A Liberal Catholic's View." In *The Problem of Abortion,* edited by Joel Feinberg, 2d ed., 15–20. Belmont, Calif.: Wadsworth.

Doppelt, Gerald
1978 "Walzer's Theory of Morality in International Relations." *Philosophy and Public Affairs* 8(1): 3–26.
1980 "Statism Without Foundations." *Philosophy and Public Affairs* 9(4): 398–403.

Dubik, James M.
1982 "Human Rights, Command Responsibility, and Walzer's Just War Theory." *Philosophy and Public Affairs* 11(4): 354–71.

Duff, R. A.
1973 "Intentionally Killing the Innocent." *Analysis* 34(1): 16–19.
1976 "Absolute Principles and Double Effect." *Analysis* 36(2): 68–80.
1982 "Intentions, Responsibility and Double Effect." *Philosophical Quarterly* 32(126): 1–16.

Dworkin, Ronald
1993 *Life's Dominion: An Argument About Abortion, Euthanasia, and Individual Freedom.* New York: Alfred A. Knopf.

Dyck, Arthur J.
1977 *On Human Care: An Introduction to Ethics.* Nashville, Tenn.: Abingdon.

Engelhardt, H. Tristram, Jr.
1974 "The Ontology of Abortion." *Ethics* 84(3): 217–34.

210   BIBLIOGRAPHY

1983   "Viability and the Use of the Fetus." In *Abortion and the Status of the Fetus,* edited by William Bondeson, H. Tristram Engelhardt, Jr., Stuart F. Spicker, and Daniel H. Winship, 183–208. Dordrecht: D. Reidel.
1986   *The Foundations of Bioethics.* New York: Oxford University Press.

Evans, Donald
1968   "Love, Situations, and Rules." In *Norm and Context in Christian Ethics,* edited by Gene Outka and Paul Ramsey, 367–414. New York: Charles Scribner's Sons.

Feezell, Randolph M.
1987   "Potentiality, Death, and Abortion." *Southern Journal of Philosophy* 25(1): 39–48.

Feinberg, Joel
1974   "The Rights of Animals and Unborn Generations" and "The Paradoxes of Potentiality." In *Philosophy and the Environmental Crisis,* edited by William T. Blackstone, 43–68. Athens: University of Georgia Press.
1976   "Is There a Right to Be Born?" In *Understanding Moral Philosophy,* edited by James Rachels, 346–57. Encino, Calif.: Dickenson. Reprint, 1980. In Joel Feinberg, *Rights, Justice, and the Bounds of Liberty: Essays in Social Philosophy.* Princeton: Princeton University Press, 183–216.
1980a   "Abortion." In *Matters of Life and Death: New Introductory Essays in Moral Philosophy,* edited by Tom Regan, 183–217. New York: Random House.
1980b   "Voluntary Euthanasia and the Inalienable Right to Life." In *Rights, Justice, and the Bounds of Liberty: Essays in Social Philosophy,* 221–51. Princeton: Princeton University Press.
1984   *Harm to Others: The Moral Limits of the Criminal Law.* New York: Oxford University Press.
1986   "Abortion." In *Matters of Life and Death: New Introductory Essays in Moral Philosophy,* edited by Tom Regan, 2d ed., 256–93. New York: Random House.

Feinberg, Joel, and Barbara Baum Levenbook
1993   "Abortion." In *Matters of Life and Death: New Introductory Essays in Moral Philosophy,* edited by Tom Regan, 3d ed., 195–234. New York: McGraw-Hill.

Feldman, David M.
1974   *Marital Relations, Birth Control, and Abortion in Jewish Law.* New York: Schocken Books.

Finnis, John
1988   "The Consistent Ethic—A Philosophical Critique." In *Consistent Ethic of Life,* edited by Thomas G. Feuchtmann, 141–81. Kansas City, Mo.: Sheed and Ward.

1991   *Moral Absolutes: Tradition, Revision, and Truth.* Washington, D.C.:
         Catholic University of America.

Finnis, John, Joseph Boyle, and Germain Grisez
    1987   *Nuclear Deterrence, Morality, and Realism.* New York: Oxford Univer-
            sity Press.

Fischer, John Martin, Mark Ravizza, and David Copp
    1993   "Quinn on Double Effect: The Problem of 'Closeness.'" *Ethics* 103(4):
            707–25.

Fletcher, George P.
    1980   "The Right to Life." *Monist* 63(2): 135–55.

Fletcher, J. C.
    1979   *Humanhood: Essays in Biomedical Ethics.* Buffalo, N.Y.: Prometheus
            Books.

Foot, Philippa
    1978   *Virtues and Vices and Other Essays in Moral Philosophy.* Berkeley and
            Los Angeles: University of California Press.
    1981   "Killing, Letting Die, and Euthanasia: A Reply to Holly Smith Goldman."
            Analysis 41(3): 159–60.
    1983a   "Moral Realism and Moral Dilemma." *Journal of Philosophy* 80(7):
            379–98.
    1983b   "Utilitarianism and the Virtues." Presidential address to the American
            Philosophical Association, Pacific Division. *Proceedings and Addresses of
            the A.P.A.* 57(2): 273–83.
    1984   "Killing and Letting Die." In *Abortion: Moral and Legal Perspectives,*
            edited by Joy L. Garfield and Patricia Hennessey, 177–85. Amherst: Uni-
            versity of Massachusetts Press.
    1985   "Morality, Action, and Outcome." In *Morality and Objectivity: A Tribute
            to J. L. Mackie,* edited by Ted Honderich, 23–38. London: Routledge and
            Kegan Paul.

Ford, John C.
    1970   "The Morality of Obliteration Bombing." In *War and Morality,* edited by
            Richard A. Wasserstrom, 15–41. Belmont, Calif.: Wadsworth. Originally
            published 1944, *Theological Studies* 5(3): 261–309.

Frankena, William K.
    1955   "Natural and Inalienable Rights." *Philosophical Review* 64(2): 212–32.

Frey, R. G.
    1975   "Some Aspects to the Doctrine of Double Effect." *Canadian Journal of
            Philosophy* 5(2): 259–83.
    1983   "Killing and the Doctrine of Double Effect." Chap. 13 in *Rights, Killing,*

     and Suffering: Moral Vegetarianism and Applied Ethics. Oxford: Basil
     Blackwell.

Fried, Charles
    1978   *Right and Wrong.* Cambridge, Mass.: Harvard University Press.

Fullinwider, Robert K.
    1975   "War and Innocence." *Philosophy and Public Affairs* 5(1): 90–97.

Geddes, Leonard
    1972   "On the Intrinsic Wrongness of Killing People." *Analysis* 33(3): 93–97.

Gendler, Everett E.
    1978   "War and the Jewish Tradition." In *Contemporary Jewish Ethics,* edited
        by Menachem Marc Kellner, 189–210. New York: Sanhedrin Press.

Gert, Bernard
    1977   Review of Alan Donagan, *The Theory of Morality. Journal of Medicine
        and Philosophy* 2(4): 410–19.
    1993   "Transplants and Trolleys." *Philosophy and Phenomenological Research*
        53(1): 173–79.

Gewirth, Alan
    1978   *Reason and Morality.* Chicago: University of Chicago Press.
    1982a "Starvation and Human Rights." In *Human Rights: Essays on Justifica-
        tions and Applications,* 197–217. Chicago: University of Chicago Press.
    1982b "Are There Any Absolute Rights?" In *Human Rights: Essays on Justifica-
        tions and Applications,* 218–33. Chicago: University of Chicago Press.
    1993   "Common Morality and the Community of Rights." In *Prospects for a
        Common Morality,* edited by Gene Outka and John P. Reeder Jr., 29–52.
        Princeton: Princeton University Press.

Gibson, Roger F.
    1984   "On an Inconsistency in Thomson's Abortion Argument." *Philosophical
        Studies* 46(1): 131–39.

Gillespie, Norman C.
    1977   "Abortion and Human Rights." *Ethics* 87(3): 237–43.

Gilligan, Carol
    1982   *In a Different Voice: Psychological Theory and Women's Development.*
        Cambridge, Mass.: Harvard University Press.

Glover, Jonathan
    1977   *Causing Death and Saving Lives.* New York: Penguin Books.

Gorr, Michael
    1985   "Some Reflections on the Difference Between Positive and Negative Du-

ties." In *Positive and Negative Duties*. Tulane Studies in Philosophy, vol. 33, 93–100. New Orleans: Tulane University Press.

Green, Michael B., and Daniel Wikler
1980   "Brain Death and Personal Identity." *Philosophy and Public Affairs* 9(2): 105–33.

Green, O. H.
1979   "Refraining and Responsibility." In *Studies in Action Theory*. Tulane Studies in Philosophy, vol. 28, 103–13. New Orleans: Tulane University Press.
1980   "Killing and Letting Die." *American Philosophical Quarterly* 17(3): 195–204.

Green, Ronald M.
1974   "Conferred Rights and the Fetus." *Journal of Religious Ethics* 2(1): 55–75.
1983   "Toward a Copernican Revolution in Our Thinking About Life's Beginning and Life's End." *Soundings* 66(2): 152–73.

Greenberg, Moshe
1978   "Rabbinic Reflections on Defying Illegal Orders: Amasa, Abner, and Joab." In *Contemporary Jewish Ethics,* edited by Menachem Marc Kellner, 211–20. New York: Sanhedrin Press.

Griffin, Leslie
1989   "The Problem of Dirty Hands." *Journal of Religious Ethics* 17(1): 31–62.

Grisez, Germain G.
1970a "Towards a Consistent Natural Law Ethics of Killing." *Natural Law Forum (American Journal of Jurisprudence)* 15: 64–96.
1970b "Ethical Arguments." Chap. 6 in *Abortion: The Myths, the Realities, and the Arguments*. New York: Corpus Books.

Grisez, Germain G., and Joseph M. Boyle Jr.
1979   *Life and Death with Liberty and Justice: A Contribution to the Euthanasia Debate*. Notre Dame, Ind.: University of Notre Dame Press.

Gruzalski, Bart K.
1988   "Death by Omission." In *Moral Theory and Moral Judgments in Medical Ethics,* edited by Baruch A. Brody, 75–86. Dordrecht: Kluwer Academic Publishers.

Gustafson, James M.
1981   *Ethics from a Theocentric Perspective*. Vol. 1, *Theology and Ethics*. Chicago: University of Chicago Press.
1988   "The Consistent Ethic of Life: A Protestant Prospective." In *Consistent*

Ethic of Life, edited by Thomas G. Feuchtmann, 196–209. Kansas City, Mo.: Sheed and Ward.

Hanink, James G.
1975   "Some Light on Double Effect." *Analysis* 35(5): 147–51.

Hare, R. M.
1972   "Rules of War and Moral Reasoning." *Philosophy and Public Affairs* 1(2): 166–82.
1975   "Abortion and the Golden Rule." *Philosophy and Public Affairs* 4(3): 201–22.

Harman, Gilbert
1977   *The Nature of Morality: An Introduction to Ethics.* New York: Oxford University Press.
1993   "Stringency of Rights and 'Ought.'" *Philosophy and Phenomenological Research* 53(1): 181–85.

Harris, John
1980a   *Violence and Responsibility.* London: Routledge and Kegan Paul.
1980b   "The Survival Lottery." In *Killing and Letting Die,* edited by Bonnie Steinbock, 149–55. Englewood Cliffs, N.J.: Prentice-Hall. Originally published 1975, *Philosophy* 50(191): 81–87.
1982   "Bad Samaritans Cause Harm." *Philosophical Quarterly* 32(126): 60–69.

Harrison, Beverly Wildung
1983   *Our Right to Choose: Towards a New Ethic of Abortion.* Boston: Beacon Press.

Hart, H.L.A.
1968   "Intention and Punishment." Chap. 5 in *Punishment and Responsibility.* Oxford: Oxford University Press.

Hauerwas, Stanley
1992   *Against the Nations: War and Survival in a Liberal Society.* Notre Dame, Ind.: University of Notre Dame Press.

Hoffman, Robert
1984   "Intention, Double Effect, and Single Result." *Philosophy and Phenomenological Research* 44(3): 389–94.

Hollenbach, David
1979   *Claims in Conflict: Retrieving and Renewing the Catholic Human Rights Tradition.* New York: Paulist Press.

Holmes, Robert
1989   *On War and Morality.* Princeton: Princeton University Press.

James, Susan
1982   "The Duty to Relieve Suffering." *Ethics* 93(1): 4–21.

Johnson, James Turner
1973   "Toward Reconstructing the *Jus ad Bellum.*" *Monist* 57(4): 461–88.

1981   *Just War Tradition and the Restraint of War: A Moral and Historical Inquiry.* Princeton: Princeton University Press.
1984   *Can Modern War Be Just?* New Haven: Yale University Press.
1991a "Historical Roots and Sources of the Just War Tradition in Western Culture." In *Just War and Jihad: Historical and Theoretical Perspectives on War and Peace in Western and Islamic Traditions,* edited by John Kelsay and James Turner Johnson, 3–30. New York: Greenwood Press.
1991b "Just War in the Thought of Paul Ramsey." *Journal of Religious Ethics* 19(2): 183–207.

Jung, Patricia Beattie, and Thomas A. Shannon, eds.
1988   *Abortion and Catholicism: The American Debate.* New York: Crossroads.

Kadish, S.
1976   "Respect for Life and Regard for Rights in the Criminal Law." *California Law Review* 64: 871–901.
1977   "Justification and Excuse in the Judaic and Common Law." *NYU Law Review* 52: 173–77.

Kagan, Shelly
1987   "Donagan on the Sins of Consequentialism." *Canadian Journal of Philosophy* 17(3): 643–53.
1988a "Causation and Responsibility." *American Philosophical Quarterly* 25(4): 293–302.
1988b "The Additive Fallacy." *Ethics* 99(1): 5–31.
1989   *The Limits of Morality.* Oxford: Oxford University Press.
1991a "Précis of *The Limits of Morality.*" *Philosophy and Phenomenological Research* 51(4): 897–901.
1991b "Replies to My Critics." *Philosophy and Phenomenological Research* 51(4): 919–28.

Kamm, F. M.
1982   "The Right to Abortion." In *Ethics for Modern Life,* edited by R. Abelson and M. L. Friquegnon, 103–16. New York: St. Martin's Press.
1986   "Harming, Not Aiding, and Positive Rights." *Philosophy and Public Affairs* 15(1): 3–32.
1989   "Harming Some to Save Others." *Philosophical Studies* 57(3): 227–60.
1991a "The Doctrine of Double Effect: Reflections on Theoretical and Practical Issues." *Journal of Medicine and Philosophy* 16(5): 571–85.
1991b "Shelly Kagan's *The Limits of Morality.*" *Philosophy and Phenomenological Research* 51(4): 903–7.
1992   *Creation and Abortion: A Study in Moral and Legal Philosophy.* New York: Oxford University Press.
1993   *Morality, Mortality.* Vol. 1, *Death and Whom to Save from It.* New York: Oxford University Press.

Kenny, Anthony
1966   "Intention and Purpose." *Journal of Philosophy* 63(20): 642–51.
1975   *Will, Freedom and Power.* Oxford: Basil Blackwell.

1985   *The Logic of Deterrence: A Philosopher Looks at the Arguments for and Against Nuclear Disarmament.* Chicago: University of Chicago Press.

Kilner, John
1990   *Who Lives, Who Dies.* New Haven: Yale University Press.

Kleinig, John
1976   "Good Samaritanism." *Philosophy and Public Affairs* 5(4): 382–407.

Kluge, Eike-Henner W.
1975   *The Practice of Death.* New Haven: Yale University Press.

Konvitz, Milton R.
1978   "Conscience and Civil Disobedience in the Jewish Tradition." In *Contemporary Jewish Ethics,* edited by Menachem Marc Kellner, 239–54. New York: Sanhedrin Press.

Kuhse, Helga
1987   *The Sanctity-of-Life Doctrine in Medicine: A Critique.* Oxford: Clarendon Press.

Ladd, John
1979   "Positive and Negative Euthanasia." In *Ethical Issues Relating to Life and Death,* edited by John Ladd, 164–86. New York: Oxford University Press.

Lammers, Stephen E.
1983   "Area Bombing in World War II: The Argument of Michael Walzer." *Journal of Religious Ethics* 11(1): 96–113.
1990   "Approaches to Limits on War in Western Just War Discourse." In *Cross, Crescent, and Sword: The Justification and Limitation of War in Western and Islamic Tradition,* edited by James Turner Johnson and John Kelsay, 51–78. New York: Greenwood Press.

Langan, John
1979   "Direct and Indirect—Some Recent Exchanges Between Paul Ramsey and Richard McCormick." *Religious Studies Review* 5(2): 95–101.

Langerak, Edward
1973   "Correspondence." *Philosophy and Public Affairs* 2(4): 410–16.

Levi, Don S.
1987   "Hypothetical Cases and Abortion." *Social Theory and Practice* 13(1): 17–48.

Levine, Michael P.
1988   "Coffee and Casuistry: It Doesn't Matter Who Caused What." In *Moral*

Theory and Moral Judgments in Medical Ethics, edited by Baruch A. Brody, 87–98. Dordrecht: Kluwer Academic Publishers.

Levine, Susan
   1984   "The Moral Permissibility of Killing a 'Material Aggressor' in Self-Defense." *Philosophical Studies* 45(1): 69–78.

Levy, Sanford S.
   1985   "Richard McCormick and Proportionate Reason." *Journal of Religious Ethics* 13(2): 258–78.

Lichtenberg, Judith
   1982   "The Moral Equivalence of Action and Omission." *Canadian Journal of Philosophy* suppl. vol. 8: 19–35.
   1994   "War, Innocence, and the Doctrine of Double Effect." *Philosophical Studies* 74: 347–68.

Little, David
   1986   "Natural Rights and Human Rights: The International Imperative." In *Natural Rights and Natural Law: The Legacy of George Mason,* edited by Robert P. Davidow, 67–122. Fairfax, Va.: George Mason University Press.
   1993   "The Nature and Basis of Human Rights." In *Prospects for a Common Morality,* edited by Gene Outka and John P. Reeder Jr., 73–92. Princeton: Princeton University Press.

Lomasky, Loren E.
   1984   "Being a Person—Does It Matter?" In *The Problem of Abortion,* edited by Joel Feinberg, 2d ed., 161–72. Belmont, Calif.: Wadsworth.
   1987   *Persons, Rights, and the Moral Community.* New York: Oxford University Press.

Luban, David
   1985a "Just War and Human Rights." In *International Ethics: A Philosophy and Public Affairs Reader,* edited by Charles R. Beitz, Marshall Cohen, Thomas Scanlon, and A. John Simmons, 195–216. Princeton: Princeton University Press.
   1985b "The Romance of the Nation-State." In *International Ethics: A Philosophy and Public Affairs Reader,* 238–43. Princeton: Princeton University Press.

Lyons, David, ed.
   1979   *Rights.* Belmont, Calif.: Wadsworth.

McCloskey, H. J.
   1975   "The Right to Life." *Mind* 84(335): 403–25.

McCormick, Richard A.
   1968   "Past Church Teaching on Abortion." *Proceedings of the Catholic Theological Society of America* 23: 131–51.
   1978a "Ambiguity in Moral Choice." In *Doing Evil to Achieve Good: Moral*

Choice in Conflict Situations, edited by Richard A. McCormick and Paul Ramsey, 7–53. Chicago: Loyola University Press.

1978b   "A Commentary on the Commentaries." In *Doing Evil to Achieve Good: Moral Choice in Conflict Situations,* edited by Richard A. McCormick and Paul Ramsey, 193–267. Chicago: Loyola University Press.

1981a   *How Brave a New World? Dilemmas in Bioethics.* Garden City, N.J.: Doubleday. Reprinted 1985. Washington, D.C.: Georgetown University Press.

1981b   *Notes on Moral Theology 1965–1980.* Lanham, Md.: University Press of America.

1984   *Notes on Moral Theology 1981–1984.* Boston: University Press of America.

1989   "The Consistent Ethic of Life: Is There a Historical Soft Underbelly?" In *The Critical Calling,* 211–32. Washington, D.C.: Georgetown University Press.

Macdonald, I. A.
1984   "The Principle of Double Effect." *South African Journal of Philosophy* 3(Fall): 1–7.

McInerney, Peter K.
1994   "Does the Fetus Already Have a Future-Like-Ours?" In *The Abortion Controversy: A Reader,* edited by Louis P. Pojman and Francis J. Beckwith, 339–42. Boston: Jones and Bartlett.

MacIntyre, Alasdair
1984   *After Virtue.* 2d ed. Notre Dame, Ind.: University of Notre Dame Press.

McMahan, Jeff
1993   "Killing, Letting Die, and Withdrawing Aid." *Ethics* 103(2): 250–79.

Mack, Eric
1976   "Causing and Failing to Prevent." *Southwest Journal of Philosophy* 7: 83–90.

1980   "Bad Samaritanism and the Causation of Harm." *Philosophy and Public Affairs* 9: 230–59.

1984   "Deontologism, Negative Causation, and the Duty to Rescue." In *Gewirth's Ethical Rationalism: Critical Essays with a Reply by Alan Gewirth,* edited by E. Regis Jr., 147–66. Chicago: University of Chicago Press.

1985   "Three Ways to Kill Innocent Bystanders: Some Conundrums Concerning the Morality of War." *Social Philosophy and Policy* 3(1): 1–26.

1988   "Moral Rights and Causal Casuistry." In *Moral Theory and Moral Judgments in Medical Ethics,* edited by Baruch A. Brody, 57–74. Dordrecht: Kluwer Academic Publishers.

1993   "Of Transplants and Trolleys." *Philosophy and Phenomenological Research* 53(1): 163–67.

Macklin, Ruth
1984   "Personhood and the Abortion Debate." In *Abortion: Moral and Legal*

Perspectives, edited by Jay L. Garfield and Patricia Hennessey, 81–102. Amherst: University of Massachusetts Press.

Malm, H. H.
1989   "Killing, Letting Die, and Simple Conflicts." *Philosophy and Public Affairs* 18(3): 238–58.
1990   "Directions of Justification in the Negative-Positive Duty Debate." *American Philosophical Quarterly* 27(4): 315–24.

Mangan, Joseph T.
1949   "An Historical Analysis of the Principle of Double Effect." *Theological Studies* 10(1): 41–60.

Marquis, Donald B.
1989   "Why Abortion Is Immoral." *Journal of Philosophy* 86(4): 183–202.
1991   "Four Versions of Double Effect." *Journal of Medicine and Philosophy* 16(5): 515–44.
1994   "A Future Like Ours and the Concept of Person: A Reply to McInerney and Paske." In *The Abortion Controversy: A Reader,* edited by Louis P. Pojman and Francis J. Beckwith, 354–68. Boston: Jones and Bartlett.

Mavrodes, George I.
1975   "Conventions and the Morality of War." *Philosophy and Public Affairs* 4(2): 117–31.

Meilaender, Gilbert C.
1987.   *The Limits of Love: Some Theological Explorations.* University Park: The Pennsylvania State University Press.
1991   "'Love's Casuistry': Paul Ramsey on Caring for the Terminally Ill." *Journal of Religious Ethics* 19(2): 133–56.

Melden, A. I.
1977   *Rights and Persons.* Berkeley and Los Angeles: University of California Press.

Mele, Alfred R.
1988   "Against a Belief/Desire Analysis of Intention." *Philosophia* 18(2 and 3): 239–42.

Michaels, Meredith W.
1984   "Abortion and the Claims of Samaritanism." In *Abortion: Moral and Legal Perspectives,* edited by Jay L. Garfield and Patricia Hennessey, 213–70. Amherst: University of Massachusetts Press.

Miller, Richard B.
1991   *Interpretations of Conflict: Ethics, Pacifism, and the Just-War Tradition.* Chicago: University of Chicago Press.

Montague, Phillip
1981   "Self-Defense and Choosing Between Lives." *Philosophical Studies* 40(2): 207–19.

Montaldi, Daniel F.
1986   "A Defense of St. Thomas and the Principle of Double Effect." *Journal of Religious Ethics* 14(2): 296–332.

Montmarquet, James
    1982   "On Doing Good: The Right and the Wrong Way." *Journal of Philosophy* 79(8): 439–55.

Morillo, Carolyn R.
    1977   "Doing, Refraining, and the Strenuousness of Morality." *American Philosophical Quarterly* 14(1): 29–39.

Murphy, Jeffrie G.
    1973   "The Killing of the Innocent." *Monist* 57(4): 527–51.

Nagel, Thomas
    1972   "War and Massacre." *Philosophy and Public Affairs* 1(2): 123–44.
    1980   "The Limits of Objectivity." In *The Tanner Lectures on Human Values,* vol. 1, edited by S. M. McMurrin. Salt Lake: University of Utah Press.
    1986   *The View from Nowhere.* New York: Oxford Unviversity Press.

Nelson, James A.
    1985   "Recent Studies in Animal Ethics." *American Philosophical Quarterly* 22(1): 3–24.

Newman, Louis E.
    1987   "The Quality of Mercy: On the Duty to Forgive in the Judaic Tradition." *Journal of Religious Ethics* 15(2): 155–72.
    1989   "Law, Virtue and Supererogation in the Halakha: The Problem of 'Lifnim Mishurat Hadin' Reconsidered." *Journal of Jewish Studies* 60(1): 61–88.
    1990   "Woodchoppers and Respirators: The Problem of Interpretation in Contemporary Jewish Ethics." *Modern Judaism* 10(1): 17–42.

Nicholson, Susan Teft
    1978   *Abortion and the Roman Catholic Church. Journal of Religious Ethics: Studies in Religious Ethics,* vol. 1. Knoxville: University of Tennessee.

Nielsen, Kai
    1973   *Ethics Without God.* Buffalo, N.Y.: Prometheus Books. Revised ed., 1990.

Noddings, Nel
    1984   *Caring: A Feminine Approach to Ethics and Moral Education.* Berkeley and Los Angeles: University of California Press.

O'Brien, William V.
    1981   *The Conduct of Just and Limited War.* New York: Praeger.

O'Neill, Onora
    1977   "Lifeboat Earth." In *World Hunger and Moral Obligation,* edited by William Aiken and Hugh LaFollette, 148–64. Englewood Cliffs, N.J.: Prentice-Hall.
    1986   *Faces of Hunger: An Essay on Poverty, Justice and Development.* London: Allen and Unwin.
    1993   "Ending World Hunger." In *Matters of Life and Death: New Introduc-*

tory Essays in Moral Philosophy, 3d ed., edited by Tom Regan, chap. 7. New York: McGraw-Hill.

Otsuka, Michael
1994   "Killing the Innocent in Self-Defense." Philosophy and Public Affairs 23(1): 74–94.

Otten, James
1976   "Even If One Were Letting Another Innocent Person Die." Southern Journal of Philosophy 14(3): 313–22.

Outka, Gene
1968   "Character, Conduct, and the Love Commandment." In Norm and Context in Christian Ethics, edited by Gene Outka and Paul Ramsey, 37–66. New York: Charles Scribner's Sons.
1992   "Universal Love and Impartiality." In The Love Commandments: Essays in Christian Ethics and Moral Philosophy, edited by Edmund N. Santurri and William Werpehowski, 1–92. Washington, D.C.: Georgetown University Press.

Outka, Gene, and John P. Reeder Jr., eds.
1993   Prospects for a Common Morality. Princeton: Princeton University Press.

Pahel, Kenneth R.
1987   "Michael Tooley on Abortion and Potentiality." Southern Journal of Philosophy 25(1): 89–107.

Palmer-Fernandez, Gabriel
1993   "Heaven's Fall: Michael Walzer on Killing the Innocent." International Journal of Applied Philosophy 8(1): 57–63.

Parent, W. A.
1980   "Judith Thomson and the Logic of Rights." Philosophical Studies 37(4): 405–18.

Parsons, Kathryn Pyne
1979   "Moral Revolution." In The Prism of Sex: Essays in the Sociology of Knowledge, edited by Julia A. Sherman and Evelyn T. Beck, 189–227. Madison: University of Wisconsin Press.

Paske, Gerald H.
1994   "Abortion and the Neo-Natal Right to Life: A Critique of Marquis's Futurist Argument." In The Abortion Controversy: A Reader, edited by Louis P. Pojman and Francis J. Beckwith, 343–53. Boston: Jones and Bartlett.

Petchesky, Rosalind P.
1984   Abortion and Woman's Choice: The State, Sexuality and Reproductive

Freedom. New York: Longman. Reprint, 1990. Boston: Northeastern University Press.

Quinn, Warren S.
1989a "Actions, Intentions, and Consequences: The Doctrine of Doing and Allowing." *Philosophical Review* 98(3): 287–312.
1989b "Actions, Intentions, and Consequences: The Doctrine of Double Effect." *Philosophy and Public Affairs* 18(1): 334–51.
1991   "Reply to Boyle's 'Who Is Entitled to Double Effect?'" *Journal of Medicine and Philosophy* 16(5): 511–14.

Rachels, James
1975   "Active and Passive Euthanasia." *New England Journal of Medicine* 292 (9 January): 78–80.
1979   "Killing and Starving to Death." *Philosophy* 54(208): 159–71.
1986   *The End of Life: Euthanasia and Morality.* New York: Oxford University Press.

Ramsey, Paul
1961   *War and the Christian Conscience.* Durham, N.C.: Duke University Press.
1968   *The Just War: Force and Political Responsibility.* New York: Charles Scribner's Sons.
1970a *The Patient as Person.* New Haven: Yale University Press.
1970b "Reference Points in Deciding About Abortion." In *The Morality of Abortion: Legal and Historical Perspectives,* edited by John T. Noonan Jr., 60–100. Cambridge: Harvard University Press.
1971   "The Morality of Abortion." In *Moral Problems: A Collection of Philosophical Essays,* edited by James Rachels, 3–27. New York: Harper & Row.
1973   "Abortion: A Review Article." *Thomist* 37(1): 174–226.
1978a *Ethics at the Edges of Life: Medical and Legal Intersections.* New Haven: Yale University Press.
1978b "Incommensurability and Indeterminacy in Moral Choice." In *Doing Evil to Achieve Good,* edited by Richard A. McCormick and Paul Ramsey, 69–144. Chicago: Loyola University Press.
1988   *Speak Up for Just War or Pacifism: A Critique of the United Bishops' Pastoral Letter "In Defense of Creation."* Epilogue by Stanley Hauerwas. University Park: Pennsylvania State University Press.

Reeder, John P., Jr.
1979   "Respect for Rational Creatures." [Review of Donagan, *The Theory of Morality*] *Journal of Religion* 59(1): 94–103.
1982   "Beneficence, Supererogation, and Role Duty." In *Beneficence and Health Care,* edited by Earl Shelp, 83–108. Dordrecht: D. Reidel.
1990   "Individualism, Communitarianism, and Theories of Justice." In *Ethics, Wealth, and Salvation: A Study in Buddhist Social Ethics,* edited by Russell Sizemore and Donald Swearers, 235–52, 273–80, 291–96. Columbia: University of South Carolina Press.
1992   "Analogues to Justice." In *The Love Commandments: Essays in Christian Ethics and Moral Philosophy,* edited by Edmund N. Santurri and William Werpehowski, 281–307. Washington, D.C.: Georgetown University Press.

1994   "Three Moral Traditions." *Journal of Religious Ethics* 22(1): 75–92.

Regan, Donald H.
1979   "Rewriting Roe v. Wade." *Michigan Law Review* 77: 1569–1646.

Regan, Tom
1983   *The Case for Animal Rights*. Berkeley and Los Angeles: University of California Press.

Rescher, Nicholas
1978   "The Allocation of Exotic Medical Lifesaving Therapy." In *Contemporary Issues in Bioethics,* edited by Tom L. Beauchamp and LeRoy Walters, 378–89. Encino, Calif.: Dickenson.

Reynolds, Terrence
1985   "Moral Absolutism and Abortion: Alan Donagan on the Hysterectomy and Craniotomy Cases." *Ethics* 95(4): 866–73.

Richards, David A. J.
1971   *A Theory of Reasons for Action*. Oxford: Clarendon Press.

Richards, Jerald H.
1980   "Alan Donagan, Hebrew-Christian Morality, and Capital Punishment." *Journal of Religious Ethics* 8(2): 302–29.

Richards, Norvin
1984   "Double Effect and Moral Character." *Mind* 93(371): 381–97.

Rosner, Fred
1978   "The Jewish Attitude Toward Abortion." In *Contemporary Jewish Ethics,* edited by Menachem Marc Kellner, 257–69. New York: Sanhedrin Press.

Russell, Bruce
1977   "On the Relative Strictness of Positive and Negative Duties." *American Philosophical Quarterly* 14(2): 87–97.
1978   "Still a Live Issue." *Philosophy and Public Affairs* 7(3): 278–81.
1979   "Presumption, Intrinsic Relevance, and Equivalence." *Journal of Medicine and Philosophy* 4(3): 263–68.
1993   "Exploring *The Realm of Rights.*" *Philosophy and Phenomenological Research* 53(1): 169–72.

Ryan, Cheyney C.
1983   "Self-Defense, Pacifism, and the Possibility of Killing." *Ethics* 93(3): 508–24.

Santurri, Edmund N.
1987   *Perplexity in the Moral Life: Philosophical and Theological Considerations*. Charlottesville: University of Virginia Press.
1992   "Who Is My Neighbor? Love, Equality, and Profoundly Retarded Humans." In *The Love Commandments: Essays in Christian Ethics and*

Moral Philosophy, edited by Edmund N. Santurri and William Werpehowski, 104–37. Washington, D.C.: Georgetown University Press.

Santurri, Edmund N., and William Werpehowski
1982   "Substituted Judgment and the Terminally-Ill Incompetent." *Thought* 57(227): 484–501.

Scholz, Franz
1977   "Objekt und Umstände, Wesenswirkungen und Nebeneffekte." In *Christlich Glauben und Handeln,* edited by Klaus Demmer and Bruno Schüller, 243–60. Düsseldorf, Germany: Patmos.

Schüller, Bruno
1970   "Zur Problematik allgemein verbindlicher ethischer Grundsätzen." *Theologie und Philosophie* 45: 1–23.
1978   "The Double Effect in Catholic Thought: A Reevaluation." In *Doing Evil to Achieve Good,* edited by Richard A. McCormick and Paul Ramsey, 145–64. Chicago: Loyola University Press.
1979   "Various Types of Grounding for Ethical Norms." In *Readings in Moral Theology No. 1: Moral Norms and Catholic Traditions,* edited by Charles E. Curran and Richard A. McCormick, 184–98. New York: Paulist Press.

Schwartz, Adina
1979   "Review of Alan Gewirth, *Reason and Morality.*" *Philosophical Review* 88(4): 654–56.

Sen, Amartya
1982   "Rights and Agency." *Philosophy and Public Affairs* 11(1): 3–39.

Sheehan, Neil
1988   *A Bright Shining Lie: John Paul Vann and America in Vietnam.* New York: Random House.

Shue, Henry
1980   *Basic Rights: Subsistence, Affluence, and U.S. Foreign Policy.* Princeton: Princeton University Press.

Shun, Kwong-Loi
1985   "Intending as a Means." *Pacific Philosophical Quarterly* 66 (1 and 2): 216–23.

Singer, Peter
1977a   "Famine, Affluence, and Morality." In *World Hunger and Moral Obligation,* edited by William Aiken and Hugh LaFollette, 22–36. Englewood Cliffs, N.J.: Prentice-Hall.
1977b   "Reconsidering the Famine Relief Argument." In *Food Policy: The Responsibility of the United States in the Life and Death Choices,* edited by Peter Brown and Henry Shue, 36–53. New York: Free Press.

1979   *Practical Ethics*. Cambridge: Cambridge University Press.

Slote, Michael
1991   "Shelly Kagan's *The Limits of Morality*." *Philosophy and Phenomeno-logical Research* 51(4): 915–17.

Smart, J.J.C., and Bernard Williams
1973   *Utilitarianism: For and Against*. London: Cambridge University Press.

Steffen, Lloyd
1994   *Life Choice: A Theory of Just Abortion*. Cleveland: Pilgrim Press.

Steinbock, Bonnie
1980   "The Intentional Termination of Life." In *Killing and Letting Die*, edited by Bonnie Steinbock, 69–77. Englewood Cliffs, N.J.: Prentice-Hall.

Stout, Jeffrey
1990   "Justice and Resort to War: A Sampling of Christian Ethical Thinking." In *Cross, Crescent, and Sword: The Justification and Limitation of War in Western and Islamic Tradition*, edited by James Turner Johnson and John Kelsay, 3–33. New York: Greenwood Press.
1991   "Ramsey and Others on Nuclear Ethics." *Journal of Religious Ethics* 19(2): 209–38.

Sullivan, Joseph V.
1975   "The Immorality of Euthanasia." In *Beneficent Euthanasia*, edited by Marvin Kohl, 12–33. Buffalo, N.Y.: Prometheus Books.

Sumner, L. W.
1981   *Abortion and Moral Theory*. Princeton: Princeton University Press.
1984   "A Third Way." In *The Problem of Abortion*, edited by Joel Feinberg, 2d ed., 71–93. Belmont, Calif.: Wadsworth.

Taurek, John M.
1977   "Should the Numbers Count?" *Philosophy and Public Affairs* 6(4): 293–316.

Taylor, Paul W.
1986   *Respect for Nature: A Theory of Environmental Ethics*. Princeton: Princeton University Press.

Thomson, Judith Jarvis
1973   "Rights and Deaths." *Philosophy and Public Affairs* 2(2): 146–59. Reprinted 1986, in Judith Jarvis Thomson, *Rights, Restitution and Risk: Essays in Moral Theory*, edited by William Parent, 20–32. Cambridge: Harvard University Press.
1975   "Killing, Letting Die, and the Trolley Problem." *Monist* 59(2): 204–17. Reprinted 1986, in Thomson, *Rights, Restitution and Risk*, edited by William Parent, 78–93. Cambridge: Harvard University Press.

1976   "Self-Defense and Rights." University of Kansas: The Lindley Lecture: 3–18. Reprinted 1986, in Thomson, *Rights, Restitution and Risk,* edited by William Parent, 33–48. Cambridge: Harvard University Press.
1980   "Rights and Compensation." *Nous* 14(1): 3–15. Reprinted 1986, in Thomson, *Rights, Restitution and Risk,* edited by William Parent, 66–77. Cambridge: Harvard University Press.
1984   "A Defense of Abortion." In *The Problem of Abortion,* edited by Joel Feinberg, 2d ed., 173–87. Belmont, Calif.: Wadsworth. Originally published 1971, *Philosophy and Public Affairs* 1(1): 47–66. Reprinted 1986, in Thomson, *Rights, Restitution and Risk,* edited by William Parent, 1–19. Cambridge: Harvard University Press.
1986   "The Trolley Problem." In *Rights, Restitution and Risk,* edited by William Parent, 44–116. Cambridge: Harvard University Press.
1990   "The Trolley Problem." Chap. 7 in *The Realm of Rights.* Cambridge: Harvard University Press.
1991   "Self-Defense." *Philosophy and Public Affairs* 20(4): 283–310.
1993a   "Précis of *The Realm of Rights.*" *Philosophy and Phenomenological Research* 53(1): 159–62.
1993b   "Reply to Commentators." *Philosophy and Phenomenological Research* 53(1): 187–94.

Tooley, Michael
1973a   "Correspondence." *Philosophy and Public Affairs* 2(4): 419–32.
1973b   "A Defense of Abortion and Infanticide." In *The Problem of Abortion,* edited by Joel Feinberg, 51–91. Belmont, Calif.: Wadsworth.
1980   "An Irrelevant Consideration: Killing Versus Letting Die." In *Killing and Letting Die,* edited by Bonnie Steinbock, 56–62. Englewood Cliffs, N.J.: Prentice-Hall.
1983   *Abortion and Infanticide.* New York: Oxford University Press.
1984   "In Defense of Abortion and Infanticide." In *The Problem of Abortion,* edited by Joel Feinberg, 2d ed., 120–34. Belmont, Calif.: Wadsworth.

Trammel, Richard L.
1975   "Saving Life and Taking Life." *Journal of Philosophy* 72(5): 131–37.
1976   "Tooley's Moral Symmetry Principle." *Philosophy and Public Affairs* 5(3): 305–13.
1978   "The Presumption Against Taking Life." *Journal of Medicine and Philosophy* 3(1): 53–67.
1979   "The Nonequivalency of Saving Life and Not Taking Life." *Journal of Medicine and Philosophy* 4(3): 251–62.
1980   "Saving Life and Taking Life." In *Killing and Letting Die,* edited by Bonnie Steinbock, 166–71. Englewood Cliffs, N.J.: Prentice-Hall.

Tribe, Laurence H.
1993   Review of Ronald Dworkin, *Life's Dominion.* In *New York Times Book Review,* May 16, 1993, 1, 41.

Tubbs, James, Jr.
1990   "Recent Theological Approaches in Medical Ethics: McCormick, Ramsey, Hauerwas, and Gustafson." Ph.D. dissertation, University of Virginia.

Uniacke, Suzanne M.
1984   "The Doctrine of Double Effect." *Thomist* 48(2): 188–218.

Walter, James J.
1990   "The Foundation and Formulation of Norms." In *Moral Theology: Chal-*

lenges for the Future. Essays in Honor of Richard A. McCormick, edited by Charles E. Curran, 125–54. New York: Paulist Press.

Walzer, Michael
  1973   "Political Action: The Problem of Dirty Hands." *Philosophy and Public Affairs* 2(2): 160–80.
  1977   *Just and Unjust Wars: A Moral Argument with Historical Illustrations.* New York: Basic Books. 2d edition, 1992.
  1985   "The Moral Standing of States: A Response to Four Critics." In *International Ethics: A Philosophy and Public Affairs Reader*, 217–37. Princeton: Princeton University Press.

Warren, Mary Anne
  1977   "Do Potential People Have Moral Rights?" *Canadian Journal of Philosophy* 7(2): 275–89.
  1984   "On the Moral and Legal Status of Abortion." In *The Problem of Abortion*, edited by Joel Feinberg, 2d ed., 102–19. Belmont, Calif.: Wadsworth.

Wasserman, David
  1987   "Justifying Self-Defense." *Philosophy and Public Affairs* 16(4): 356–78.

Wasserstrom, Richard
  1978   Review of *Just and Unjust Wars* by Michael Walzer. *Harvard Law Review* 92: 536–45.

Wegner, Judith Romney
  1988   *Chattel or Person? The Status of Women in the Mishnah.* New York: Oxford University Press.

Weinryb, Elazar
  1980   "Omissions and Responsibility." *Philosophical Quarterly* 30(118): 1–18.

Werpehowski, William
  1991   "Covenant Love and Christian Faithfulness." *Journal of Religious Ethics* 19(2): 103–32.

White, Alan R.
  1984   *Rights.* Oxford: Clarendon Press.

Wicclair, Mark R.
  1981   "The Abortion Controversy and the Claim That This Body Is Mine." *Social Theory and Practice* 7(3): 337–46.

Wolterstorff, Nicholas
  1983   *Until Justice and Peace Embrace.* Grand Rapids, Mich.: W. B. Eerdmans Publishing Co.
  1984   "Reply by Wolterstorff." *Reformed Journal* 34(12): 23–29.

Zimmerman, Michael
  1981   "Taking Some of the Mystery out of Omissions." *Southern Journal of Philosophy* 19(4): 541–54.

Index

on euthanasia, 47n.4; on yielding, 53; on right to refuse treatment, 46n.2

Brody, Baruch A.: on nonvoluntary and involuntary pursuit, 88–93, 95–97; nothing is lost and, 59–60, 62–63, 74; yielding, 55–56

Brown, Robert M., on structural violence, 42n.50

bystander: in human shield case, 151–53; nonvoluntary and involuntary pursuit and, 105n.37; in trolley case, 119n.21, 125–27, 139n.47

Cahill, Lisa Sowle, 2n.2; "counterproductive" means concept, 108n.4; on divine dominion, 200n.35; nonmoral evil/moral evil distinction, 109n.6; on teleological ethics, 107–8

cancer scientist, usefulness of, in selecting whom to kill, 65

cancerous uterus case: double effect and, 109–13; intention and, 141n.50, 142–43; proleptic yielding in, 117n.18, 118n.19

capital punishment, 157

Catholic tradition: direct vs. indirect killing and, 135–36; divine dominion in, 200; double effect in, 106n.1, 113–17

"causal casuistry" principle, 129n.22

causation: letting die and, 31–33; non-preventing and, 33n.36, 33n.37

charity: as basic virtue or right, discussion of, 14–17; killing–letting die and, 14n.11, 35

Childress, James F.: on just war, 81n.8; on right to life, 3n.6

chocolate box case, Minimal Samaritanism and, 16–17

Christian ethics: fatal-use doctrine and, 107–8; regarding euthanasia, 48

commission, killing as, 6–7, 6n.2

common morality, concept of, 3n.5, 174–76

"commonsense" criterion, moral status and, 180–81, 201n.37

community, saving of, 70–74. See also political community case

complicity, starvation and, 42–43

"considered moral judgments," agreements on killings and, 1

constraints on aid, cost-based considerations, 16–17

continued existence, moral status and, 181–87

contraceptive failure, abortion and, 18, 21–29

convoy case, double effect, 136–37

"cooperation," coercion and, 86

Costa, Michael J.: missile cases, 130n.34; on trolley case and double effect, 126n.28

cost-benefit analyses, absolutism and, 154–57; constraints on aid and, 16–17; value of continuing life and, 46n.3, 50

counterattack, voluntary aggressor and, 79–82

"counterproductive" means, Cahill's concept of, 108n.4

craniotomy: cancerous uterus and, 109–13; causal priority approach to, 112n.11; as direct killing, 132–34; double effect and, 143–44; intention in, 133n.39; nonvoluntary and involuntary pursuit and, 93–94, 102–4

Curran, Charles E., on Ramsey, 103n.34

Damoflis, George, on abortion, 24n.27

Daube, David, on "collaboration with tyranny," 66–74

Davis, Lawrence, 193

Davis, Nancy: on double effect, 141n.52; on "Negative/Positive Duty Doctrine," 34; nonvoluntary and involuntary pursuit and, 97–100; rock climbing and ice-fishing cases, 31–33; on trolley case, 120n.23

"deadly causal process," killing–letting die and, 6n.1

"death throes," ethics of euthanasia in face of, 48–49

defense of others, vs. self-defense, 80–82

defilement, guilt of selection and, 68–69. See also rape

deity, concept of, euthanasia and, 49n.7

LaVergne, TN USA
04 December 2009

165966LV00002B/21/A